MARGARET OLIPHANT

By the same author

THOMAS HARDY AND RURAL ENGLAND

PREFACE TO HARDY

WOMEN IN THE ENGLISH NOVEL, 1800–1900

MARGARET OLIPHANT

A Critical Biography

Merryn Williams

MACMILLAN

First published 1986

Published by
THE MACMILLAN PRESS LTD
Houndmills, Basingstoke, Hampshire RG21 2XS
and London
Companies and representatives
throughout the world

Printed in Hong Kong

British Library Cataloguing in Publication Data
Williams, Merryn
Margaret Oliphant: a critical biography.
I. Title
823'.8 PR5114
ISBN 0–333–37647–1

To my parents

Contents

List of Illustrations

Introduction

'I am in very little danger of having my life written', Margaret Oliphant wrote towards the end of her career. Until recently, her life would probably not have seemed worth writing, and some people may still think so. Though one of the most popular Victorian novelists, she slipped into obscurity very soon after her death in 1897. She has had scarcely any attention from critics and most of her work, including some of the best, is out of print. Recently, though, more people have begun to see that she was an important novelist and a most remarkable woman.

Part of the reason why she failed to make an enduring reputation was that she never had quite enough time to 'labour with an artist's fervour and concentration to produce a masterpiece', to use her own words. She called herself a 'general utility woman', turning her hand to anything, producing a baby every year of her short-lived marriage and then writing an almost unbelievable number of novels, articles, travel books, histories and other pot-boilers to support a tribe of hangers-on. However, she also managed to write some extraordinarily good books. Perhaps our own generation, more aware than hers of the special problems of women, will sympathise.

This book began as a study of her major novels, some of which are now in print again. At the time I knew no more about her than anyone may read in the fragmentary *Autobiography*. However, a few years ago a large collection of her family papers was made available by her great-niece, the late Miss Margaret Valentine, and with their help I have been able to piece together the story of her life, which is as fascinating as any of her novels. It is a tragic story, but not, ultimately, a depressing one. This is therefore the first full biography.

I have been greatly helped by the only other study of Margaret Oliphant, *The Equivocal Virtue*, by Vineta and Robert A. Colby. I do not agree with all their literary judgments, but their work has made my task much easier.

I would particularly like to thank Mr Danvers Valentine, Margaret's great-great-nephew, for allowing me to print copyright material, and for helpful information. I am also most grateful to staff at the National Library of Scotland; the British Museum; the Bodleian and Cambridge University Libraries; the Public Record Office; Register House, Edinburgh; the University of Glasgow; the Durham and Northumberland County Record Offices; Windsor Castle library, and public reference libraries at Windsor, Reading, Liverpool, Birkenhead, Edinburgh and Glasgow. Also to my family and friends, who read some of the novels and short stories, and assured me that they were worth writing about.

M. W.

THE OLIPHANTS AND THE WILSONS

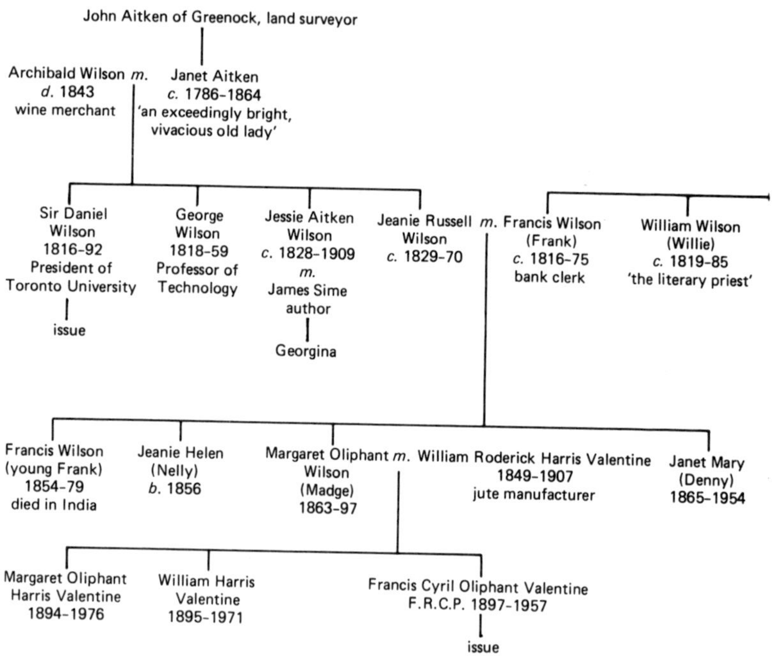

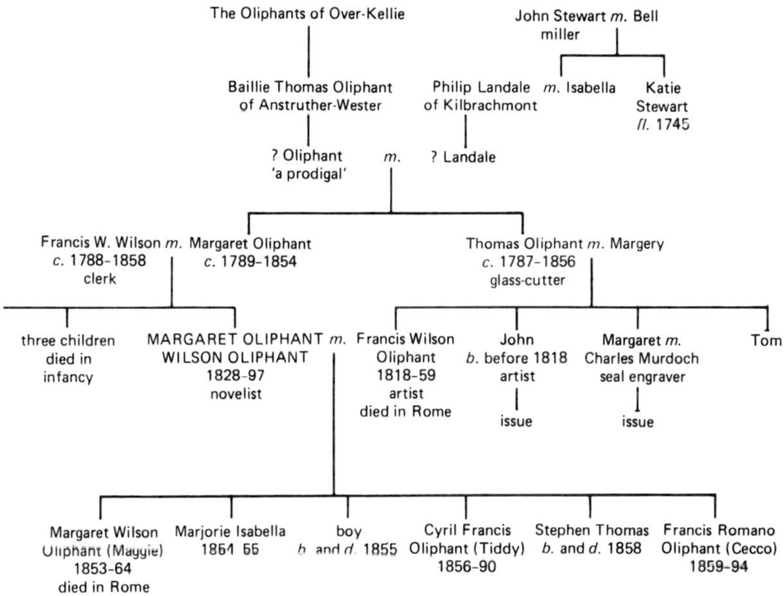
The Oliphants of Over-Kellie
John Stewart *m.* Bell
miller
Baillie Thomas Oliphant
of Anstruther-Wester
Philip Landale
of Kilbrachmont
m. Isabella
Katie
Stewart
fl. 1745
? Oliphant
'a prodigal'
m.
? Landale
Francis W. Wilson *m.*
c. 1788–1858
clerk
Margaret Oliphant
c. 1789–1854
Thomas Oliphant *m.* Margery
c. 1787–1856
glass-cutter
three children
died in
infancy
MARGARET OLIPHANT *m.*
WILSON OLIPHANT
1828–97
novelist
Francis Wilson
Oliphant
1818–59
artist
died in Rome
John
b. before 1818
artist
issue
Margaret *m.*
Charles Murdoch
seal engraver
issue
Tom
Margaret Wilson
Oliphant (Maggie)
1853–64
died in Rome
Marjorie Isabella
1854–55
boy
b. and *d.* 1855
Cyril Francis
Oliphant (Tiddy)
1856–90
Stephen Thomas
b. and *d.* 1858
Francis Romano
Oliphant (Cecco)
1859–94

1 Oliphants and Wilsons (1828–52)

Margaret Oliphant Wilson was born on 4 April 1828 at Wallyford, Midlothian; the youngest child of Francis Wilson and his wife Margaret, who had been an Oliphant before her marriage. Her mother was proud of her unusual name. 'She had a very high idea', wrote her daughter, '... of the importance of the Oliphant family, so that I was brought up with the sense of belonging (by her side) to an old, chivalrous, impoverished race. I have never got rid of the prejudice, though I don't think our branch of the Oliphants was much to brag of.'

Long before this time, their ancestors had lived in Kellie Castle (which is still standing, and can be seen by summer visitors) near the fishing village of Pittenweem in Fife. Their motto was 'À tout pourvoir' – to provide for all – a saying which came to mean a great deal to Margaret. But the Lords Oliphant had become extinct in the eighteenth century; the castle had been abandoned 'to the rooks and the owls who built in its crumbling chimneys'[1] and the family had 'died down into landlessness and obscurity many generations ago'.[2]

One of the few things we know about Francis Wilson is that he definitely did not come from a fine old family. He had a cousin, Archibald Wilson, who was a wine merchant in Edinburgh, and he himself was a clerk. He seems to have been a withdrawn and rather bad-tempered man, who took little notice of his children, and Margaret had to be very quiet when he was around. Her mother had a much more vivid personality:

> She was taller than I am, not so stout as I have grown. She had a sweet fresh complexion ... and beautiful liquid brown eyes, full of light and fun and sorrow and anger, flashing and melting, terrible to look at sometimes when one was in disgrace .... She had grown very early grey like myself ....

> Though her kindness was inexhaustible and her love boundless, yet she could drive her opponent of the moment half frantic with half-a-dozen words, and cut to the quick with a flying phrase. On the other side, there was absolutely nothing that she would not have done or endured for her own; and no appeal to her generosity was ever made in vain. She was a poor woman all her life, but her instinct was always to give.

Mr and Mrs Wilson were both approaching forty when their daughter was born. They had two boys, Frank and Willie, who were about twelve and nine, and in between there had been three other children who had died. For this reason the little girl was particularly loved and valued.

Wallyford is a hamlet on the edge of the Midlothian coalfield, set in rich farming country. 'The land is the finest', wrote Cobbett in 1832, 'that I ever saw in my life'.[3] The port of Musselburgh was only a mile or two away and the fisherwomen in their striped petticoats used to walk through the village to sell oysters in Edinburgh. The Wilsons lived in a picturesque old house with a cosy brick-floored kitchen and a drawing-room upstairs which looked out on Arthur's Seat. As a toddler Margaret fell into the fireplace and badly burned her arm. Her mother called in the local doctor, David Macbeth Moir (1798–1851), who also wrote poems and essays, under the name of Delta, for *Blackwood's Magazine*. Twenty years later he was to congratulate himself on having saved the life of a promising young author.

Soon afterwards the family moved to Lasswade, a village six miles from Edinburgh. There was a paper mill, a cluster of houses, and one street, surrounded by hills and fields. The little girl watched the coaches go over the bridge and gathered primroses on the banks of the river Esk. She was a dark-haired child, rather small for her age, with her mother's striking brown eyes and beautiful complexion. Unfortunately her teeth stuck out, as her mother's had done, and in those days that was uncorrectable.

In many ways living conditions in the 1830s were primitive. Operations had to be done without anaesthetic and houses became almost completely dark when the sun went down. Margaret recalled, in 1897, how terrifying it had been to creep along an unlighted passage. The country was still ringing with stories about Burke and Hare, the body-snatchers, and 'almost every child in Scotland trembled for the possibility of something pouncing upon it out of every dark corner, a dreadful hand upon its mouth'.[4] There were no daily papers, except in London, and the cost of receiving a letter was prohibitive for most people. Relatives who went away or abroad were not heard of for months, often years. The Firth was full of splendid white-sailed ships; railways were in their infancy and the usual way of travelling was by coach or on foot. 'The world was wrapt in perpetual silence, as when Columbus sailed into the unknown', wrote the elderly Margaret Oliphant, summing up the vast technological changes she had seen in her lifetime. 'Now it thrills with sound around all the spheres'.[5]

As a child she was dimly aware of enormous excitement about the Reform Bill. Scotland at this time had a population of 2.4 million people, less than five thousand of whom had a vote. The Bill gave the franchise to all male ten-pound householders, probably including Margaret's father, and when it was passed, in 1832, her brothers took her into Edinburgh to see a mammoth victory procession. The Wilsons were 'tremendously political and Radical', especially her mother and the elder boy Frank.

Another early memory was of being held up to put her penny in the Plate at the church door. On Sundays all normal activity stopped – even going for a walk was thought to be rather frivolous – so that respectable families like her own could go to the kirk. Like other Scottish children, she was brought up on the legends of the heroic Covenanters. They impressed her deeply, particularly the story of her namesake, Margaret Wilson, a girl of eighteen who had been drowned in Solway Firth for refusing to recognise the King as the head of the Church. The services were plain, austere and bare, but that did not matter. 'The passion of ritual has never taken root on Scotch soil ... but the passion of earnest religious feeling ... has been a universal charm'.[6]

Margaret tells us that her parents were not well off, but her mother kept everything going comfortably, probably with the help of one servant. She remembered the cheerful fire and candles in their Lasswade home, the snowy tablecloth, the kettle always on the boil and her mother getting up early to make breakfast for Frank before his long walk to work. Frank was a reliable boy, very kind to his little sister; Willie was a great charmer, 'with eyes that ran over with fun and laughter'. Everyone assumed that he was the cleverest of the family.

Both boys were left behind when the family moved again, to Glasgow, where Mr Wilson became a clerk at the Royal Bank. The long cold journey along the Union and Forth and Clyde canals took them most of a day. Margaret, aged six, astonished her fellow-passengers by reading aloud from a newspaper. She already felt that 'books were the most precious objects in existence',[7] although they were too expensive to be bought regularly. She seems not to have been very happy in Glasgow, where they lived for four years at 75 Bath Street; however, her mother took her regularly to a circulating library where she was caught, at about nine, reading *Ernest Maltravers*, an immoral novel by Bulwer Lytton.

It is not clear whether she ever went to school, although she may have, as education was highly valued in Scotland and there was a school in every parish for children of both sexes. But, more importantly, she had the chance to read the English and Scottish classics and the constant company of her highly intelligent mother. Mrs Wilson was a great raconteur and she passed on everything she knew to her daughter – Bible stories, bits of family history, ballads, tales of the saintly Queen Margaret who had brought the arts of civilisation to Scotland, Shakespeare, Pope, Wordsworth, Burns and Scott.

'She was trained, as many a Scotch girl for generations after her was trained, in the homeliest narrow round of duties', Margaret wrote of the mathematician Mary Somerville, 'yet with so much movement of intelligence in the minds around her ... full of mother-wit and independent original thought, as to neutralise the crushing effect of that narrowness.... We wonder if this was such a bad education after all.'[8]

Around 1838 Margaret and her parents went to Liverpool, where her father worked in the Customs House as a clerk in the export department of the Excise Office. It is not easy to trace her brothers' movements. Frank soon joined them, finding work as a clerk in the Bank of England, Willie remaining in Scotland. Margaret used to go down to the quay where she waited for hours, admiring the 'mighty river with all its ships, and the wonderful landscape',[9] until the Glasgow–Liverpool steamboat came in. When the passengers had come out the stewardess would give her a parcel containing Willie's letters, and also some long extracts from *Nicholas Nickleby* which he had kindly copied out for his little sister. A letter sent in the ordinary way would have cost them the enormous sum of 1s 11d. 'Nobody thought it wrong in those days to cheat the Post'.[10]

Over the last few years the city of Liverpool had been growing rapidly. The Wilsons were part of a great influx of people who sent the population up by forty-three per cent in the 1830s; over the next decade it went even higher as starving Irish refugees from the potato famine poured in. Poverty was worse than in any other English city; the average age of death, for manual workers, was fifteen. At the same time the merchants of Liverpool made great fortunes and the public buildings, like the new St George's Hall, were particularly splendid. To a child who had spent her early years in the Midlothian countryside, it was 'full of din and ceaseless activity'.[11] The streets were shrouded in yellow mist, and cholera haunted the filthy courts and cellars where the poorest people lived and died. On the pavements, merchants and clerks rubbed shoulders with sailors, prostitutes, children playing out late at night and poorly-dressed young women gazing wistfully into the expensive shops. Margaret grew used to seeing the innumerable ships unloading bales of cotton, and the workmen going to the foundries in their white moleskin suits, which were black by the end of the week. Across the Mersey, the 'magnificent skeleton town' of Birkenhead was 'striding out every year'.[12] What had been a tiny village on a 'headland of birches' at the beginning of the century was transformed, during Margaret's time in Liverpool, into a big industrial centre with its own iron works and docks.

The Wilsons lived in Everton, where there was a large Scottish community, moving house, as their habit was, every few years. We find them at 36 Lawrence Street in 1839; in 1843 at 30 Beau Street; at 22 Juvenal Street in 1845 and at 121 and later 115 Great Homer Street in 1849. Margaret tells us very little about these years except that she helped collect signatures for an anti-Corn Law petition, and that her father was the treasurer of a church relief fund set up at a time of great distress. Her mother probably shielded her as much as possible from the corruption all around them, but she very soon found out about the seamy side of life. Mrs Wilson believed that the answer to the problem of poverty was for every family to try to help another family worse off than itself. Accordingly, her daughter helped her make a new gown for the Irish charwoman, whose dress had been torn off her back by her husband's mistress.

Margaret was about twelve when Willie came to Liverpool, and very soon afterwards she began to sense that something was wrong. She gives few details, but it is clear that her much-loved brother could never keep a job for long and that every so often he broke out drinking. A friend described him as 'good-natured, affectionate, docile, incurably weak, hopelessly foredoomed'.[13] He was sincerely religious and fond of his family, and each time he promised faithfully that it would never happen again. Everyone said he was 'nobody's enemy but his own'. None the less, Mrs Wilson was deeply hurt and shocked that any son of hers could behave in that way.

Time and again in her early novels Margaret returns to this situation, which overshadowed all her years as a teenager and young woman. There are several hints that Willie had 'borrowed' money from his employer (he certainly kept getting into debt), and she constantly drew the picture of a mother waiting through the night for her son to come home. Later, when she read the *Life of Charlotte Brontë*, she was struck by the similarities between Willie and Branwell, but felt that the Brontës should not have revealed their family troubles to strangers. She herself learned at an early age to say as little as possible about Willie.

However, after a long illness, he really seemed to have reformed, and this was connected with one of the most important events in Margaret's early life, the Disruption of the Church of Scotland. The Presbyterians had always said that the only head of their church was Christ and that they would not tolerate any secular interference. The radical wing wanted each congregation to have the right to choose its own minister while the State insisted that a group of local magnates should appoint him. In May 1843 one-third of the membership walked out and set up the Free Church of Scotland. They included some five hundred clergymen who 'sacrificed by one general act their position, their homes and their living'.[14]

In later life Margaret regretted the Disruption, saying that it had split every Scottish village into two warring factions. As an idealistic fifteen-year-old who believed everything her parents told her, she passionately identified with the Free Church. The Liverpool Scots divided, with the Wilsons and many others leaving the established church in Rodney Street and building their own chapels. Willie is said to have been involved in this, and soon afterwards he decided that he wanted to be a minister. He took Greek and Latin lessons and then went to London to study at the English Presbyterian College. Probably his parents could only just afford to pay his fees and, although this is unprovable, there are hints in Margaret's novels that she and her mother took in sewing to make some extra money.

About this time she began to realise that she was very attractive. 'She photographed very badly', we are told, 'and indeed only colour could have shown the beauty of her eyes and complexion',[15] but the earliest known photograph of her shows a pleasant-looking girl. She had an 'always-troublesome mouth, imperfect in any face that is good for anything', and was probably very self-conscious about her teeth. However, a young Irish minister hinted before she was sixteen that he wanted to marry her. Then there was a brief engagement to someone else, whom she identifies only as J. Y. He was going to the States for three years, and was to marry her when he came back, but apparently he was not very clever, and Margaret was. They quarrelled by letter and he stopped writing. 'My poor little heart was broken. I was just over seventeen, I think.'

This seems to have been Margaret's only serious relationship before she met her husband, and she could certainly never have been accused of being too preoccupied with men. As a teenager she had a very quiet life, never went to dances or parties, and saw no one at home because her father hated strangers. 'Our pleasures were books of all and every kind, newspapers and magazines.' Just after the break-up of Margaret's little romance her mother became ill, and she had to sit beside her for hours without speaking. It was then that she wrote her first novel, a very crude one, about an angelic elder sister who takes care of her family after her lover dies, and a brother who falls into dissipated ways but reforms and becomes a clergyman. It was published years later as *Christian Melville*. 'And very silly I think it is, poor little thing', Margaret said.

From then on she got into the habit of writing, working at a corner of the sitting-room table and reading out her stories to her family. There was no question of her having a room to herself. 'My mother, I believe, would have felt her pride and rapture much checked, almost humiliated, if she had conceived that I stood in need of any artificial aids of that or any other description.' At first she did not try to find a publisher. Life went on uneventfully until the beginning of 1849, when she made a mysterious note, half-rubbed out, in the old book where her autobiography was later written:

> 1849 23d of January a Black Day
> a day to be remembered[16]

There is no clue to what this meant. Perhaps it was trouble with a boy friend; more likely, though, it had to do with Willie.

By this time Willie had almost completed his theological studies. Mrs Wilson had a brother, Thomas Oliphant, whose sons, Frank and Tom, were in London, and all three young men had rooms in a house at 27 Burton Street, St Pancras. Some time in 1849 he sent his parents a 'dreadful letter of misery and humiliation',[17] confessing that he was in trouble again. Mrs Wilson went straight to London and brought him home, though without telling her nephews the full story. The family had long anxious discussions about whether they had any right to let him be a minister. He assured them that he had finally given up his bad habits, but they were beginning not to believe him.

Before this happened, he had taken the MS of his sister's novel, *Passages in the Life of Mrs Margaret Maitland, of Sunnyside*, to the London publisher Henry Colburn. The Wilsons were still deeply depressed when Margaret got a letter offering to publish it on the half-profit system. 'The delight, the astonishment, the amusement of this was not to be described', she wrote. 'First and foremost, it was the most extraordinary joke that ever was. Maggie's story!' The contract was signed on 24th August, when she was still only twenty-one.

Soon afterwards, Willie returned to London. His parents had agreed, after much hesitation, to let him go on with his studies, but Margaret, although she had hardly ever left home before, went with him to guard him against drink and debt. They stayed in the same house as their Oliphant cousins for three months. As it would not have been proper for Margaret to roam about London by herself, she sat in the parlour all morning while Willie was at lectures. In the afternoons they explored the parks and bookshops. Margaret found that one of his debts was still unpaid and dealt with it with her usual energy. On certain days they gave up their midday meal and went for a long walk, eating only a bun until supper-time – 'and the little bill was paid and never known of at home'.

She was too preoccupied, and perhaps too inexperienced, to realise that Frank Oliphant admired her. Although they were first cousins, they hardly knew each other. He was an artist and stained-glass designer, ten years older than herself, who was working with Pugin on the windows for the new House of Lords. He took her to meet his friends and to the National Gallery, but Margaret knew nothing about pictures and was disappointed.

Margaret Maitland was published in November, and the young author read her first, on the whole very friendly review one wintry afternoon in the *Athenaeum* magazine:

> It has given us much pleasure of a quiet and wholesome kind ... Had the passages been condensed within a single volume, the tale would have taken a very high rank. Its imaginary writer is, of her single self, sufficient to sweeten the tempers of all who have maintained a traditional antipathy to the genus Spinster.... There are Mistress Maitlands in real life, but we are not aware that the Maiden Aunt has ever before found so favourable a representative in print.[18]

It was rather an unusual book for a girl of twenty. Instead of a love story, as might have been expected, Margaret had described the life of a Scottish spinster, a 'quiet eldern woman' who finds her greatest pleasure in watching over other people's children. The novel quickly went into a third edition, after which Colburn gave her £150. Margaret was overwhelmed; it was probably more than her father earned in a year. She sent a copy to the aged Lord Jeffrey, the first editor of the *Edinburgh Review*, who wrote back that he had been 'captivated'.[19] Mudie's lending library put it on their list, ensuring a large readership, and it continued to be popular for the next twenty years.

But although she was delighted with her small triumph there was no question of being too pleased with herself. She tells us that she was young for her age and very shy, having mixed with hardly anyone outside her family, and her books were written mainly to please her mother and her brother Frank. After she and Willie returned home she wrote another Scottish novel, *Merkland*, which was published by Colburn at the end of

1850. But other things seemed more important, particularly the problem of finding Willie a job. He had to wait for several months but eventually, on 24 October 1850, he was ordained in the Presbyterian church at Etal, Northumberland.

It was a very pretty village on the River Till, near the site of Flodden Field. There was a large Presbyterian congregation who, rather strangely, called their minister 'the priest'. Margaret and her mother went to see him and made him promise to write home regularly. They left him there 'with thankful hearts, yet an ache of fear'. Around the same time the family moved across the river to a large house in Kenyon Terrace, Grosvenor Road, Birkenhead.[20]

Probably early in 1851 her cousin Frank Oliphant came for a visit and suggested that they should get married and build up the vanished glories of the family again. Margaret was alarmed, never having thought of this, and said no. In the spring of that year she and her mother visited Edinburgh, probably staying with the Wilson family, her second cousins on her father's side.

In many ways this family was very like her own – liberal in politics, nonconformist in religion, and with a great love of books. Their mother, the widowed Mrs Janet Wilson, was a vivacious old lady who had encouraged her children to study natural history and make their own museums. It was entirely due to her that her sons, though starting with no advantages, had done so well. Daniel Wilson (1816–92) was an archaeologist and English scholar who emigrated to Canada two years later and eventually became President of Toronto University and a knight. George Wilson (1818–59) was a chemist and a popular scientific writer who did pioneering work on colour-blindness. Four years later he became Professor of Technology at Edinburgh University and founded what is now the Royal Scottish Museum. There were also two girls of Margaret's age, Jessie and Jeanie.

George Wilson was a delightful character, 'writing very amusing letters and talking very amusing talk, which was all the more credit to him as he was in very bad health'. He had had a foot amputated, without anaesthetic, and walked with a stick. He joked endlessly about his health and did not allow it to interfere with his serious interests, science and religion. He gave courses for disadvantaged groups like working men and girls, and believed that women should be encouraged to use their minds. Whether on principle, or because he realised that his young cousin was exceptionally intelligent, he gave her every encouragement to go on with her writing. Over the next year he sent her letters praising her not very promising early novels for their 'picturesque descriptions', humour, and understanding of male characters.[21]

Margaret remembered that visit to Edinburgh all her life. She had been in Fife as a girl, but she had certainly not had many chances to go back to Scotland or to meet people who shared her intellectual interests. They saw Dr Moir, with whom they had kept in touch, and after her mother had gone home Margaret stayed behind with him and his family and had 'a kind of introduction to Edinburgh literary society' which had far-reaching results.

Blackwood's Edinburgh Magazine – known to its contributors as 'Maga' – had been launched in 1817 by the first William Blackwood as a Tory counterblast to the Whiggish *Edinburgh Review*. Prominent contributors were James Hogg, John Gibson Lockhart, and John Wilson (1785–1854) who used the pen-name of Christopher North. It became famous almost at once when it published the 'Chaldee Manuscript', which satirised several local personalities and which, as some pious people thought, verged on blasphemy. 'My mother was a fervent Liberal', Margaret wrote, 'and therefore completely opposed to *Blackwood's Magazine*; also a woman much out of the world, living in the country ... yet her laugh over it, and her remembrance of it, made it familiar to me long before I saw a word of it in print. It was one of the old brilliant things "such as you never hear of nowadays" of her youth'.[22] In its first years it printed some unpleasant attacks on Leigh Hunt and the 'Cockney school' of poets, including Keats. Later it became milder and more literary, or, at any rate, Margaret liked to think so. It published work by Galt and by Susan Ferrier, 'the Scottish Jane Austen', and Christopher North was one of the first to praise the poetry of Wordsworth. Coleridge, himself a victim of 'Maga's' bile in its early days, wrote in 1832 that it was 'an unprecedented Phenomenon in the world of letters, and forms the golden – alas! the only – remaining link between the Periodical Press and the enduring literature of Great Britain'.[23]

William Blackwood was succeeded by several of his sons. In 1851 the editor was John Blackwood, who had taken on the job

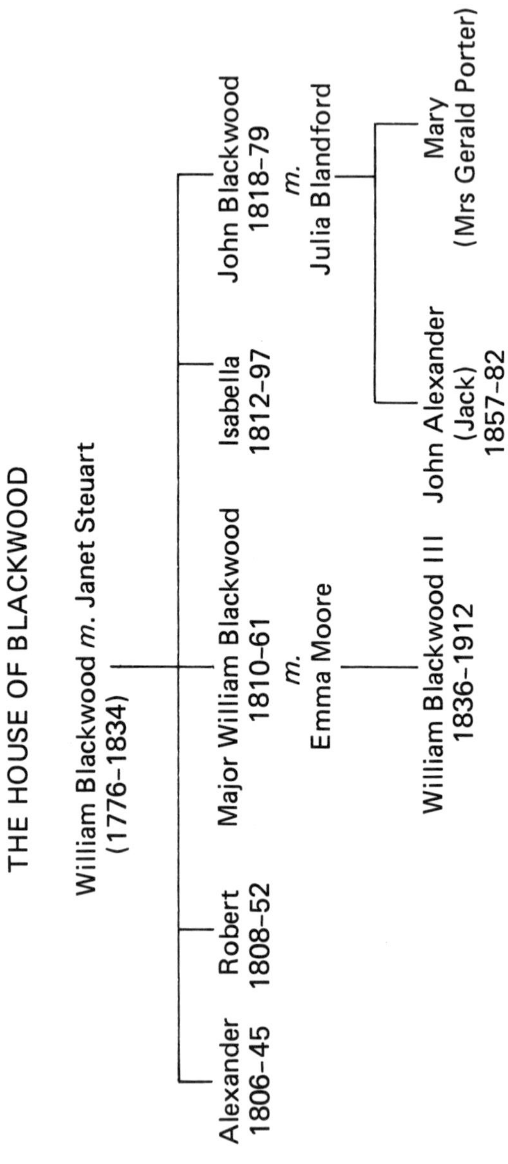
THE HOUSE OF BLACKWOOD
William Blackwood *m*. Janet Steuart
(1776–1834)
Alexander
1806–45
Robert
1808–52
Major William Blackwood
1810–61
m.
Emma Moore
Isabella
1812–97
John Blackwood
1818–79
m.
Julia Blandford
William Blackwood III
1836–1912
John Alexander
(Jack)
1857–82
Mary
(Mrs Gerald Porter)

in his twenties and was assisted by his elder brother, Major William Blackwood, who had spent most of his adult life in India. He was a 'mild and courteous' man whom Margaret liked immensely. John Blackwood, like his father, was an active Tory, but 'always welcomed, whether as editor or publisher, what he considered to be literary ability, without regard to the political or religious opinions of its possessors',[24] and he cultivated good relationships with his writers:

> A magazine with him was a magazine, meaning a collection of everything, where authors, professional or non-professional, soldiers, politicians, clergymen, travellers – all might exhibit their wares, and hence to a great extent the cause of its and his own popularity.[25]

A typical number of *Blackwood's* might contain ninety thousand words. There would be a serial, commentaries on current affairs, book reviews, miscellaneous essays, perhaps a poem or a short story. Selling about seven thousand copies a month, it never had the mass circulation of some Victorian periodicals, but for a long time it was one of the most influential. In the 1890s, Margaret called it 'almost the last really literary magazine'.[26]

During that spring of 1851 she met the Major and Christopher North, now a tall old man with white hair 'falling picturesquely about his ears'. Margaret gazed up at him reverently while Dr Moir explained that she had already published some novels and would have to be warned against overwork. 'No need of that', said North, 'so long as she is young and happy work will do her no harm'.[27]

She returned to Birkenhead thinking it would be a great thing to be a Blackwood's author. It was the last time she saw 'Delta', who died on 6 July. Back at home she threw herself into her work. Colburn had published a third novel, *Caleb Field*, in April, and his successors, Hurst and Blackett, were to take several more, but she was already finding that one publisher was not enough for her. That summer she approached Richard Bentley with a new book, *John Drayton, The Liverpool Engineer*. She had been impressed by the 'condition of England' novels which had appeared recently and thought she might use her experience of industrial towns to write something similar. Liverpool and Birkenhead had gone through a severe depression in the late

1840s, and although the Chartists had never been really strong there, there had been some talk of riots in 1848. Margaret's attitude was much the same as that of the Christian Socialists, for whom she kept a certain tenderness all her life. Employers must show more sympathy for their workmen; the workers must reject the doctrine of class war, and things will get better. There are rather crude attacks on an employer, called Hardman, and a Chartist leader, called Wyld. The book is a failure artistically (and was not very successful commercially) because Margaret did not actually know much about working-class life. Bentley published it in August and expressed his willingness to see more of her work.

The summer and autumn were a crucial time for Margaret and Frank Oliphant. In the *Autobiography* she tells us only that she had rejected his first proposal, 'but in six months or so things changed'. Possibly the Wilsons went to London for the Great Exhibition, where Pugin was in charge of the Medieval Court and where several of the firms for which Frank worked were displaying stained glass.[28] She may well have seen his work and talked to him about the future, but there are no details.

On 15 September the twenty-two year old Jeanie Wilson left Edinburgh to visit her Birkenhead cousins, bringing Margaret a letter from her brother George. By the time he wrote again, on 11 October, both girls were engaged. What apparently happened was that, early in October, Margaret changed her mind and agreed to marry Frank Oliphant. There was general delight and rejoicing. Mrs Wilson declared that she loved him like her own son and began making plans to live near the young couple in London or wherever else they went. Margaret's brother, Frank Wilson, was still living at home at thirty-five and seems to have been upset by his parents' decision to leave him. Very soon afterwards he proposed to Jeanie, whom he hardly knew, and was accepted, 'and so two new houses were formed out of the partial ruins of the old'.

It was arranged that Frank and Jeanie should get married in the following March, and Margaret and the other Frank in May. Meanwhile she decided to do as much writing as possible. She gave Bentley *The Melvilles*, another novel about social problems in Liverpool, and also wrote to Major Blackwood asking him to consider a short novel, *Katie Stewart*, for serialisation in the *Magazine*. Going back to Scotland seems to have given her a sense of her own roots, and this book is better than anything else she wrote as a very young woman. Her mother had told her a great deal about her girlhood in Fife – 'I know my mother's youth better than my own',[29] she used to say – including the story of her great-aunt, whose maiden name was Katie Stewart. Katie had been born about 1727 and taken up by the Erskine family who at that time owned Kellie Castle. She had seen Prince Charlie ride into Edinburgh (but, as a Whig, had not supported him) and had waited ten years for her lover, who had been press-ganged, to come back and marry her. Margaret's mother had known her as a very old lady and had heard the story from her own lips.

Katie Stewart, A True Story, was accepted and became the first of several hundred contributions to *Blackwood's Magazine*. It seemed likely to be her seventh published novel, and she was still only twenty-three. But while she was happily planning her wedding, and congratulating herself on her blossoming career, came a disaster.

Willie had now been in Etal for about eighteen months. He was popular, having converted a local 'wild man' by his eloquent preaching, and his mother and sister had allowed themselves to hope that there would be no more trouble. But the congregation soon found out about his drinking habits and early in 1852 rumours reached the church authorities in Berwick, who decided to hold an ecclesiastical trial. At about the same time Mrs Wilson got an anonymous letter and set off for Northumberland at once. She decided that as he was certain to be unfrocked in any case, it was better for him not to appear at the trial. After a few miserable days, the mother and son left for home. There was a feeling in Etal, for some time afterwards, that Willie had been treated with a certain lack of Christian charity.

Before they came back Margaret wrote to her fiancé telling him the full story. She had not done so before, but there could be no concealment now:

> My dear Frank, you do not know Willie – sober, rational, sensible and affectionate at home – away from home his life seems inevitably to merge into this madness. He is no hypocrite – do not think so – my dear, dear Willie.

They had decided that Willie must come home 'to be guarded

and provided for as if disease had disabled him'. 'A year ago', Margaret wrote, 'I should have seen my duty clearly to devote myself to my brother – now the position of all of us is complex and difficult – yet I do not and cannot regret dearest Frank the engagement which has united us to each other. I gave you my promise when I was not secure of my heart – I give you my heart now without reserve, with joy and thankfulness, even in this affliction.'

It is worth quoting at length from this letter because, apart from one short note, it is the only one written by Margaret to Frank which survives. Whatever she may have felt, before or afterwards, she was wholeheartedly in love with him then, if only because he had assured her that Willie's behaviour made no difference to his feelings. 'In my heart nothing can ever come between us', she told him, '– your letter is to me the dearest comfort – your love the strongest support. I lean upon you, I trust to you with all my heart . . . but such a terrible calamity as this must leave its mark in our family history – it cannot pass away as if it had not been.'[30]

Willie himself seemed perfectly content with the situation. He settled down at home, smoked, read old novels and the newspapers, and made absolutely no effort to find work. Margaret could hardly bear to watch him. After a while it occurred to her that if he were to copy out some of her novels and take a share of the profits, this might give him an illusion of being employed. He seems to have written the clean manuscripts of *The Melvilles* (1852), *Ailieford* (1853), and *Christian Melville* (1856). All of them came out anonymously, but they, and *John Drayton*, are attributed to William Wilson to this day.

Evidently Frank persuaded Margaret that there was no reason to put off the wedding, and it was agreed that her parents and Willie would move to London later in the summer. They were married at St Andrew's Presbyterian Church, Birkenhead, on 4 May 1852. It was an odd choice of date, since Margaret had already noted, in her first novel, the old Scottish superstition that 'ill fortune ever follows them that are married in May'.[31]

2 General Utility Woman (1852–59)

Francis Wilson Oliphant had been born on 28 September 1818 at Gateshead, where his parents, Thomas and Margery, were then living.[1] On his marriage certificate, he described his father as a 'gentleman', and Margaret gave the impression that her uncle came from 'an ancient but fallen family'.[2] All the contemporary records, though, make it clear that Thomas Oliphant was a glass-cutter. Frank grew up among skilled workmen – 'well paid, educated in their way, thinking themselves a kind of artists' – and probably learned about the qualities of glass from a very early age. At some point the family moved back to Edinburgh, where his brother John was working as an artist, and Frank studied drawing at the Trustees' Academy under Sir William Allan, a well-known painter of scenes from Scottish history. The Academy was not an art school in the modern sense. Founded with public money, it existed to prepare boys for a trade, and most of them went on to become craftsmen. A few decided that they wanted to be full-time painters, including Frank. But as a young man he spent most of his time on stained-glass windows because they 'had the advantage of paying at once'.[3]

In the 1830s, following a religious revival, there was a phenomenal increase in the demand for stained glass. Frank worked first in Edinburgh and then in Newcastle for the firm of William Wailes, which supplied glass to Pugin. He moved to London around 1846 and became Pugin's second designer two years later. Afterwards he liked to give the impression that Pugin (who went mad and died in 1852) had been a close personal friend, but the great man's surviving letters sound much more like those of an employer.[4] By the time he married Margaret he was a very experienced artist, had visited several European countries and could say that 'the number of windows that have been executed from my designs is past counting and are in nearly every county and cathedral in England'.[5]

Frank Oliphant is, unfortunately, a shadowy figure. No photograph of him survives, nor any of his letters to his wife, and in her *Autobiography* she says almost nothing about their relationship. But it is clear that he had what is usually called a poetic temperament and was enthusiastic about his work. Like Pugin, he believed there had been no really good stained glass since the Middle Ages and wanted to revive the art: 'I honestly think I can compete with the old works'.[6] He was ambitious in the sense of wanting to get to the top of his profession, but basically he was uninterested in money. 'Every true artist likes and longs to see the best made of the art he professes', he wrote, and he was sure that any glass painter would 'rather work at a lower rate of remuneration, if he felt that he was working to the advancement of his craft'.[7] The windows he left behind, with their brilliant colours and careful drawing, suggest that he was a distinctly better worker than average.

If Margaret's feelings were ambiguous, his were not; all the evidence is that he was devoted to her, though perhaps not very sensitive to her feelings. He admired her work and never suggested she should give it up, although naturally he assumed that she and not he would be responsible for running the home. In later life she came to feel that perhaps she had been too intolerant, demanding that Frank should measure up to some impossible ideal rather than appreciating the good qualities he really had. Her novel *At His Gates* (1872) contains an artist's wife who is discontented because her husband's work has no 'spark of divinity':

> 'Why was he not a Raphael, a Titian?' she wondered.... Her mind had wanted something more than his easy talent, his exquisite skill, the gentle, modest pitch of imagination which was all that common life moved him to.

Perhaps, she reflects, she ought to have married Michelangelo. 'She could have understood the imperfection which is full of genius; what she was slow to understand was the perfection in which no genius was'.[8] That sums up the difference between the Oliphants. Frank was an artist without genius who laboured hard to produce perfect work; Margaret was a genius, whose work is shot through with imperfection.

After the wedding the young couple moved into 6 Harrington Square, St Pancras. It was an unfashionable neighbourhood, but with several 'modest circles of art and literature in London which in those days made, far more than now, a little world for themselves'.[9] Their way of life was probably more Bohemian than anywhere else in mid-Victorian England. The atmosphere was jolly, informal, relaxed. They used to drop in on other painters in the evenings and sometimes sit up until midnight, the men having long arguments about art while Margaret, with her alert mind, soaked up information about her husband's work.

From time to time they went to literary parties. Frank was a better mixer than his wife and tried in vain 'to form me and make me attend to my social duties'. Hostesses who had picked her up as a rising young novelist were disappointed to find that she was very shy. Possibly it was at this time that Margaret learned to be rather reticent about her background. Later novels prove that she knew what it was like to be uncertain of one's exact social position. She and her husband had a fine old Scottish name and could have said, with one of her characters, 'We are a family of artists. We are everybody's equal, and we are nobody's equal. We have a rank of our own'.[10] However, she soon realised that Free Presbyterians ranked below members of the Established Church, and Frank's vagueness about his father's occupation suggests that he wanted to make their background seem grander than it really was.

Among the writers she met were Mr and Mrs Samuel Carter Hall, Irish authors, and Mary Howitt (1799–1888), who had written several books, independently or with her husband William. She was a 'mild, kind, delightful woman', who gave Margaret a great fright by telling her that she had lost several babies through a heart defect 'which she said was somehow connected with too much mental work on the part of the mother'. Another literary acquaintance was Dinah Mulock, a tall, thin, intense young woman who had been living alone and supporting herself by novel-writing for years.

To be a young married woman, in charge of her own household, was an exhilarating sensation. It was 'the first smack of absolute freedom', Margaret wrote later, 'which women ever taste'.[11] Any middle-class family in those days could afford at least one servant, and Margaret seems to have realised, early on, that she could use this system to free herself for writing. They probably employed a cook and housemaid, and later a nurse, but she still had to do a fair amount herself.

In August her parents came to London with Willie to look for a home. Mrs Wilson wrote to Frank's father that so far as London was concerned 'I know very little about it and care less, we are in it but not of it, and were it not for these young people at Harrington Square I would greatly prefer Constantinople'. It is easy to see where Margaret got her way with words. She went on to tell him proudly that *Katie Stewart*, which was appearing anonymously in *Blackwood's Magazine*, had made 'a great sensation ... Fife is in a ferment – that is, not our Fife but literary Fife.... I like Fife with all its faults and vulgarities which are neither few nor small and it is a great pleasure to think my little Maggie has made herself a name among the magnates of it.'

'With regard to certain speculations of yours', the old lady added, 'I believe they are premature ... if you please to time we will leave this subject'.[12] Frank and Margaret were then just about to go to Germany for a 'wedding journey'. When they came back, around the end of September, they were expecting their first baby.

We can assume that up to then the marriage had been completely happy. The trouble began only after the Wilsons joined them, settling round the corner in a small house near the railway in Park Village East. Willie got no better after the move. He shut himself into his room, smoking, copying out Margaret's books, and sometimes drinking. Separated from one son and bitterly disappointed in the other, Mrs Wilson expected to see a great deal of the daughter who had been born after so much suffering and to whom she had always been exceptionally close. On the other hand Frank wanted his wife to himself and had what Margaret called 'foolish ideas about a mother-in-law'. 'I have gone through many sorrows since', she wrote long afterwards, 'but I don't know that any period of life has ever contained more intolerable moments than those first years that should have been so happy'.[13]

Well before the baby was born, the family was in a state of extreme tension. Frank made it clear, without actually saying so, that he objected to Mrs Wilson constantly coming to the house, and she may well have retaliated with one of her stinging phrases. Margaret, taken completely by surprise, tried unhappily and unsuccessfully to reconcile them. Mr Wilson read his paper and appeared not to know what was going on.

When her daughter was born, on 21 May 1853, there was a brief truce. The baby was named Margaret Wilson Oliphant, Maggie for short. Margaret and her mother both loved this child with a passion which they never seem to have felt for their male partners. She always thought that the birth of a baby was 'the most exquisite moment of a woman's life'.[14] But some time in the next year there was a horrible argument. Mrs Wilson came no more to Harrington Square, but Margaret stole out to visit her every day.

It was ironic that this should have happened just when everything was looking hopeful for the young couple. Frank had got the job of designing the windows for the east end of Ely Cathedral, and Margaret was still writing novels at high speed. Bentley had broken off relations after finding that her 'condition of England' novels did not pay, but she remained on excellent terms with Hurst and Blackett, who published *Harry Muir*, a novel based on Willie's career, in 1853. *Blackwood's Magazine* had taken more of her work and agreed to serialise another novel, *The Quiet Heart*. An American woman writer who met her that summer described her as

> a fair Scotchwoman ... a modest, quiet, lovable person, who seems far from having made up her mind to accept the fact of her own genius. Having wakened one morning to find herself famous, she believes the world to be labouring under some strange delusion, and counts herself an immensely overrated little woman after all.[15]

Although Margaret remained composed in public, *The Quiet Heart*, which began to appear in December 1853, shows that the Oliphants' marriage was in deep trouble after only eighteen months. The heroine is a naïve girl, in love with a writer whom she believes to be a genius but who turns out to be lazy and shallow. She breaks off their engagement because he is hostile to her mother – a dignified Scottish lady – and becomes a self-supporting painter. Although they eventually come together again the girl has some bitter experiences, fears that she is going mad and learns the hard lesson that she cannot rely upon the man she loves. This novel marks Margaret's transition from a protected child to a suffering adult, and in a sense her relationship with Frank never recovered.

Yet both of them knew that they had to make the best of things. There was Maggie to think of, and another baby was on the way. Margaret dramatised her state of mind during this wretched time in *The Days of my Life*. The narrator turns against her husband (who is her cousin, and takes her on an idyllic honeymoon in Germany) and very nearly wrecks her marriage. Basically she did not want to leave Frank, but for a time she could not conceal her hostility, and she had certainly picked up her mother's unspoken message that he was not good enough for her.

On 22 May 1854, the Oliphants had a second daughter, Marjorie. The next day, Mrs Wilson collapsed. Apparently she had been suffering for some years from a disease of the rectum, but had told no one about it, and had kept it off until after the baby was born 'by sheer stress of will'. Margaret nursed her through the summer, probably having hardly any time for the two tiny children. She did not realise how serious it was until one day, in front of her mother's door, 'all in a green shade with the waving trees', the doctor made it clear that she was going to die. Margaret had had no experience of death before. She had to cope, not just with the heavy nursing, but also with new and painful emotions – the need to keep a secret from her mother for the first time, the desire to give up and go to sleep of which she was bitterly ashamed. Mrs Wilson died at Harrington Square on 17 September. 'And, oh me! when all was over, mingled with my grief there was – how can I say it? – something like a dreadful relief.'

It was not surprising. There were no longer two people for her to please (she noted in a cancelled section of the *Autobiography*), only one. After this, the family drifted apart. Willie is said to have gone to a clachan on the shores of Loch Lomond, where over the next few years he wrote some novels which earned him the nickname, around Etal, of 'the literary priest'. Mr Wilson, while remaining on perfectly good terms with Margaret, went off by himself, and from then until his death four years later she had little to do with him.

At the beginning of 1854 Frank had rented a small house at

14 Salisbury Place for a studio/workshop. His idea was to have his painted windows made there under his own supervision, partly because he had never been happy with the way his designs were done into glass and partly because he hoped to get a settled income and so have more time for painting.

Setting up the business took all the money they had got, and slightly more. In March, with her baby due in two months, Margaret was writing to Blackwood, 'I should like very much if you would employ me in some miscellaneous work, reviews or essays of a lighter sort, by which I might make fifty pounds'.[16] A few months later, sending a new novel, *Zaidee*, she begged to be paid straight away, 'It happens that just at this present time I am considerably in want of money.... It pains me to ask for such favours so often, and I trust never to have the same occasion again as I have now – but your past kindness leads me to apply to you'.[17]

Her relationship with the Blackwoods was becoming steadily closer. Although she used other publishers (Hurst and Blackett brought out one of her novels almost every year in the 1850s) she always felt a particular loyalty and affection for them. She met the genial John Blackwood, the head of the firm, who apparently heard her talking so brilliantly about Dickens and Thackeray that he asked her to write down her thoughts for the *Magazine*. In the twelve months of 1855 he took no less than nine of her articles and another long novel, and nine in 1856 – hefty articles of about ten thousand words each. For the rest of her life, with one short interruption, Margaret was, in her own words, a 'general utility woman'[18] for *Blackwood's*.

This meant that, while leading a fairly normal life with her husband and children, and without knowing many people in the literary world, she was able to reach a wide and distinguished audience. It was a remarkable *coup* for a young woman under thirty. The reason probably was that she could write competently, if not profoundly, about almost anything. In one short series, for instance, she dealt with theology, science, history, travel books, art and poetry. One subject which she left alone was politics; Blackwood probably thought this was too important to be entrusted to a woman and in any case Margaret, who still called herself a Radical, did not pretend to share his views. But she was ready to tackle most other things. We find her defending Christianity against the sceptics, and arguing that Scottish

Presbyterians did not deserve to be called fanatics or persecutors. In an article of May 1855 she drew attention to the fact that this was an 'age of female novelists' and discussed several of them, including the two greatest then living, Charlotte Brontë and Elizabeth Gaskell. As she was finishing it she heard the news of Charlotte Brontë's death. 'We repeat again over her grave', she wrote, 'the great admiration with which we have always regarded her wonderful powers'.

Only once did she ask for a month's postponement. The baby, Marjorie, died on 8 February 1855, when her mother was struggling to finish an essay on Dickens:

> My dear little Marjorie was always pale and delicate, but with glorious eyes – to think of an eight months' old baby having these! But I remember that as she died she opened them widely and seemed to fix them on me as she lay on my knee, giving up her little soul in that look of consciousness.

The guilt feelings she had experienced at the time of her mother's death came back when she realised that her grief for her baby went deeper. 'I miss my mother till this moment when I am nearly as old as she was . . . I dream constantly of being a girl with her at home. But at that moment her loss was nothing to me in comparison with the loss of my little child.'

She went on writing doggedly, taking comfort from the fact that she was pregnant again. In November she gave birth prematurely to a boy, but he died after only one day. After that she went into a serious depression. She must have asked herself whether she had been responsible for the babies' deaths by doing 'too much mental work' as Mary Howitt had suggested. The two-year-old Maggie was still alive, but at one time she feared that she would lose her too. When she read a newspaper report about a mother who had killed her baby, she broke down. And one of the worst things was that everyone, including Frank, assumed that it was a very minor tragedy and that she would soon get over it.

However, she began to feel better at the beginning of 1856 when they moved to 7 Ulster Place, near Regent's Park. Another baby was expected at the end of the year. Around this time her publisher, Henry Blackett, had asked her to introduce him to Dinah Mulock. Margaret invited them both to dinner and he arranged to publish the book which became *John Halifax, Gentleman.* It is said that Margaret helped her friend correct the proofs and was amused by the blameless hero. To her astonishment, it became one of the great Victorian best-sellers, quite eclipsing any mild success that Margaret had had. From then on Dinah was in an unassailable position. For all her sentimentality, she stood out for a good price and got 'more with a few books, and these of very thin quality, than I with my many'.

Early in 1856 Mary Howitt asked her to sign a petition for a Married Woman's Property Act and sent her a pamphlet, 'A Brief Summary, in Plain Language, of the most Important Laws concerning Women', by Barbara Leigh-Smith. This pointed out, in a calm and unemotive style, that married women could own nothing, were not allowed to leave their husbands, and had no right to the custody of their children. As it happened, Margaret had been thinking about these subjects for some time, and had spoken disparagingly of the feminist movement in *Merkland.*[19] Her quarrel with women's rights activists was that they exposed other women to the sneers of men, and this offended her always very strong sense of personal dignity. She was to come back to this question time and again throughout her life. Now she used the pamphlet as the basis for an article, 'The Laws Concerning Women', which was published in *Blackwood's* in April. Her tone is moderate; she did not want women to be treated unjustly; she was not prepared to say that they were inferior to men. But she doubted whether the law could interfere between married people. Her view of the husband/wife relationship sounds disenchanted for a young woman who had been married only four years:

> Let us grant that in most cases they have their differences; that they do a little private fighting quietly under their own roof.... We may chafe and strain at the chain that binds us; but sober thought and cooler temper say what the law says.... The 'marriage of true minds' may be as rare as it is lofty and fortunate. The marriage of interests, hopes, and purposes is universal.

All the signs are, though, that her relationship with Frank improved after her mother died and especially after the move to Ulster Place. She called this 'the bright time of my early life'.[20]

He got several orders for windows, and also painted some pictures which were hung at the Royal Academy. But what was best of all was that the baby, Cyril, arrived safely on 16 November. Margaret begged the doctor to tell her if he was healthy and got a reassuring answer, '"That fellow!" he said, "he has lungs like a sponge."'

The winter of 1856–7 was happy and cheerful. Margaret used to write all morning in the small back drawing-room, jumping up occasionally to have a word with Frank in his studio, or to play with the children when they came in from their walk – 'my dear little Maggie, my baby-boy, two beautiful children, fresh and sweet, well and strong, reviving my heart, that had been so heavy and sore with the loss of my two infants, by the sight of their beautiful shining faces'.

During the last year Frank had had a young assistant, Sebastian Evans, who had given up his career in the Church because of religious doubts. This did not shock Margaret now, although it probably would have a few years ago. She thought his cheerful company was good for her husband, who was not very well, and worried because his workmen were not finishing the windows on time. The young man wanted to become a partner, so his brother came to inspect Frank's accounts to see if the business was a paying proposition. When he had done so 'he congratulated my husband that his circumstances permitted him to be so indifferent to profit. And there was an end of the partnership'.

The young Oliphants ignored the danger signals for some time longer. Both of them were too unworldly to be really worried about money. Frank was 'an artist and not a man of business';[21] Margaret was absorbed in her children and her writing. She was getting about four hundred pounds for each novel, not to mention articles, and as has been seen she was publishing at least one novel a year. Four hundred a year was a comfortable income in the 1850s. Frank was selling a picture occasionally, and producing several windows for about two hundred pounds each. They should certainly have been able to manage on their joint earnings. No doubt they were paying something towards the support of Willie, but that was not the main problem. What was swallowing almost everything they had was the expenses of the workshop.

Margaret's labour was essential to support the family. 'I hope you will not be quite shocked to find me resuming so soon my natural weapons of warfare', she wrote to Blackwood soon after the birth of Cyril. '... I find I cannot quite afford this year the luxury of keeping quiet'.[22] Their correspondence reveals that she was always in debt and offering articles or a new novel to clear it up. This worried her, for she had been brought up to be scrupulous about money, and every debt she ever contracted was eventually paid. But she was not a good manager as her mother had been. Throughout her life we find her spending more than she had got and protesting that she had 'never been extravagant'. John Blackwood disliked the situation but always lent her money when she needed. it.

It is not very surprising, in the circumstances, that none of the novels she produced during her married life was especially good. She was living through all kinds of intense experiences which she put to creative use later on, but while they were happening she had very little emotional energy to invest in her work. Her novel *The Athelings*, written before and after Cyril's birth, compares very badly with *Scenes of Clerical Life*, which was appearing in *Blackwood's Magazine* at the same time. When it came out in book form George Meredith reviewed it:

> We have to look through her three volumes again and again to discover how it is she can possibly have contrived to spin out dreary conversation to such an extent.... The Authoress is clever: she can describe society.... Her main fault has killed the most charmingly written books, and this lady has only to practise compression to become an excellent novelist.[23]

One evening in the early summer of 1857 she went out to the shops, leaving Frank with a close friend. When she came back it was clear that something unusual had happened, but the two men told her not to worry; Frank had only coughed up a little blood.

'And so', wrote Margaret, 'the happy time came to an end.'

After the first shock, she was not seriously worried. But it was soon clear to her that the stained-glass workshop was becoming too much for Frank. He got on very well with the men (not surprisingly since his father had been a glass-worker) but Margaret thought, rightly or wrongly, that they had no sympathy with his problems and could never be trusted to get the work done on time. She had been 'brought up with a high idea of the honour and virtue of working men', and was bitterly hurt. They decided, reluctantly, that he ought not to spend another winter in England and that they should get rid of the business within a year. Before they had made up their minds he went to see a specialist in Harley Street; Margaret waiting outside in a terrible state of suspense.

Frank came out smiling and said the report was excellent; he was suffering mainly from overwork and would be better once he got away. But later, in Rome, a friend told her that Frank had been warned in that interview that he was dying of tuberculosis, but had not had the courage to say so. Margaret could not believe that he would have deceived her, or dragged her overseas with the children if he had known he was not coming back. Perhaps, with his usual optimism, he simply did not believe it.

She had another baby that spring, but the child, Stephen Thomas, died on 28 May, aged nine weeks. Apparently the cause of death was a hole in the heart, and again Margaret must have wondered if it had been her fault. Two months later, on 29 July, her father died very suddenly at his son's home in Birkenhead. An inquest could find no obvious reason and decided that it had been 'the visitation of God'. Margaret evidently recalled the shock she had felt when, seven years later, she was writing *Miss Marjoribanks*. Possibly the old doctor in that novel, with his friendly but detached relationship with his daughter, owes something to the enigmatic figure of Francis Wilson.

One of Frank's last jobs in England was to make the chancel windows for St Mary's parish church in Aylesbury. They had all been paid for by local donors except one, which looked as if it would have to remain blank. He could not bear the thought of leaving his work unfinished and presented the window to the church as a gift. 'The reader will probably think that this was as ingenious a mode of doing away with the profits of that particular piece of work as could well be invented', Margaret commented, 'though to us it seemed the most natural and pleasant thing in the world.'[24] That was in August 1858. Today the windows are still in place, one of them with a Latin memorial to Frank.

They left England in January 1859, intending to go to Florence, of which they knew nothing except that it was warm. With Margaret now the sole breadwinner, John Blackwood had agreed to send her twenty pounds a month in return for articles. Travelling with them were Maggie and Cyril, aged five and two, and the nursemaid, Jane Hockey, a very big young woman with ox-like brown eyes. Over the next few years she was to be a tower of strength.

Tom Oliphant came with them as far as Paris and then turned back. 'It was my first experience of having to take the management of things myself, and all was new to me.' They went on a slow train to Lyons, keeping Frank warm with piles of coats and rugs, and then found that they had mislaid their luggage and run out of money. Everyone, though, was very kind to the helpless party. It was probably clear to most people that Frank was unlikely to get well.

They travelled next to Marseilles, sharing the train with groups of peasants in blouses going to draw their tickets for conscription, and then to Nice in a *diligence*. It was an uncomfortable journey, twenty-four hours over bumpy roads. Maggie slept sweetly in her mother's arms while Cyril kicked and cried. When they got to Nice the sun was shining and Margaret was delighted by the blue sea and the gardens of oranges. In the morning they met an Englishman who casually mentioned that the French had invaded Italy. They tried to get a *Times* to check the story, but failed to find one and decided to go on anyway.

As it happened they had chosen the worst possible time to go to Italy. Ever since the Napoleonic wars the country had been divided into several small states, with Austria dominating the north, the Papal States stretching across the centre, and the Kingdom of Naples and Sicily in the south. But the movement for unity had been building up for years, and Victor Emmanuel II of Sardinia, with the help of Louis Napoleon, was about to drive the Austrians out of Lombardy. This was the first war in western Europe for nearly half a century.

They heard more rumours of fighting as they travelled on through Alassio, Genoa, and by sea to Leghorn, arriving at Florence at night and in a thick fog. Margaret's first reaction was that it might have been Manchester rather than the sunny south. In the morning it was fine, but very cold; everyone in the streets seemed to be carrying little pans of hot charcoal. The spring flowers were already out but the hills were covered with snow. They found lodgings in the Via Maggio, a narrow street with tall houses where the rooms were freezing and quite unsuitable for an invalid. 'There is nothing but stone and marble, and universal chill.'[25] Margaret realised afterwards that, because of her inexperience, she had managed badly. She sat at one end of the room, forcing herself to write, while Frank crouched over the little stove, too depressed to speak. It did not exactly help that, almost every night, a funeral procession passed under their windows. Looking down, as if into a deep gorge, they could see bands of white-robed monks with blazing torches, chanting as they carried the corpse out of the town to be thrown into a common grave.

As the weather improved, they grew more cheerful. Florence was extremely cheap, and they could get a good meal from the *trattoria* almost every evening. Jane took the children to the Boboli gardens and brought them back carrying handfuls of anemones. Maggie was a beautiful child, with brown curly hair; Cyril, who called himself Tiddy, was a lively toddler, always singing and shouting. Their parents went out occasionally and met some of the English inhabitants. Margaret asked Blackwood to send her a copy of *Adam Bede*, the new novel by the anonymous author of *Scenes of Clerical Life*. Frank thought that Trollope might have written it; Margaret was sure that, whoever it was, it could not be a woman.

Frank went to the Pitti and Uffizi galleries and was 'profoundly, depressingly ... impressed by the pictures at first – and all the glory of them', realising that he could never now hope to paint masterpieces like that. Margaret used to wander into a small room where Albertinelli's huge picture, 'The Visitation', hung alone. It shows Mary, the mother of Jesus, embracing her cousin Elizabeth. The point is that both women are pregnant and by this time, April 1859, Margaret suspected that another baby was on the way.

Living as quietly as they did, they had had no idea that Florence was on the eve of a revolution. On 27 April they looked out of their second-floor window and saw an Italian tricolour unfurled on the house opposite. Suddenly everyone seemed to be rushing into the street, wearing green, white and red rosettes and shouting 'Viva l'Italia!' The two-year-old Cyril immediately began to shout too. Margaret, in a state of great excitement, persuaded her husband to come out and join the crowd in front of the Pitti Palace, where at that moment the Grand Duke of

Tuscany was negotiating with representatives of the people. Typically, she wanted to be in the middle of the revolution, but Frank was nervous and said that it was no business of theirs. What they were witnessing was the end of despotism in Florence. The province was taken under Victor Emmanuel's protection and became part of the kingdom of Italy in 1861.

In May they moved on to Rome, much against Margaret's will as she was afraid of the children catching the dreaded Roman fever. But Frank overruled her because he wanted to be near an artist friend, Robert Macpherson, and his wife, 'Geddie'. In the end the two couples became very close.

Gerardine Bate had met her husband when, as a teenager, she was travelling on the continent with her aunt, Anna Jameson, one of the first self-supporting literary women. Her family had opposed the marriage, as he was a Catholic convert, and it had not turned out very well. Robert had developed an eye problem and given up painting for photography, taking some of the 'first and finest'[26] photographs of Rome. Geddie was a pretty, charming woman with a Bohemian life-style – 'untidy, disorderly, fond of gaiety of every kind'. She and Margaret both quarrelled with Robert, who sided with the Pope against the nationalists, and every so often he would storm out of the house, pulling his red beard.

It was probably through them that Margaret met Robert and Elizabeth Browning, whom Geddie knew well. At this time the older woman was completely preoccupied with the liberation of Italy, and Margaret warmly sympathised. She sent Blackwood an article about the Florentine revolution, which he did not use. Liberal opinions were not welcome then or at any other time in the *Magazine*. Most of the English tourists had left Rome because of the 'distant echoes of French cannon',[27] and they decided to go with the Macphersons to Nettuno, a primitive little seaside town.

There were a few good days, when they went bathing or sat on the broom-covered cliffs while Frank sketched. Margaret was concerned, though, because Blackwood was not printing her articles. She begged him to take no notice of 'such crude opinions as I may have formed on the politics of the time . . . I shall be glad to return to miscellaneous literature'.[28] A little later she wrote, 'I feel extremely uneasy and troubled to think that while you have felt able to use so few of my papers I am under the necessity of continuing to ask you for money'.[29] At the end of June they moved on to a villa in Frascati, which offered a fine view over the Campagna. There were spectacular sunsets, 'in the vault of sky which covered in that melancholy waste with its specks of ruin',[30] and they could see the dome of St Peter's, 'the only sign of the existence of Rome'. When she went into the cathedral, Margaret was startled to find herself looking at the tomb of Bonnie Prince Charlie.

As the summer went on Frank grew visibly weaker. He was very thin, with great hollows around his eyes, and could not eat. On 1 October they returned to Rome and got an apartment in the Via Babuino. The city was 'mute with political tension; empty, for the most part, of English and American visitors'.[31] They called in a French specialist, who examined Frank and told Margaret that there was no hope. She went back to him in tears, thinking that he already knew, but found that he had not been told and 'it was I in my misery who was taking him the news'.

'Well, if it is so, that is no reason why we should be miserable', Frank said eventually. Margaret could not understand his calmness. And she wondered how it was that he could be standing, as she believed, on the threshold of eternity, without being at all altered in himself. Several times she came back to this theme in her novels:

> To see him so individual and characteristic, with all the notable features and even faults of his mind as distinct and apparent as if he had been in the strongest health, and yet so near the end, was the strangest spectacle. What was it the end of?[32]

She nursed him night and day, going about in a dazed state after the doctor had given her laudanum, often reading to him in the middle of the night, only occasionally leaving the room for a moment to cry. At one of these times Cyril 'came up and stood at my knee and pulled down my head to him, and smiled all over his beaming little face – smiled though the child wanted to cry too, but would not'.

Frank died on 20 October 1859, 'quite conscious, kissing me when his lips were already cold'. He was just forty-one. Afterwards Margaret's clearest memory was of Cyril in the next room singing a popular children's hymn, 'Oh that will be joyful, when we meet to part no more'.

The Macphersons did everything they could throughout this time. After Frank had been buried, in the English cemetery, there were more offers of help. John Blackwood told her to draw on him for as much money as she needed, and Henry Blackett offered to come out and bring her home. But Margaret could not leave Rome yet, as her baby was due in a few weeks. In everyone's mind was the thought that she might die and that the children would have to be taken back to England. After a while Frank's sister, Margaret Murdoch, the wife of an Edinburgh seal-engraver, came out to her.

Meanwhile she systematically set her affairs in order, writing to Blackwood:

> My debt to you is now very large. If I live I will repay as much as is possible in money ... and the rest in work with the least delay and the best skill I have. If on the other hand I should not live, enough will be left nearly if not altogether to discharge this.... In such a case late precedents make me hope that perhaps a pension might be got for my children.[33]

The baby, a boy, was born on 12 December. She named him Francis Romano, after his father and his place of birth.

3 The Salt and Bitter Waves (1860–65)

Margaret left Rome in February 1860 with Mrs Murdoch, Jane and the children. Maggie was six, Cyril three, and the baby two months. She also took the Macphersons' little boy, who was going home to England. It is very noticeable, at every stage of her life, how willing other people were to leave their children in her charge.

They went almost at once to Birkenhead to stay with her brother, Frank Wilson, at 13 Balls Road, Claughton. His hasty marriage to his cousin Jeanie had turned out surprisingly well and there were two children, Frank junior and Nelly, aged five and four. After the mild climate of Rome, Birkenhead felt like 'one of the windiest corners in all England',[1] and the visit was not a success. On one occasion Margaret picked up her book and inkstand and walked out of the family drawing-room so that she could do her work in peace. Her relations were quite offended. She had never hinted that she needed privacy before.

The real problem was that she was in no state to mix with happy people. She 'had learned the first hard lesson of grief, which is that it must not fatigue others with its eternal presence – that they who suffer most must be content often to suffer silently, and put on such smiles as are possible'.[2] When her brother came home from work and her children, as well as his, ran to meet him she was upset to see how quickly they had got over the loss of their own father. It is also possible, though she does not say so, that Frank or Jeanie made her feel unwelcome. In a novel written a few years later, *Madonna Mary*, she describes a woman whose husband has died abroad and who has come back to England 'with all those helpless children to be, most likely, a burden on her friends':

'If Mary had been a sensible girl, and had married a man who

> could make proper settlements upon her, and make a provision for his family, do you think she would have required to come here to seek a shelter?'

Mary's situation, as a young widow with no money and whose children are too little to understand her problems, is strikingly similar to Margaret's in those Birkenhead days. 'The others had all someone to consult, someone to refer to, but Mary was alone'.[3]

Quite apart from her grief, which was very bitter in the first year, she was anxious about the future. She owed debts of £1000, and had only an insurance of £200 on Frank's life, some furniture in a warehouse, and her professional skills, such as they were. John Blackwood remained kind, and tried unsuccessfully to get her a pension, but he printed only a few of her articles. In order to find work for her he suggested that she should translate Count Charles de Montalembert's book *Les Moines d'Occident*, a massive study of monastic orders in Europe which in the end came to seven volumes. She gladly accepted, although her French was not particularly good.

Now that there was no longer any reason to live in one place rather than another she hesitated about where to go after she left Birkenhead. However, in the summer she moved with Jane and the children to Elie, one of a string of fishing villages on the south coast of Fife, her mother's country. John Blackwood and his family were staying nearby and she saw a good deal of him, although they already had 'that curious kind of intimacy which is created by a publisher's knowledge of all one's affairs'. He had gone out of his way to help Margaret, and over the years she came to value him greatly as a friend and critic, but she could hardly forget that in the last resort their relationship was that of employer and employee. He had to tell her that Montalembert was displeased with her translation, and she agreed to take lessons to improve her French. 'I know it was nothing but a kind impulse which prompted you to give me this to do – the only thing that would really wound my pride would be the feeling that you had got an imperfect and unsatisfactory piece of work by employing me.'[4]

She had another project which interested her more deeply. Just before leaving England she had published an article on the charismatic Scottish preacher Edward Irving (1792–1834) which had led to the suggestion that she should write his biography.

She had not been able to work on it in Italy but now, as she wrote in the preface, 'I hoped to get personal consolation amid heavy troubles out of a life so full of great love, faith and sorrow.' During that summer in Scotland she began systematically collecting information.

Irving's name is unlikely to mean much to moderns; however, he made a deep impression on those who knew him personally, including Thomas and Jane Welsh Carlyle. He had begun his career as a schoolmaster in Haddington, where he tutored Jane Welsh and came very near to marrying her, although of course Margaret's book does not say so. After being ordained in the Church of Scotland he moved to London, where his dramatic oratory transformed a small and poor congregation into a large and rich one. But the Church accused him of heresy and in the end he was excommunicated. He also got involved with some strange individuals who claimed they could speak, like the apostles, in 'unknown tongues', and was removed from his pulpit for allowing them to interrupt services. He died soon after he had founded the Catholic Apostolic Church, which still had a fairly large following in 1860.

It is easy to see why his character appealed to Margaret. She admired him not because she agreed with him on all points but because he seemed to her a great man pulled down by bigots. Like Savonarola, of whom she also wrote with enthusiasm, Irving had wanted 'a higher style of Christianity, something more magnanimous, more heroical than this age affects'.[5] His generosity, affection for children and lack of self-interest were all qualities she could find in herself. Irving's career, as well as Willie's, influenced several of the novels which she wrote about clergymen in the next few years. At the same time she had little sympathy for the people who surrounded him ('If I had married Irving', Jane Carlyle said, 'the tongues would never have been heard.'[6]). The paradox was that Irving could not speak in tongues himself and believed that God had not found him worthy of it, but had been punished for defending those who could – and then been snubbed by the same people because he was no longer a priest. Margaret's later novels are rich in this kind of irony.

Her researches brought her several new friends. She was advised to visit Thomas Carlyle, and made a quick trip to London in the summer of 1860. Rather nervously, she called at

5 Cheyne Row where the great man received her kindly. He had been a close friend of Irving's when they were young, although he had become alienated from him on religious questions, but he told Margaret only that his wife knew more than he did. A few days later she was called to the door and 'found in a homely little brougham a lady with bright eyes and very hollow cheeks, who told me she had to be out in the open air for certain hours every day, and asked me to come and drive with her that we might talk about Irving'. They drove round the park for hours and found that they had much in common.

Jane Welsh Carlyle was nearly sixty at this time, 'but she was one of those women whom one never thinks of calling old; her hair was black without a grey hair in it'. What attracted Margaret at once was her strong resemblance, not in looks but in personality, to her own mother. She had grown up in East Lothian, where Mrs Wilson had lived for years, and she had the same 'wonderful talk ... flashes of keen wit and sarcasm, occasionally even a little sharpness', which Margaret had heard nowhere else. Probably she told her all about her romance with Irving. They met several more times before Margaret returned to Scotland.

She had decided to settle, at least for the time being, in Edinburgh. By October 1860, a year after Frank's death, she had moved into the ground floor and basement of 17 Fettes Row, on the fringes of the New Town. She had always liked this part of Edinburgh – 'the squares and crescents and connecting lines of streets in this quarter still form a city of palaces, ample and lofty houses in all the solidity of grey stone',[7] with its panoramic views of the sea and the Fife shore. It was not smart but there was a wide view of houses, waste land and sky. Maggie went to school while Jane and Margaret looked after the two little boys. The younger was beginning to be called Cecco (pronounced Chekko), the Italian diminutive of Francis. Perhaps extravagantly, she hired a cook and housemaid to live in.

In November she was visited by a young man of twenty-five, the Reverend Robert Herbert Story, who had just returned from Montreal to succeed his father as the minister at Rosneath. He had heard about her work and came to tell her that he had several of Irving's letters to his father. Having heard of her only as a successful author and a widow, he was not prepared for what he saw:

> A slight figure, draped in black; a very calm and gentle manner; a low and pleasant voice, marked with that homely Scottish accent which she never lost or wished to lose; a pair of the most delicate and beautiful hands I had ever seen; and such eyes as I had never looked into, large, intensely dark, and lambent, with a pure and steady flame. The upper part of her face, with these wonderful eyes, and crowned with what was then very dark brown hair, bore a singular resemblance to the Madonna di San Sisto. Indeed, 'Madonna Mia' was a name she was not unused to hear.[8]

Margaret saw a rather striking-looking young man with a distinct resemblance to the pictures of John Knox. He did not make the deep impression on her which she obviously did on him, but she agreed to come to Rosneath and read the letters soon.

The winter of 1860–61 was bitterly cold, even by Edinburgh standards. Margaret worked away at the Irving biography, the Montalembert translation, and a dreary novel, *The Last of the Mortimers*. On Sundays she went for a long walk across the town to see her Wilson cousins. George Wilson had died in 1859, only a month after Frank, and his mother, now in her seventies and very deaf, was living in a cottage on Blackford Road with her unmarried daughter Jessie. Margaret had always liked the amusing old lady, who in spite of many sorrows (she had survived eight of her eleven children) was still interested in everything that went on. She appears as Mrs Proctor in *The Rector*, one of the first *Chronicles of Carlingford*.

In February, reluctantly as she hated to leave her children, she visited Story and his mother in the manse at Rosneath. Perhaps the young man had urged her to come, rather than posting Irving's letters, because he was anxious to see more of her. However that may have been, she enjoyed herself much more than she had expected. The village is on a tiny peninsula, known locally as 'the island', between the Gareloch and Loch Long. 'I did not know anything about the West of Scotland, and, winter as it was, the lovely little loch was a revelation to me.' Story told her how in 1830 a local girl, Mary Campbell, had miraculously recovered from a near-fatal illness and had been the first person on the island to speak in 'tongues'. He also introduced her to an elderly neighbour, John Campbell of Row (1800–72), a friend of Irving's who had been excommunicated by the Church of Scotland for not believing in eternal damnation. He was a little shocked to find that Irving's biographer was quite a young woman and that she and Story, who had a 'witty and profane' tongue, kept laughing. Margaret said apologetically that 'a sort of convalescent as I was from such trouble and sorrow', she could not help being amused when she got into cheerful society, although she had 'honestly expected never to laugh again'.

The rest of the winter, though, was far from cheerful. Over the last two years the Blackwoods, who had published so much of her work during the 1850s, had clearly lost faith in her. They remained personally friendly, and used her articles when they were short of material, but during the early months of 1861, from February to May, they took none of her work. One day, probably in March, she went to their offices at 45 George Street to offer them a serial:

> They shook their heads: they were very kind, very unwilling to hurt the feelings of the poor young woman, with the heavy widow's veil hanging about her like a cloud. No; they did not think it was possible. I remember very well how they stood against the light, the Major tall and straight, John Blackwood with his shoulders hunched up in his more careless bearing, embarrassed and troubled by what they saw and no doubt guessed in my face, while on my part every faculty was absorbed in the desperate pride of a woman not to let them see me cry.[9]

George Street is at the top of a hill which runs steeply down through the New Town to Fettes Row. Margaret walked home, with the north-east wind blowing in her face, occasionally catching glimpses of the Forth and the blue hills of Fife. Years afterwards she remembered a street organ playing 'Charlie is my darling' as she passed. She was absolutely desperate. She must have wondered how she was going to support her small family if her talent was really drying up, as it seemed to be; whether she would be reduced to living off her relations, an idea that appalled her. When she got home the children ran to the door to meet her. She played with them for the rest of the day, then sat up all night and wrote a short story, 'The Executor', feeling that this was her last chance. It was accepted, and became the first of the once-famous Carlingford series.

From then on there were no more problems about getting her work in the *Magazine*. The Major died soon afterwards but John Blackwood had become convinced that she had a real talent for fiction. During the summer and autumn, the happiest she had known for a long time, she finished the Irving book and wrote two long short stories, *The Rector* and *The Doctor's Family*, which were published in *Blackwood's* under the general title of *Chronicles of Carlingford*. With these stories, for no obvious reason, she suddenly made the breakthrough from hack-work into literature.

Feeling greatly relieved, and very ready to enjoy herself, she took the children to Rosneath for the summer. During the last year she had made several close friends. Story was one of them; another was Blackwood's sister Isabella, a stout lady in her fifties who liked to remember the days when she had been called a sylph. She too was at Rosneath that summer, as were Principal John Tulloch of St Andrew's and his wife, the former Jane Anne Hindmarsh. Margaret had met them before, but it was only now that she got to know them well.

The Principal was an enormous man with tawny hair, inherited from his Scandinavian ancestors, and a 'big delightful spontaneous laugh'.[10] He had risen rapidly through a depleted Church of Scotland and at thirty-one, to his own great surprise, had become professor of theology at St Andrew's University and principal of the tiny St Mary's college. Like Story, he was a liberal Christian who wanted to get rid of the old shibboleths, like sabbatarianism and eternal damnation, and to bring the Church into line with modern thought. He could hardly have been accused of being too pious; when a friend postponed a game of golf several times in order to go to church the Principal remarked, 'It is quite clear that his brain is softening'.[11] He and his wife were a devoted couple with a large family – eventually three sons and seven daughters – and the two eldest girls, Sara and Fanny, became friends of Maggie's. Of Mrs Tulloch, whom Margaret called 'the padrona', she wrote long afterwards with deep emotion:

> I do not know whether I have been able to convey to the reader any just idea of the wonderful and beautiful character of this entirely unobtrusive and often unnoticed woman. Her

> self-forgetfulness and lifelong adoption of the part of caring for others were so complete ... 'Oh, what does it matter about me?' had been the half-impatient sentiment of her mind throughout her life.[12]

They were a very cheerful party, going on pleasant walking and boating trips and taking long drives in the rain. But Margaret and Mrs Tulloch felt older than the rest, 'in our maturity of motherhood and experience', and another bond was that Mrs Tulloch had lost two babies. One day they took their children for a picnic on a heathery upland with a view of the two lochs. There was a wonderful vista of mountains, sky and 'the dazzle of the great Clyde sweeping downwards towards Arran and the glowing west'. 'We talked, very likely, of our nurseries and the children's little ailments. Why not? These things were more to us than the movements of the spheres. We were two women together, with nobody to note whether we were silly or wise ... we were friends from that day.'[13]

The holiday was a turning-point for Margaret. 'I doubt if I had ever been so gay. I was still young, and all was well with the children. My heart had come up with a great bound from all the strains of previous trouble and hard labour and the valley of the shadow of death.'

Readers may well feel that Margaret recovered rather quickly from the loss of Frank. At the time of which she writes, 'I doubt if I had ever been so gay', he had been dead for less than two years. During those two years, though, she had been intensely miserable. She had reacted like any happily married woman to his illness and death – she was terrified about his bad health, determined to nurse him to the end, and probably felt that she only kept going afterwards for the children's sake. Yet before that time her feelings had been more complex. She had wanted her husband to be a great man, a Michelangelo or an Edward Irving, and it had been a painful shock to discover that he had faults. She knew perfectly well that it was dangerous to idealise anyone, and there was quite enough loyalty and affection to have kept the marriage going if Frank had not died. But gradually, as the first pain grew duller, she began to feel that there were some advantages in being in control of her own life. Frank had almost ruined the family by his financial carelessness. After mid-

1861, Margaret realised that she was managing fairly well. Her work was once again appearing regularly; she had several friends and, above all, there were the children. There was no complexity in her feelings for them; she quite simply loved them.

It has been suggested that Story fell in love with her at about this time and proposed marriage.[14] Neither of them ever said so, but it is perfectly possible. In 1861 Margaret was thirty-three and still very attractive, although over the next few years her hair turned quite grey. Some of her fiction shows that she could enter into the feelings of a young widow who is attracted to a man although she knows it is highly unsuitable.[15] During the happy summer at Rosneath she read the manuscript of Story's book – a biography of his father – and tried to get Blackwood to publish it. She had, she said, a 'maternal interest in the young man'[16] and his work. What happened may perhaps be guessed at from her novel *The Three Brothers*, written some years later. Mrs Severn, an artist's widow, is an obvious self-portrait. 'Everybody knew that she had been very fond of poor Severn ... and that she was very desolate when he was gone', but she has gradually grown happy – 'happy in her work, and her freedom, and her independence, and her children.'[17] When a younger man wants to marry her she tells him decisively that the children mean more to her than he does. The Victorians had a strong prejudice against the remarriage of widows and Margaret seems to have shared this. Whatever problems she had had with Frank, it was not possible for her to look on any other man as her husband.

She was seven years older than Story and considered him almost as a member of another generation. By this time her way of life was fixed and her character set. Her writing had changed drastically in the early 1860s; after years of producing very indifferent novels she was now doing work of distinction, and her personality had changed too. The rather naïve, romantic girl, with a simple religious faith, who had stood by helplessly while her mother and husband fought over her, disappears around this time; in her place we find a mature, sceptical and disenchanted woman. In another novel, *Madonna Mary*, she hints that she now saw herself primarily as a mother:

> Mary, in the calm and silence of her loneliness, felt herself put back as it were into history, along with Ruth and Rachel, and

> her own mother, and all the women whose lives had been and were over.[18]

In October she moved into a small house with a big garden at Cambridge Villas, Uxbridge Road, Ealing, to be near the publisher Henry Blackett and his wife Ellen. In those days Ealing was a small village some way from London. Soon afterwards John Blackwood agreed to serialise another Carlingford story. Margaret told him that she meant to write a full-length novel about Dissenters, 'hoping that no one will imagine me to be copying George Eliot'.[19]

In fact people were already beginning to link the two names. Blackwood, who had published all George Eliot's work so far and given her lavish encouragement in the days when she needed it, believed that Margaret might turn out to be an equally eminent author. She was 'a wonderfully clever little woman',[20] he wrote privately in January 1862. The following month, *Salem Chapel* began to appear in the *Magazine*. This was to become Margaret's best-known and most popular novel, though not for any good reason.

There were some wild speculations about the author's identity. The *Saturday Review* suggested George Eliot, much to her annoyance:

> I am NOT the author of 'The Chronicles of Carlingford'. They were written by Mrs Oliphant, author of 'Margaret Maitland' etc. ... I have not read 'The Chronicles of Carlingford' but from what Mr Lewes tells me, they must represent the Dissenters in a very different spirit from anything that has appeared in my books.[21]

Margaret reacted in a more relaxed way. 'A high compliment to me, no doubt; but women, you know, according to the best authorities, never admire each other, and ... the faintest idea of imitating or attempting to rival the author of 'Adam Bede' never entered my mind.'[22]

She was not herself convinced that *Salem* was a good novel. 'I need not repeat that I am much encouraged by your plaudits', she wrote to Blackwood, ' – it is however a marvel to me how or why I have done better than ordinary in this series of stories.'[23]

The Life of Edward Irving came out in April 1862. Margaret was rather nervous about this, her first biography, but on the whole the reviews were encouraging. Thomas Carlyle was particularly impressed and said that she was 'worth whole cartloads of Mulocks, and Brontës, and THINGS of that sort'.[24] Since the move she had become very friendly with him and his wife, though without endorsing his more bizarre opinions. She insisted, then and afterwards, that despite his public image Carlyle was personally the kindest of men. She read George MacDonald's *David Elginbrod* for Hurst and Blackett and strongly recommended publication; he, too, became a lifelong friend.

After the success of *Salem Chapel* Blackwood was keen to have another Carlingford novel about the clergy. This was *The Perpetual Curate*, which began to appear in 'Maga' in June 1863. He gave her £1500 for it, an enormous sum in those days. In fact, this was the most she ever got for a book.

However, what gave her the deepest satisfaction was not her career but the three children. Cyril and Cecco were both attractive little boys. But the child to whom she felt closest was Maggie, the firstborn, the only one who remembered her father, already 'a little mother in her way'. Unconsciously, she relied on her for help and emotional support. She was 'a bright, handsome, loving little girl',[25] a friend said. Margaret occasionally had poems published in *Blackwood's* (not especially good ones; she had no talent for poetry), and one of them, written when Maggie was ten, describes a sunny day when she was reading to the children on the lawn:

> Green grass beneath, green leaves above,
> That rustle like a running stream,
> And sunshine that with tender gleam
> Touches the little heads I love –
>
> The little heads, the dewy eyes,
> That shine and smile through sun and shower,
> That are my portion and my dower,
> My sum of wealth beneath the skies.
>
> The white doves flutter on the wall,
> Amid the rose-tree's crimson pride;
> The small house opes its windows wide,
> Fearless, whatever may befall.

Whate'er befalls – oh, instinct strong
Of this strange life, so sad and dear,
That still foresees some coming tear,
And of its joy still asks – how long?[26]

If any further trouble was on the way, she concluded, she was thankful not to know what it was.

During the spring of 1863 she had grown very worried about the Tullochs. The Principal, apparently the most sane and cheerful of men, had suddenly become dangerously depressed. It had been triggered off by some articles in an Edinburgh paper attacking his scholarship, although Margaret thought this was not the true cause. Depression was very little understood at the time, and perhaps she, with her buoyant temperament, was the last person to understand it. But there was no doubt about the Principal's extreme distress. He and his wife visited her at Ealing and they walked under the elm trees discussing his problem. The large, dignified-looking man was 'like a child in his abandonment and self-pity'.[27] Eventually he was told to stop work and it was arranged that he should go to Greece with his teenage son William and get a complete break.

Around the same time Geddie Macpherson came to stay. They had kept in touch after Frank's death, and a year or two earlier had found work for Willie, who was now living near them in Rome and helping Robert with the business side of the studio. It was Geddie's idea that Margaret should come back with her and see how he was getting on. Probably she told her friend that she ought to see Rome under happier circumstances. Between them they persuaded Mrs Tulloch to come with them and meet her husband on his way back. To finance the holiday, Margaret made a bargain with Alexander Macmillan for a Scottish novel, *A Son of the Soil*.

That summer Story became engaged to Miss Janet Leith Maughan, from a wealthy Edinburgh family, who, like Margaret, was seven years older than himself and a novelist. A lady with a very definite personality, she is said to have been the original of Miss Marjoribanks in the novel of that name.[28] Margaret may have been surprised, but she certainly was not upset.

The party left England at the end of November – Geddie, Mrs Tulloch with Sara and Fanny, and Margaret with Jane and the three children. They had a long but merry journey by train and steamboat, Margaret keeping her companions going in her usual lavish style with meat, wine and champagne. The children were all well and happy; the three women, all about the same age, thoroughly enjoyed themselves. When they arrived the Oliphants and Tullochs got a house at 68 Via di Capo le Case. The Italians were baffled by such a large female party. 'I am more than ever confirmed in my idea that men are a nuisance in travelling', Margaret wrote to her publisher, 'by the perfect and triumphant success of our journey.'[29]

Everything went smoothly for several weeks. Willie seemed to have settled happily and the Principal, when he joined them in December, was obviously much better. Margaret was the life and soul of the party, taking the children for little expeditions. She had got well ahead with both her novels, which were appearing simultaneously, *The Perpetual Curate* in *Blackwood's* and *A Son of the Soil* in *Macmillan's Magazine*.

The twenty-second of January was Mrs Tulloch's birthday, and that evening there was a party for the children.

The next day, Maggie went down with gastric fever. Her mother was alarmed, but at first not seriously. She did not leave any record of the next four days, except that the little girl did not know how ill she was. On 27 January 1864 Maggie died, aged ten years and eight months. Within a week of the party she was buried beside her father in the English cemetery.

'I had escaped, I thought, from the valley of the shadow of death, and had been happy, in sheer force of youth and health and the children', Margaret wrote afterwards, 'now I was plunged again under the salt and bitter waves.' Frank's death had at least been expected, and had been followed quickly by the birth of Cecco. But Maggie's death had been a total shock, and there would be no more children. For much of the rest of her life, and especially over the next few months, she tried to work out why it had been allowed to happen. Her Presbyterian upbringing had left her convinced that Christianity proved itself; she did not doubt the Principal when he told her that her child was in heaven. What she wanted to know was why she had been singled out from others for such exceptional suffering.

After the funeral Geddie took her to the villa in Frascati where she and Frank had stayed in the summer of 1859. They camped out in a huge cold room, which brought back horrible memories of that first journey to Italy. She had a great longing for Frank, as the one person who could have shared her misery. The boys were too little to understand, and her friends, distressed and considerate as they were, were not suffering in the same way. Their kindness only emphasised the fact that they would have spared her this blow, but God had not.

On 13 February the Principal wrote to Blackwood that Margaret would soon be sending him the next instalment of *The Perpetual Curate*. 'She goes on with her work which is perhaps the best thing she can do, but she continues in a very sad and unhappy state .... She cannot as yet see anything but what appears to her the bitter cruelty of the bereavement, and it will be long I fear till she regains anything of the comparative happiness she has enjoyed for a year or two.'[30] There was a month's break in the publication of her novels, but afterwards they went on appearing regularly. *The Perpetual Curate* had only a few more months to go, and was not changed drastically. But *A Son of the Soil*, which had begun as a novel about social mobility, abruptly became a novel about death. The work seems to have been therapeutic; this book, which mingles memories of Frank's last illness and vivid impressions of Italy with the fundamental questions she was asking about human suffering, was the most powerful she had written yet.

During the winter and spring, while she moved about with Mrs Tulloch and the children from Frascati to Albano and then to Naples and Capri, she made several jottings in her notebook. Deliberately left out when the *Autobiography* was published, they show that her bitterness against God went much deeper than she normally admitted:

> *Albano, March 13th.* I keep on always upbraiding and reproaching God – I can't help thinking of the question somebody once asked a grieving woman – Have you not yet forgiven God? – I feel like that myself .... How he sows children broadcast about the world – how they swarm untaught uncared for by the score in these Italian villages, living in beggary and wretchedness – Oh my Lord why didst thou grudge to me the one blossom of womankind that I thought my own .... I am neither better nor worse than my brother Frank who has never known a trouble in his family – I am neither better nor worse than my dear friend who is so much happier, so much more

> blessed than I, but I am smitten and they are spared – Why is it? – God has put upon me a great many things to do – Frank left me not only with my children to work for but with many encumbrances to clear off – and W. is entirely dependent both for his living and for such guidance as is possible upon me – I have been wilful and extravagant in many things but I have not shrunk from any of my duties – I have faced the burden and borne it and never tried to put off any part of it upon the shoulders of others – God help me – does this make me think that I had a right to demand from him that divine cordial of happiness which I have been enjoying for these years past, but which now he has deprived me of?[31]

Nevertheless, over the next few months she convinced herself that God had decided to take Maggie because, for some reason, this was best for the child. A review of Renan's *Life of Jesus* which she wrote later that year expresses the views which she held for the rest of her life. 'Christianity itself does not undertake to satisfy all the questions of the wistful spirit, but there is nothing else which makes any response at all out of the awful darkness in which, one time or other, every living soul loses some precious thing.' Agnosticism might appeal to 'the intellectual classes', but not to ordinary people, because it offered them no hope.[32]

But although in theory she might hope, her religion gave her very little actual comfort. 'Now in the innermost chamber of the heart', she wrote, 'which no man except a husband can enter and he but little I am alone.'[33]

Capri was particularly beautiful in the early spring. Oranges, lemons and figs grew everywhere; there were 'great green fresh vine-leaves bursting out of every patch of soil'. There were hardly any English visitors. Margaret made friends with the hunchbacked maidservant, with whom she felt an affinity, and noticed how it was mainly the old and poor who crowded into the churches. Across the bay they could see Vesuvius, which was unusually calm that year. 'The enchantment of those wonderful seas as blue as heaven, scarcely fretted by the great rocks, into all the crevices of which the little tideless waves played with a dazzling ripple, brought a certain calm even to the sick heart.'[34]

The party went back briefly to Rome, leaving it for the last time on 29 May. Not surprisingly, Margaret could never face it again. They spent the summer in Switzerland, and then the Tullochs went home, leaving Sara and Fanny with Margaret. They moved on to Paris and settled in a pleasant flat on the sunny side of the Champs-Elysées. 'It was at the height of the gaiety and prosperity of the Empire', and Napoleon and Eugénie drove past their windows daily. On New Year's Eve she wrote to John Blackwood:

> I cannot say much of myself except that I keep on living and working without having much interest in either, but my little boys are well which is the source of all blessing .... It is a long time now since we first knew each other, and I think I have lived out all my individual existence in those years, but still with so much heart as is left me I thank you for all your many kindnesses.[35]

She had finished *The Perpetual Curate* and *A Son of the Soil*, but at the beginning of 1865 was busy with two more novels. One was *Agnes*, which is semi-autobiographical, and in which she tried to write directly about Maggie's death. The other was a Carlingford story, *Miss Marjoribanks* (pronounced Marchbanks), for *Blackwood's Magazine*. John Blackwood was so impressed with the early chapters that he praised her work rather more than she was prepared for:

> Don't frighten me, please, about 'Miss Marjoribanks' [she wrote]. I will do the very best I can to content you, but you make me nervous when you talk about the first rank of novelists, etc.: nobody in the world cares whether I am in the first or sixth .... But all the same, I will do my best, only please recognise the difference a little between a man who can take the good of his reputation, if he has any, and a poor soul who is concerned about nothing except the most domestic and limited concerns.[36]

Few would suspect from reading *Miss Marjoribanks*, her finest comic novel, that it was written at a time of great grief. Her reputation was now so high that she got a flattering offer from the religious magazine *Good Words*, who suggested a thousand pounds for a novel. She was tempted, but first got Blackwood's permission, feeling that her connection with the *Magazine* was 'my sheet-anchor'.[37]

In Paris she met the Comte de Montalembert and agreed to translate the third volume of *The Monks of the West*. He was the leader of the more liberal French Catholics and his views were a strange mixture of progressive and anti-democratic sentiments. Margaret had become interested in Catholicism during her travels but found it odd that 'a man so acute and keenwitted can receive with such perfect simplicity so vast an array of fables'.[38]

From Rome the Macphersons sent reports that Willie had had his worst bout so far. This went on for several more years, with Margaret paying to keep him out of prison when necessary. When Robert heard that he was 'incapable at his lodging'[39] he usually sent the servant to confiscate his clothes so he could not go out. No one could understand where he got the money.

Between May and September they wandered through Brittany and Normandy, where they met Story and his new wife. By this time Margaret could speak passable French and knew a great deal about the civilisation of the country, and the little boys were practically bilingual. Although she was in no hurry to go back to England, she felt that she should do so soon for the sake of their education. Finally, at the end of September 1865, they crossed the Channel and took rooms in Kensington while Margaret looked around for a permanent home.

4 The Most Remarkable Woman of her Time

'While I cheerfully recognise that the imaginative force of Charlotte Brontë and George Eliot is in certain respects inimitable', wrote a critic in 1883, 'I am often inclined to maintain that Mrs Oliphant is the most remarkable woman of her time .... Each of these great romance writers concentrated all her faculties for months (I might say for years) upon a single work. Mrs Oliphant has never had leisure for this absorbing devotion, this almost fierce concentration .... Had Mrs Oliphant concentrated her powers, what might she not have done?'[1]

There is every reason to regret the fact that she only occasionally 'concentrated her powers'. As we have seen, Margaret got into the habit, very early in her career, of writing a book every few months and often two at once. Altogether she turned out ninety-two long and short novels; eight collections of stories and twenty-five works of non-fiction including the *Autobiography*. There were also literally hundreds of articles, most published in *Blackwood's* but some in other magazines. She was not, perhaps, the most prolific writer the world has ever seen, but she was much more prolific than any other Victorian with any claim to distinction. Trollope once claimed that he had written more novels than she had, but when they counted titles she was found to be far ahead. No one who wrote at that speed could work at a consistently high level. 'When people comment upon the number of books I have written', she noted, 'and I say that I am so far from being proud of that fact that I should like at least half of them forgotten, they stare – and yet it is quite true'. The really surprising thing is not that she produced a great deal of hack-work, but that so much is so good.

> One mistake which many of her critics make [wrote Howard Sturgis, who knew her in later life] is the supposition that her

> work at its best was injured by her immense productiveness. Her best work was of a very high order of merit. The harm that she did to her literary reputation seems rather the surrounding of her best with so much which she knew to be of inferior quality, that her high peaks of achievement, instead of rising out of the plain, as it were, suffer diminution by the neighbourhood of so many foothills.

He commented, 'I cannot help thinking that much grain will be left when Time has winnowed out the chaff'.[2]

One of the aims of this book is to separate the chaff from the grain, and I do not propose to spend much time on the inferior work which neither she nor anyone else took seriously. Most of her novels are entertaining stories, worth reading for addicts of Victorian fiction, but certainly not great works of art. A few are downright bad. There remain perhaps fifteen that seem to me worth reprinting, which does not mean that all of them are perfect. We find great differences of quality within, as well as between, her novels. Many of them have been overstretched to fill three volumes; her shorter works (*The Doctor's Family*, *The Curate in Charge*, *A Beleaguered City*) are often among her best. Others (*The Wizard's Son*, *A Poor Gentleman*) begin well, but 'there comes a lapse of mood; the situations flag, the aim of the book becomes hazy and uncertain'.[3] But even in a weak novel there is often a page or paragraph where the writing suddenly comes to life. Margaret was well aware of this and in her great autobiographical story, 'Mr Sandford', shows an artist reflecting on the unevenness of his work:

> It stood out upon the picture like something by another hand, painted in another age. Had he done that only an hour ago – he with the same brushes that had produced the rest of the picture which looked so pale and insignificant beside it? How had he done it? it made all the rest of the picture fade.

After reading the life of George Eliot Margaret wondered whether she would have been a better writer if, like her, she had been protected from normal stress and strain. She had never had 'a room of her own' and had always been expected to stop working when the family needed her. It was impossible not to feel that 'the men who have no wives, who have given themselves up to their art, have had an almost unfair advantage over us'. The conditions of the market were against her too. She felt compelled to write a great deal of the sort of fiction which she despised and which did not come naturally to her, but which the public was eager to read. Love stories were particularly uncongenial to her, and her young lovers are almost invariably boring. 'I have learned to take perhaps more a man's view of mortal affairs', she wrote, 'to feel that the love between men and women, the marrying and giving in marriage, occupy in fact so small a portion of either existence or thought.' In one of the last things she wrote, she confessed that she had often begun a book determined to 'kill or part' the lovers, but that public opinion would not let her. She also praised the youthful Kipling for his 'perception of life as something more than love-making'.[4]

This was one kind of novel which she often wrote without being deeply committed to it. Another was the sensation novel, which became extremely popular in the 1860s after the appearance of Miss Braddon's *Lady Audley's Secret* and Wilkie Collins' *The Woman in White*. She admired the latter very much, calling it 'a marvel of workmanship'.[5] But when she tried to write melodrama herself, as she did in two of her Carlingford novels, it fell flat. Dozens of her works employ the stock ingredients of the popular novel – long-lost heirs, unjust wills, mystery and murder – and this is always a weakness. The reason is that, although she wrote a famous series of supernatural stories, she was essentially a realist.

Margaret Wilson had grown up seeing life in glaring black and white. Her childhood heroes had been the Covenanters and the men of the Disruption who, as she saw it, had sacrificed their homes and jobs for a principle. Her teenage novel, *Christian Melville*, presents a cliché-ridden world of absolute good and evil, in which the existence of God is taken for granted and only the bad have 'doubts'. At some stage, though, this 'visionary girl', as she called herself, realised that she had been over-simplifying, and her mature novels are set in the 'sphere of mental and moral complication in which most of us have our home'.[6] Her best work is faintly disillusioned, though not cynical. She continued to believe in objective standards of good and evil, and she remained all her life a slightly unorthodox Christian. But she did not believe in Providence, in the sense of a power which handed out rewards for good conduct. 'The good and weak die and suffer', observed a critic, 'and the bad and strong get on, as far as this life is concerned, pretty well .... She has, as the reader of any work of hers might be aware, no very conventional feelings or sentiments'.[7]

This is illustrated by a late and good novel, *Old Mr Tredgold* (1896). Mr Tredgold is a selfish old plutocrat who has two daughters, Katherine and Stella. Katherine is older, plainer and much less attractive than her sister, who ruthlessly grabs everything she wants. After she has run away to get married Katherine spends the best years of her life nursing her unpleasant father because she thinks it is her duty. Although well aware that he does not care for her, she assumes she will inherit his money and makes affectionate plans to share it with her sister. But in fact Stella gets all the money and refuses to give up any of it. It is natural that 'everything that was pleasant and amusing and extravagant and brilliant' should go to Stella (30), while Katherine is 'the unlucky one, the one always left in the cold shade' (37). The inequality of rewards, and the contrast between givers and takers, are themes which dominate Margaret Oliphant's work.

Characteristically, this novel has a sting in its tail. Katherine has an admirer who has gone to India, and the reader assumes she will marry him. But it turns out that he has been married briefly to another woman who died and has a child. Katherine is hurt, although she knows this is unreasonable, and in the end it is not clear what will happen to her.

In fact the author disliked ending her novels in the traditional way, with a marriage. Sometimes they end with the break-up of a marriage (*A Country Gentleman and his Family*), or an imperfect marriage (*A Son of the Soil*), or no marriage (*Kirsteen*). She always, when she could, avoided the stock situation. 'Most people had expected a tragic scene of remorse' when old Mr Tredgold dies (31), but given the character of the man it does not happen. Her best work, though not all her work, is remarkably free from the clichés which even the greatest Victorian novelists used.

It was an age, as J. I. M. Stewart has said, 'when an element of sentimental effusion was a matter, almost, of public comportment .... The novelists, feeling their way to the elevating of fiction among the higher forms of literature, are as a body lavish in sententious utterance – no doubt to an extent which offends modern taste'. He points out that an anthology of George

Eliot's 'wise, witty and tender sayings' was printed with her approval.[8] Margaret Oliphant's great contemporary was indeed very sententious and very sentimental when she felt like it. Margaret herself went to the opposite extreme. She had a habit, most unusual among English novelists at the time, of bringing complicated and disturbing feelings to the surface. In the first chapter of *Miss Marjoribanks*, for instance, the Doctor has none of the expected reactions when his 'faded helpless' wife dies:

> The widower was tearless, indeed, but not from excess of emotion. On the contrary, a painful heaviness possessed him when he became aware how little real sorrow was in his mind, and how small an actual loss was this loss of his wife .... It was even sad, in another point of view, to think of a human creature passing out of the world, and leaving so little trace that she had ever been there. As for the pretty creature whom Dr Marjoribanks had married, she had vanished into thin air years and years ago.

He insists on behaving normally after the funeral and is irritated when his daughter assumes a grief which she does not feel. While the author is concerned to show people's real emotions, rather than those they think they ought to have, she is not being cheaply mocking about death. One of her great strengths was her ability to write ironically about serious subjects without devaluing them. Her domestic novels are not at all 'Victorian'; they belong instead to the tradition of her countrywoman, Susan Ferrier, and of Jane Austen. Writing about the latter novelist in 1870, Margaret paid tribute to her 'fine vein of feminine cynicism':

> It is something altogether different from the rude and brutal male quality that bears the same name. It is the soft and silent disbelief of a spectator who has to look at a great many things without showing any outward discomposure, and who has learned to give up any moral classification of social sins, and to place them instead on the level of absurdities. She is not surprised or offended, much less horror-stricken or indignant, when her people show vulgar or mean traits of character, when they make it evident how selfish and self-absorbed they are, or even when they fall into those social cruelties which selfish and stupid people are so often guilty of, not without intention,

but yet without the power of realising half the pain they inflict . . . . This position of mind is essentially feminine.[9]

Like Jane Austen, she did not so much draw attention to people's faults as allow them to reveal themselves through their conversation and the small details of everyday behaviour, as below:

> This sentence was concluded by some weeping, of which, however, Nettie did not take any notice. Making mourning by lamp-light is hard work, as all poor seamstresses know. Nettie had no tears in the eyes that were fixed intently upon the little coat which was to complete Freddy's outfit; and she did not even look up from that urgent occupation to deprecate Susan's tears.
>
> 'I tell you, Nettie, I never could bear this place', said Mrs Fred; 'and now, whenever I move, the dreadful thoughts that come into my mind are enough to kill me. You always were strong from a baby, and of course it is not to be expected that you can understand what my feelings are. And Mrs Smith is anything but kind, or indeed civil, sometimes; and I don't think I could live through another of these cold English winters. I am sure I never could keep alive through another winter, now my poor Fred's gone.'
>
> 'Well?' asked Nettie, with involuntary harshness in her voice.
>
> 'I don't care for myself', sobbed Mrs Fred, 'but it's dreadful to see you so unfeeling, and to think what would become of his poor children if anything were to happen to me. I do believe you would marry Edward Rider if it were not for me, and go and wrong the poor children, and leave them destitute. Nobody has the feeling for them that a mother has; but if I live another winter in England, I know I shall die.'
>
> 'You have thought of dying a great many times', said Nettie, 'but it has never come to anything. Never mind that just now. What do you want?'[10]

If we have read *The Doctor's Family* we already know that Susan is incapable of looking after her children and has practically forced her sister to do so. But it is clear enough from this conversation that one of them is doing all the work and the other, while complaining about her poor husband and poor children, is thinking mainly of herself – and incidentally is determined not to let her sister get married. People who take responsibility seem harsh because they have little time to indulge their feelings. Indeed the word 'feelings' is used rather contemptuously because it implies a refuge from duties – 'Who was to take charge of the children, and conduct those vulgar affairs for which Susan's feelings disqualified her?'[11] This is the type of humour, 'just touching a subject and leaving it',[12] which she considered essentially Scottish.

These novels, like Jane Austen's, can be appreciated on many levels. Her style is always clear, vivid and comprehensible; years of writing for a middlebrow audience had given her a respect for the reader which we do not find in some other novelists, like Henry James, who describe complex states of mind. But in other ways she is very different from Jane Austen. She had a much greater knowledge of male characters, and her novels deal less with etiquette (who dances with whom? which chain to wear at a ball?) and more with fundamental human problems (who is to look after a destitute family? how to react when someone dies?). Jane Austen, as every reader knows, wrote virtually perfect novels about a small segment of human experience. Margaret Oliphant's range is far wider, and her novels are seldom perfect. They deal with subjects like cruelty, including sexual cruelty, and fundamental doubt about the laws of the universe. Austen characters are ultimately all right if they keep the rules; in an Oliphant novel there is no such certainty.

We have seen that she called the art of Jane Austen 'essentially feminine', and the same thing has sometimes been said of her own work, although we should note that she was interested in many things apart from women's problems. 'She approached every subject from a woman's point of view', wrote a friend, 'believing and professing that a woman's estimate of life is generally to be preferred to a man's.'[13] Henry James also accused her of having a 'woman's' approach to her work:

> 'The poor soul had a simply *feminine* conception of literature: such slipshod, imperfect, halting, faltering, peeping, down-at-heel work – buffeting along like a ragged creature in a high wind, and just struggling to the goal, and falling in a quivering mass of faintness and fatuity. Yes, no doubt she was

> a gallant woman – though with no species of wisdom – but an artist, an artist!' He held his hands up and stared woefully at me.[14]

Readers will have to decide for themselves whether they think this is a fair description of her style; the point to note is that James confidently uses the word 'feminine' as a term of abuse. Margaret was quite aware that many men treated women with a mixture of aggression and condescension, and her own attitude to them was not flattering. The 1883 critic wrote that 'she treats the male sex, it must be admitted, with habitual tolerant good-humoured contempt'. Some of the men in her novels are domestic tyrants who use brute violence against the women in their power (*The Ladies Lindores, Kirsteen*). Others are weak creatures who have to be looked after by some hard-working wife or daughter (*Agnes, The Curate in Charge*). In *A Rose in June* (1874), which fizzles out after a brilliant opening, there is a refined vicar who talks pleasantly about 'the beauty of repose' while his 'rather commonplace' wife keeps the home together. 'It stands to reason that when a man must not be disturbed about bills, for example, his wife must be, and doubly; when a man cannot bear the noise of children, his wife must, and doubly .... Mr Damerel's delightful and unbroken serenity had an irritating effect on his wife, in addition to the effects produced by her burden of care.'[15]

This type of man generally believes that all women want to be married, and that they cease to be interesting when they are no longer young and pretty. The popular novel at this time assumed much the same thing. Heroines, as Margaret wrote in 1855, were 'a sadly featureless class of well-intentioned young women'.[16] They were young, beautiful, well-behaved, had no intellectual interests, and almost invariably got married on the last page. 'Strong-minded' women, 'blue-stockings', and old maids were treated as figures of fun. Margaret Oliphant's serious novels query all these assumptions. She had a respect for spinsters, based on those she had known in Scotland – 'middle-aged ladies, of the class to which Scotch society owes so much, the rural single woman, individual and strong-minded'.[17] In one of her best novels, *Kirsteen*, the heroine remains single, but achieves more than her married sisters and is a better person morally. She also sympathised and identified with older women (often pointing out that women in their thirties were not, in fact, old).

She was interested in married women and widows and their feelings for husbands and children. Most of the great women writers of her generation were childless, and in some ways this was an obvious advantage. Margaret, who had 'all the usual experiences of woman', found that this caused several problems, but in other ways, perhaps, it helped.

EARLY NOVELS

Margaret's interest in the woman who does not marry dated from very early. *Christian Melville*, the novel written when she was sixteen, is about a woman destined to be not a bride but a maiden aunt. Margaret Maitland, in the novel of that name, is a middle-aged spinster who is more interested in the love affairs of the young people around her than in any possible marriage for herself. Indeed she turns down a proposal from a man who is astonished that she does not snap him up.

'Most artistically nice', as the *Athenaeum* noted, 'is the author's avoidance of all exaggeration in the sayings and doings of the character.'[18] Both this reviewer and Lord Jeffrey noted its resemblance to Galt's *Annals of the Parish*, although naturally the twenty-year-old author could not produce anything like so fine a book. It is a story of unpretentious Scottish people whose language has been deeply coloured by the Bible and who lead quiet lives apart from one great event, the Disruption. At this time Margaret still took the theology of the Free Church for granted. She had no respect for those who stayed with the Establishment, and assumed that the singing of 'ungodly songs' on Sunday was a serious sin. Much later, she wrote:

> I cannot think why the book succeeded so well. When I read it over some years after, I felt nothing but shame at its foolish little polemics and opinions. I suppose there must have been some breath of youth and sincerity in it which touched people, and there had been no Scotch stories for a long time.

Although she had moved to England as a child and wrote several novels without a Scottish dimension, she never lost her identity as a Scottish writer. Like Lewis Grassic Gibbon in the next century, she lived in England while visiting Scotland frequently and wrote both 'English' and 'Scottish' fiction, and she believed throughout her life that there were few poets as good as Burns and no novelist as good as Scott. Her next important novel, *Katie Stewart* (1853) is a Fife story. For a young woman of twenty-three, it is rather a remarkable book.

'Want of incident I am afraid must always be a fault of mine', she wrote apologetically to Blackwood, but she assured him that the story was 'strictly and simply true'.[19] No doubt she used her imagination, but she refused to falsify the facts as she knew them, stressing, rather against the publisher's will, that Katie and her family had not welcomed the 1745 rebellion:

> 'He's maybe no a' that folk could desire, this king' [says Katie's mother] 'but he's a decent man, sae far as I can hear, and onyway, he's better than a Papish. Onything's better than a Papish. And you think the Chevalier wouldna have sanctioned a press gang? It's a' you ken: he would have sanctioned muckle waur, be you sure. Popery wi' its coloured vestments, no to speak of profane music in the kirk on Sabbath days, and prayers read out of a book, and the thumbikins and the rack in the Castle of Edinburgh, and martyrs in the Grassmarket. Eh, lassie, ye dinna ken ye're born!' (22)

Here, as elsewhere, she could write Scottish dialect which the English reader can enjoy without difficulty. Mrs Stewart is exaggerating what would happen if the Chevalier won but 'it would only be after many a man was killed' (9). Like Scott in *Waverley*, she feels that romance is no substitute for the sober virtues. Her sympathy is not for Charles Edward but for the hard-working sailors and land-dwellers of Fife whose lives are affected by events outside their control.

The story has some striking resemblances to Elizabeth Gaskell's *Sylvia's Lovers*, published ten years later. There are the same graphic descriptions of the press-gang's attack on a peaceful community and their resentment. In both books the heroine is a vain girl who grows up when her lover is taken by the press-gang, and in each case he comes back years later as a naval officer. As *Katie* was first published in the widely read *Blackwood's Magazine*, Mrs Gaskell may well have seen it.

Katie Stewart cannot stand comparison with *Sylvia's Lovers*, but it is much the best of Margaret's early books. There is a happy atmosphere (it was written during her engagement) which disappears after she had moved into the 'sphere of mental and moral complication'. Although the moral is that the light-hearted Katie has to learn the mature virtues of loyalty and endurance, it is still optimistic. 'When ye gang owre the green in the morning, Katie, mony's the gowan [daisy] ye set your bit foot upon, but the minute the footstep's past, up comes the gowan's head as blithe as ever, and naebody's the waur' (22).

The other novels of the 1850s do not deserve much attention. We can recognise the figures of her parents and Willie if we read them; several are about a much-loved son and brother who goes astray. Others (*The Quiet Heart* and *The Days of My Life*) reflect her early conflicts with Frank. Her 'conditions of England' novels have been mentioned; she also tried historical fiction (*Caleb Field*, *Magdalen Hepburn*) and conventional plots with a missing will (*Zaidee*). In this novel, written in 1855, there is a great deal of artificial sentiment – 'The pure blood came to her cheek in maidenly acknowledgement of her affianced bridegroom's name' (6). But there is some sharp observation too – 'Her face composed to that solemnity with which people bear the misfortunes of others' (31).

The last sentence, not the first, is typical of her mature style. Some novels of the late 1850s – *The Laird of Norlaw*, *Orphans*, *Lucy Crofton* – have stray gleams of insight and irony, but she wrote nothing memorable before the *Chronicles of Carlingford*, which are discussed in the next chapter, and *A Son of the Soil*.

A Son of the Soil, although it has some rough edges, was the most powerful full-length novel which Margaret had produced so far. It brings together several of her preoccupations – social mobility, the cultural differences between England and Scotland, the relevance or otherwise of religion, altruism versus egotism and the meaning of pain and death.

The book was planned, as we have seen, in the summer of 1863 when she was staying on a farm near Rosneath. The early chapters evoke the landscape – which is beautiful but spoiled for some visitors by the 'soft-falling incessant' rain – and build up a contrast between Colin Campbell, the farmer's son who is to be the hero, and his natural enemy, Harry Frankland, a brash Eton schoolboy who calls his father Sir Thomas and is only there to shoot grouse:

> 'I say, you boy, it always rains here, doesn't it? .... I'll be glad to dry my boots if you'll let me', he said, holding up a foot which beside young Colin's sturdy hoof looked preternaturally small and dainty ... (1)

Getting one's feet wet is, of course, a parable. The inhabitants ('aborigines', as the English boy calls them) take a certain amount of discomfort for granted: 'If you're fond of the hills you'll get reconciled to the rain'. Harry can expect to have everything done for him while Colin's parents can only just afford to send him to Glasgow University, where he will be expected to work hard and live frugally:

> He, trudging heavily over the muddy, lengthy road; the other, flying along in that dainty, little, bird-like boat, with those white wings of sail .... Why should one boy have such a wonderful advantage over another? (3)

However, when a storm blows up and Harry falls in the loch Colin pulls him out. This does not make the boys like each other any better, and their rivalry looks certain to be a major theme in the novel. The author points out that the local people have certain prejudices and limitations, like Sabbatarianism. But it is very clear that while the English visitors feel superior to their hosts the Campbells have the moral advantage. The farm, where 'everything was for use and nothing for show' (14), represents something of great value, as we see early on when Colin's mother is settling her baby for the night:

> The red firelight made harmless glimmers all over her figure, catching now and then a sidelong glance out of her eyes as she smoothed the little pillow, and laid the tiny coverlet over the small unconscious creature wrapt closely in webs and bands of sleep. When she had done, she still knelt watching it as mothers will, with a smile upon her face. After a while the beaming soft dark eyes turned to the light with a natural attraction, to the glimmers of the fire shooting accidental rays into all the corners, and to the steady little candle on the mantel-shelf. The mistress looked round on all the familiar objects of the homely low-roofed chamber. Outside, the rain fell heavily still upon the damp and sodden country, soaking

> silently in the dark into the forlorn wheat-sheaves, which had been standing in the fields to dry in ineffectual hopelessness for past weeks .... The Holy Loch gleamed like a kind of twilight spot in the darkness, and the house of Ramore stood shut up and hushed, no light at all to be seen but that from the open door, which the farmer suddenly extinguished as he came in. But when that solitary light died out from the invisible hillside, and the darkness and the rain and the whispering night took undisturbed possession, was just the moment when the mother within, kneeling over her cradle in the firelight, was surprised by that sudden conscious touch of happiness... (2)

There is no doubt about the importance of certain things, like crops and children, but we are always conscious that they are under threat from the darkness outside. The baby dies, emphasising that any amount of care and love can be, apparently, wasted. As the darkness suggests a menace, so the rainbows, shifting skies and gleams of sunshine over the loch suggest limitless possibilities. In the beginning Colin is convinced that he can do anything; gradually his perceptions change and he has to be satisfied to do what small amount of good he can.

'The changes that have come to pass within the recollection of the living generation', we are told, 'are almost as great though very different from those which made Scotland during last century so picturesque in its state of transition.' (3) Since the Disruption people no longer worship in the same place but can choose between Kirk, Free Church and 'English Chapel' – 'the reign of opinion and liking was established in the once primitive community'. Colin, who is destined, unenthusiastically at first, to be a minister in the Kirk, is aware that very few things can be taken for granted; none of his friends believe, for instance, that the earth was created in six days. Later he visits an English church and finds the prayers 'all but divine in their comprehension of the wants of humanity', but is amused to hear the curate preach 'how sweet it was to recollect that this was the day which had been appointed the Twentieth Sunday after Trinity' (14). Similarly he is not impressed by the ritualism of the Catholic church in Italy, but is struck to find that, for ordinary people, religion is 'absolutely a part of their daily existence' (31). It helps if the modern reader knows something about the differences between the churches which seemed so important to many Victorians; however, for Margaret, the question was not which church was the true one, but whether it was possible to believe at all.

Colin finds himself posed uneasily between his family (he feels he is too good to work with his father and brothers on the farm) and the Frankland circle, who 'knew about as much of Scotland as if it had lain in the South Seas', and no more consider him one of themselves than 'a New Zealand chief' (15). He is aware that there is no future in the Church of Scotland for an ambitious young man. But although he has enough male aggression to make him convincing, he is basically an idealist, 'To get through life easily and secure as much pleasure as possible was not the theory of existence known at Ramore .... He had something to do in his own country, in his own generation.' (16)

How the novel would have developed from here we do not know, because, after only a third had been written, Maggie died. And this transformed it; in the central and most powerful section the author is obviously struggling to come to terms with her own grief. Colin saves Harry's life for a second time (which is an artistic flaw, of course) and is badly injured:

> But as Colin lay helpless, stunned by this unlooked-for downfall, there came before his eyes, as vividly as if he saw them in actual presence, the sick people of his native district – the young men and the young women who now and then paid, even on the sweet shores of the Holy Loch, the terrible toll which consumption takes of all the nations of the north. One of them, a young man about his own age, who like himself had been in training for the Scotch Church, whom Colin had pitied with all his kind heart – with the deepest half-remorseful sense of his own superior happiness – came before him with intense distinctness .... He could almost have thought that he saw the spectral attenuated form, with its hectic cheeks, its thin, long, wasted hands, its preternatural length of limb, seated in the old, high-backed easy-chair in the farmhouse parlour. All the invalid's life appeared to him in a sudden flash of recollection; the kindly neighbours' visits; the books and papers which were lent him; the soup and jellies which the minister's wife and the other ladies of the parish ... kept him provided with. Colin could even remember his own

> periodical visits; his efforts to think what would interest the sick man; his pity, and wonder, and almost contempt, for the patience which could endure, and even take a pleasure in, the poor comforts of the fading life. God help him! was this what he himself was coming to? (19)

There is a vast difference between this kind of writing and that which she had been producing only three years earlier. Suffering seems to have 'concentrated her powers' and given her an intensely clear vision of what did and did not matter. Colin's mother, who significantly has lost her only daughter, is forced, like him, to ask some agonising questions. 'God had His reasons, but what were they? The agony of loss, in which there seemed no possible gain; the bitterness of suffering, without knowing any reason for it, overpowered her. The contrast of her own trouble with the happiness, the full possession, the universal prosperity and comfort which she saw, struck her sharply with something which was not envy of her neighbour, but the appeal of an amazed anguish to God.' (20)

Margaret does not attempt to justify God's actions, but she does, perhaps, suggest some of the answers. Somebody asks 'why Harry, who was good for nothing in particular, should have been saved, and Colin ... should have been the sufferer'. The reason is 'because of his own nature, which would not permit him to see another perish' (20). This is one of her central themes. It is inevitable, in her scheme of things, that certain people will feel obliged to help others. But goodness has to be its own reward; they must not expect God to intervene in their favour, and the weak people whom they help are unlikely to be particularly grateful.

This awareness makes the book very funny on the minor problems of the situation. 'The entire household was possessed by sensations utterly unlike those which it ought to have felt.' (24) Harry is 'sore and resentful', not 'grateful and affectionate'. His mother, who has been 'used to be petted and tended all her life', inadvertently makes it clear that she cannot be expected to be as distressed about Colin as his own family. This is not depravity, just a 'natural human appreciation of her own concerns, and unconscious, unintentional indifference to those of others' (21).

The rest of the story is told in much the same spirit; deep

feeling without the sentimentality which we find, for example, in the novels of Dinah Mulock. Colin eventually gets better, but when he goes to Italy to convalesce he meets a young man, Arthur Meredith, who is dying of tuberculosis. Meredith is an intense evangelical Christian who thinks he has a mission to save others and embarrasses everyone he meets by talking about religion. As he realises himself, his faith does not make him a saintly character:

> His thoughts were fixed on eternity, as he said and believed; but his body was profoundly sensitive to all the little annoyances of time. The light touch of his sister's foot on the floor seemed to send a cruel vibration through him, and he glanced round at her with a momentary glance of anger... (26)

He wants to set an example of how a Christian ought to die, but, like Nikolai in the yet-to-be-written *Anna Karenina*, he cannot die at what seems the most appropriate time. 'Few human creatures are strong enough, except in books, to march thus solemnly and statelily to the edge of the grave .... The last event itself was twenty-four hours later than the anxious watchers expected it to be, and wore them all out more utterly than any previous part of the patient's lingering illness .... The dying man dozed a little, and woke again less dignified and composed .... That death so clear and conscious, for which he had hoped, was not granted to him; and, when at last the deliverance came, even Alice, on her knees by the bedside, felt in her desolation a moment's relief.' (35) It is difficult to imagine any other English novelist of the time writing about death in this way.

Colin stays with Meredith to the end and will not write him off as a fanatic, but he is not able to give the same 'confident explanation of God's dealings'. (32) The one thing he is sure of is that God is a compassionate father, not a judge. The rest of the novel is as unconventional as what went before. Colin drifts into an engagement with Meredith's sister, Alice, because she is abroad with no one to protect her. She is a typical Victorian heroine – meek, gentle, and a thoroughly good person, but, the author suggests, she is also rather boring. She is 'unaccustomed to think or act for herself' (38) and, significantly, is over-concerned with the forms of religion, worrying when Colin reads the wrong lesson for the day. He is 'not the kind of man who can propose to himself to form his wife's mind, and rule her thoughts' (48), and is secretly rather relieved when her father takes her away.

Over the next few years Colin decides that he still wants to be a minister, although there are hints that he might have achieved distinction in some other sphere. 'Like other fervent young men, an eager discontent with everything he saw lay at the bottom of his imaginations; and it was the development of Christianity – "more chivalrous, more magnanimous, than that of modern times" – that he thought of.' (42) Naturally he will not achieve this but will have to put up with an ultra-critical Scottish congregation. He will also have to accept a less than ideal marriage. Meeting Alice accidentally after several years he finds her ill and miserable. 'She had seen nobody and done nothing during that dreary interval .... He seemed to find her exactly where he had left her, though with the sense of having himself travelled to an unutterable distance in the meantime.' (50) Reluctantly, he decides to marry her, although he is aware that this is not very sensible. 'He could conduct himself only according to his own nature; and this is all that there is to say.' (52)

Typically, the author refuses to provide either a happy or a tragic ending. Instead, as in *Middlemarch*, the central character has to adjust his 'ridiculous impossible ideal' to the demands of common life. Colin's wife will never completely understand him, but he will be 'as happy as most people are'. (53) But the novel has a deeper theme than the conventional one of lost illusions; it is that certain people are distinguished from their fellows by their habit of accepting responsibility. Colin is a natural priest not because he is a very orthodox Christian but because he sacrifices himself for others:

> 'I should like to do a priest's duty' [he says to the strongly Protestant Meredith] '... I believe in priests inferior – priests who need be nothing more than men...' (34)

Women cannot be priests, of course, and indeed it is argued (in Chapter 38) that at certain times a woman can get more help from another woman than from the clergyman. But in a great many cases they have to sacrifice themselves, and this is the theme of a novel written soon afterwards, *Agnes*.

Agnes was written a year after Maggie's death, around the same time as the brilliant *Miss Marjoribanks*. In this novel the emotion which is rigorously controlled in *Miss Marjoribanks* reaches the surface, and the last chapters are painful to read. Although there are some obvious differences from the author's own life there is one great similarity; Agnes loses first her husband and then – a worse blow – her eldest child.

There is evidence that the book startled its first readers, accustomed as they were to a well-understood system of rewards and punishments. Agnes is a good daughter, a loyal wife, a devoted mother, and what she gets is a series of kicks in the teeth. The opening is fairly conventional. Agnes, whose father is a blacksmith, marries Roger Trevelyan, a dissolute baronet's son. Everyone thinks she is an artful girl who has married for a title but in fact she is a stronger character than Roger and it is she who holds the family together when he proves inadequate:

> She was no longer able to admire Roger, however much she tried, nor to look up to him, nor even to trust him much ... and yet, withal, she had not ceased to love him, and stand by him with all her might, which wonderful problem of humanity is one very little discussed in works of imagination ... (30)

The conventional novel, Margaret had discovered, bore little relation to most people's experience, and she discussed this problem in the preface to *Agnes*. Life was 'full of broken threads and illogical conclusions, and lacks altogether the unity of the regularly constructed fiction, which confines itself to the graceful task of conducting two virtuous young persons through a labyrinth of difficulties to a happy marriage .... Yet at the same time everybody knows that there are many lives which only begin after that first fair chapter of youthful existence is completed.'

It is stressed that women have problems which men do not share and that, on the whole, they are likely to have a harder time. Agnes's husband is unreliable and drives a wedge between her and her father, and she loses more than one baby, a sorrow which 'counts for little in the estimation of the world' (30). She feels a great need for tender sympathy from other women but is taunted by Roger's upper-class friends because of her social background. Above all she fails to get any support from her sister-in-law Beatrice, a single woman in her thirties. This part of the novel is excellent. Like married women, spinsters have their own special kind of pain and humiliation; Beatrice is well aware that people sneer at her because she has 'never picked up a husband after twenty years' hard work' (55), and her only way to escape from her appalling father and empty life is to get married. She resents Agnes because the younger girl has apparently been more successful, and although her jealousy has evil results the author finds it understandable.

Agnes resigns herself to her marriage, 'seeing nothing better was to be made of it' (34), but this is by no means all she has to face. Roger dies, and although she suffers intensely she is aware that there has always been something unsatisfying in their relationship and begins to recover. But her eldest child, the heir to the title, is kidnapped by Beatrice, who thinks his mother is unfit to bring him up, and is fatally injured trying to escape. This brings in an unacceptably sensational element, but the issues raised by the child's death are extremely serious. As in *A Son of the Soil*, we are asked to consider the mystery of why certain people are singled out for exceptional suffering. Beatrice is not punished, as the reader has been expecting; instead she gets married, while Agnes ends up deprived of any personal happiness. 'The vicarious life in which most women spend the latter part of their days might still remain for her; but her own life was over and done.' (59)

Her suffering has been caused, not by any human agency, but by God. George Eliot, a professed agnostic, was nothing like as frank as Margaret about the difficulties of religious belief. Margaret comments that simple people think that sufferings are 'signs of God's love', but in fact, as 'most people find out sooner or later' (35), they tend to deteriorate the character. She also points out that human beings would not usually be cruel enough to deprive a mother of her child but God, who was supposed to be love, had done it. She was to come back to these questions again, nearly fifteen years later, but for the time this was her last word.

Weak and blotched though it is, *Agnes* is in some ways a highly original novel. The really fine things in it are the portrait of Beatrice, the author's ability to describe complex feelings, and her use of subject-matter which most English novelists left alone. It also contains thoroughly conventional things like the kidnapping and the theme of the young aristocrat who marries beneath him. Yet we feel strongly that she was dissatisfied with the 'woman's novel' as it then was, and was trying to remould it. *Agnes* follows the normal shape of a woman's life, including marriage problems, widowhood and the loss of children. Although the heroine suffers an appalling tragedy, we are told that she 'had in no way an exceptionally hard fate ... it was only the common lot'. (58) This can only mean that her life is closer to most women's experiences than the novel in which the heroine gets married and lives happily ever after. Agnes has to entertain her husband on his deathbed with a romantic novel; in the same way, she tells reassuring stories to her dying child. But the author had clearly begun to feel that the novel should be more than a sedative. In her later work we find the same tension between the realistic novels at which she excelled, and the pot-boilers which she had so many temptations to write.

5 Chronicles of Carlingford

Margaret Oliphant is still best remembered as the author of the *Chronicles of Carlingford*, which, as she said, 'made a considerable stir at the time'. This was not only because of their great merits. There was a vast public for religious works of all kinds, and novels about the Anglican clergy had become fashionable after *Scenes of Clerical Life* and Trollope's Barsetshire series. In fact the two best Carlingford stories, *The Doctor's Family* and *Miss Marjoribanks*, are not about clergymen or religious problems, but *Salem Chapel*, which was a best-seller, added a new dimension to the clerical novel with its comic picture of a Nonconformist congregation. Her Presbyterian background enabled her to see that in England the established church was closely involved with the status quo and that dissenters were made to feel socially inferior. Like Trollope, she wrote a series of novels set in an imaginary provincial town, and with the same characters appearing more than once, but she is not only, or even mainly, interested in the clergy. Like George Eliot in *Middlemarch*, she looks at a broad section of the middle classes in a fairly conventional country town.

'Carlingford is, as is well known, essentially a quiet place', the author tells us. '. . . There is no trade, no manufactures, no anything in particular, except very pleasant parties and a superior class of people . . . . But in every community some centre of life is necessary. This point, round which everything centres, is, in Carlingford, found in the clergy.'[1] 'A superior class of people' can be found in the 'exclusive houses in Grange Lane, where the aristocracy of Carlingford lived retired within their garden walls.'[2] But the town has a shabby underside represented by Grove Street, where the Dissenting tradesmen live and worship, and Wharfside, a rough district around the canal where the people are almost indifferent to religion.

The series began with 'The Executor', which appeared in *Blackwood's* in May 1861 and was followed by another short story, *The Rector* and then by the longer *Doctor's Family*. Afterwards came three full-length novels, *Salem Chapel, The Perpetual Curate*, and *Miss Marjoribanks. Phoebe Junior* appeared much later, in 1876. The three shorter pieces, all written in 1861, introduce most of the leading characters and also the two most important themes – the clergyman who (like Edward Irving and Willie) is tormented by personal problems, and the special burdens of women.

Margaret did not think 'The Executor' (the story she wrote in Edinburgh after a long run of bad luck) worth reprinting. On one level it is a conventional tale about a missing heir and an unjust will. But it is well written, with a characteristic note of irony:

> Only half an hour ago he had attended her funeral with decorum and perfect indifference, as was natural, and had come into this parlour without the slightest idea of encountering anything which could disturb him. Fate, however, had been lying in wait for the unsuspecting man at the moment he feared it least . . . (1)

Basically it is the story of a female breadwinner, Bessie Christian, a girl with no money and demanding parents whom she supports. The young doctor, Edward Rider, wants to marry her, but has not got the courage.

The Rector also looks realistically at human weakness and feelings of shame at one's own inadequacy. It is far better than anything she had written in the 1850s, for (*pace* Henry James) she had by this time developed a subtle and beautiful style. She could now write very vivid descriptions:

> It was such a scene as is only to be found in an old country town; the walls jealous of intrusion, yet thrusting tall plumes of lilac and stray branches of apple-blossom, like friendly salutations to the world without; within, the blossoms dropping over the light bright head of Lucy Wodehouse underneath the apple-trees, and impertinently flecking the Rev. Cecil Wentworth's Anglican coat . . . . With the white May peeping out among the green overhead, and the sweet narcissus in a great dazzling sheaf upon the grass, making all the air fragrant

> around them, can anybody fancy a sweeter domestic out-of-door scene? (1)

Mr Proctor, the Rector of the title, is a welcome guest in the comfortable houses and enclosed gardens of Carlingford. He is a man of fifty who has spent most of his life as a fellow of All Souls and had little contact with anyone except other celibate dons. But he is forced to reconsider his vocation when he finds that he does not know how to comfort a dying woman and that Wentworth and Lucy are of much more use to their fellow-creatures:

> For the first time in his life he set himself to inquire what was his supposed business in this world .... Young Wentworth knew what to say to that woman in her distress; and so might the Rector, had her distress concerned a disputed translation, or a disused idiom .... Today he had visibly failed in a duty which even in All Souls was certainly known to be one of the duties of a Christian priest. Was he a Christian priest, or what was he? (3)

He decides to return to Oxford, but this does not satisfy him, and it is hinted at the end that he will marry and become a hard-working parish priest. In this story, and in later works like *The Curate in Charge*, the author explores the tension between everyday life with its incessant demands and the life of the mind. While she always said that human beings were far more important than books there is no doubt that the world of scholarship held a deep attraction for her. She was very conscious, though, that it was not possible for people like herself to live permanently in that world.

Margaret recalled, thirty years later, that at the time of writing she had liked *The Doctor's Family*. She was not mistaken; although it has been out of print for years, and is not well known even among those who have some acquaintance with her work, it happens to be one of the best short novels in English.

Dr Rider, who in 'The Executor' allowed the girl he liked to marry someone else, is a young professional man struggling to earn a living in the unfashionable new part of Carlingford. We respect him because he is worker, but he has no heroic or saintly qualities; instead he shows 'that contemptuous hardness into which incessant personal contact with the world drives most men' (11). The author seizes our attention at once when she introduces us to 'the skeleton in Edward Rider's cupboard':

> The skeleton is not in a cupboard. It is in an upstairs room, comfortable enough, but heated, close, unwholesome – a place from which, even when the window is open, the fresh air seems shut out . . . . There is a fire, though it is not cold – a sofa near the fire – a sickening heavy smell of abiding tobacco – not light whiffs of smoke, such as accompany a man's labours, but a dead pall of idle heavy vapour, and in the midst of all a man stretched lazily on the sofa, with his pipe laid on the table beside him, and a book in his soft, boneless, nerveless hands . . . (1)

This man bears a distinct resemblance to Willie, but any emotion which she may feel is well under control. Dr Rider, much against his will, has taken in his brother Fred, a compulsive idler and alcoholic. He turns out to have a wife, as incompetent as himself, who arrives from Australia with their three children and her sister Nettie, the person who holds the family together. The situation is presented with wit and high spirits, but a note of exasperation is never far away:

> 'Be seated, please', said the doctor, with dreadful civility, 'and compose yourselves. Fred is well enough; as well as he ever is. I don't know', added poor Rider with irrestrainable bitterness, 'whether he is quite presentable to ladies; but I presume, madam, if you're his wife, you're acquainted with his habits. Excuse me for being quite unprepared for such a visit. I have not much leisure for anything out of my profession. I can scarcely spare these minutes, that is the truth . . .' (2)

The doctor leaves the responsibility of coping with the children and their feckless parents to Nettie. He falls in love with her but they both know that he could not tolerate living with her family and would take it out on her. 'Love, patience, charity, after all, are but human qualities, when they have to be held against daily disgusts, irritations and miseries.' (12) Domestic life is presented at its worst. The children are 'terrible little imps' who fight, scream, and pursue one another 'with brushes and mops' (6). We are not meant to despise Rider because he cannot stand it; the author simply takes it for granted that this is how the average man would behave.

At the same time she shows how Nettie feels obliged to look after the family because no one else will; as Margaret said in another context: 'the pressure of the *must* is strong upon her'.[3] Most Victorian novelists would have treated a young woman who gave up her marriage prospects for other people's sakes as an angel. Nettie is nothing of the sort but a 'wilful passionate creature', 'dark, eager, impetuous, with blazing black eyes and red lips' (2). Like her creator she is a born manager and is not above saying a few sharp words, 'She was not even fortunate enough to be able to persuade herself into admiring love and enthusiasm for those to whom necessity obliged her to give up her own life.' (12) She is well aware that her sister, Susan, is stupid and ungrateful – 'a creature insensate, unreasoning, whom neither argument nor fact can make any impression upon' (3) – but such people always have an enormous advantage because they have no scruples about doing what they like.

It seems there is no way for the doctor and Nettie to marry unless somebody has an unconvincing 'change of heart', but in fact the author does solve the problem successfully. Fred is drowned on his way home from the pub (significantly it is only Nettie who is really shocked) and his wife, although she moans about her hard lot, quickly marries again. There is no question of her, or Dr Rider, becoming less selfish, and the novel remains a comedy without avoiding the serious issues it has raised.

We are forced to re-examine the 'modern sentimental ethic' that goodness brings its own reward. People who sacrifice themselves for others should not expect gratitude and will probably be snubbed by those they have helped. The perennial contrast between givers and takers is seen very clearly in *The Doctor's Family*; so is the author's remarkable power of treating serious subjects with a light touch.

One element which seems old-fashioned is that Nettie has her own income and all her work is done within the home, whereas in later Oliphant novels heroines go into the labour market to support their dependants. In all of them, though, there is a pattern of strong women who carry other people's burdens, and more or less weak and selfish men.

'*Salem Chapel*', Margaret wrote, 'made a kind of commotion, the utmost I have ever attained to .... As a matter of fact I knew nothing about chapels, but took the sentiment and a few details from our old church in Liverpool, which was Free Church of Scotland, and where there were a few grocers and other such good folk whose ways with the minister were wonderful to behold. The saving grace of their Scotchness being withdrawn, they became still more wonderful as Dissenting deacons, and the truth of the picture was applauded to all the echoes. I don't know that I cared for it much myself, though Tozer and the rest amused me well enough.'

As usual, her instinct about her work was a sound one. *Salem Chapel* is not a good novel, although it is very funny when it deals with Tozer, the butterman who dominates the congregation, and other worshippers who think the minister is their paid servant. It was reprinted several times in the next fifty years and has a shadowy place in English literature, remaining probably her most famous work.

Arthur Vincent, a young man educated at a good Nonconformist college and with high ideals about his mission, comes to Carlingford as the minister of Salem Chapel. His belief that the Nonconformists are 'the party of progress' and that he has a 'high vocation as a soldier of the Cross' is shaken when he meets his flock – prosperous tradespeople, smelling of butter and bacon, who expect him to spend his evenings in tea and gossip. He falls in love with a mindless beauty, Lady Western, but soon realises that as a poor man and a Dissenter he has no hope of marrying her. When he meets the Anglican curate, Wentworth, 'a world of difference and separation lay between them', although they are both young, poor and clergymen. 'A poor widow's son, educated at Homerton, and an English squire's son, public school and university bred, cannot begin on the same level.' (2) His congregation soon realise that he prefers the local aristocracy to them and feel offended. Then his sister disappears, and is accused of murder, and while Arthur is rushing about trying to solve the mystery his mother comes to Carlingford to keep up his credit. This part of the novel is very well done; Mrs Vincent, desperately worried about her children, has to fend off impertinent questions and pretend that everything is normal – a kind of work, the author suggests, which women are well used to. The crisis is resolved, but by this time Arthur has had enough and decides to leave the ministry:

> 'I am one of those who have boasted in my day that I received my title to ordination from no bishop, from no temporal provision, from no traditionary church, but from the hands of the people. Perhaps I am less sure than I was at first, when you were all disposed to praise me, that the voice of the people is the voice of God; but however that may be, what I received from you I can but render up to you. I resign into your hands your pulpit, which you have erected with your money and hold as your property .... I am either your servant, responsible to you, or God's servant, responsible to Him – which is it?' (42)

Dissenters, understandably, were upset by this novel, and later critics have accused it of pandering to the snobbery of middle-class readers. The truth is rather more complex. Margaret had grown up in the bosom of the Free Church which upheld the absolute right of each congregation to choose its own minister; the problem was that when a congregation had become thoroughly complacent the minister might have great difficulty in following his own conscience. She was satirising not the poor, who have no place in Salem, but 'the flower of the middle classes' (21), as they like to call themselves. The problem is not that they drop their 'h's' but that they are philistine and self-satisfied. Arthur tells them, at one of their religious tea-meetings, 'how strangely they appeared to him standing on this little bright gas-lighted perch amid the dark sea of life that surged round them' (10). The light-darkness imagery, which recurs throughout the Carlingford novels, reflects his (and the author's) attempts to find meaning in a world which has become fairly frightening. When he is hunting for his sister he has to travel on Sunday, 'rushing wildly along distant railways on the day of rest', a fact which would shock his congregation if they knew about it and would also have shocked the young Margaret Wilson. 'Total disarrangement, chaos, all the old habitudes of life gone to wreck, and only desperation and misery left, was the sensation produced by that interruption of all religious use and wont.' (21) Eventually he admits that 'he is not very sure what anything means – that life is a great wonder, and that he only faintly guesses how God, being pitiful, had the heart to make man and leave him on this sad earth' (42).

The novel has some fairly glaring faults. The sub-plot, with its murder mystery, is not impressive, and another great weakness is that Arthur does not really stand for anything much better than the limited values of Salem Chapel. Although there are hints that a different kind of Christianity is what is needed, he is mainly preoccupied with a wish to rise in the world, a snobbish distaste for people who sell groceries, and his feelings for Lady Western. For these reasons it is hard for the modern reader to take the novel seriously or to have much sympathy for its hero.

Yet it is not a work which can be completely written off. The sparrings between the minister, his mother, and the congregation are excellent comedy. Much of the rest of *Salem Chapel* has the confusing effect of a bad dream:

> Through the sullen silent midnight the train dashed on, the faint light flickering in the unsteady carriage, the two speechless figures, with eyes averted, watching each other through all the ice-cold hours. It was morning when they got out, cramped and frozen, at the little station, round which miles and miles of darkness, a black unfathomable ocean, seemed to lie, and which shone there with its little red sparkle of light among its wild waste of moors like the one touch of human life in a desert . . . (20)

While a Margaret Maitland or a Katie Stewart had been at home in their environment, the sensitive and complicated characters in later Oliphant novels are almost completely alienated from theirs.

The Perpetual Curate began to appear in *Blackwood's* only a few months after *Salem Chapel* had ended, and in some ways the two novels are very similar. Once again the hero is a clergyman, although Frank Wentworth, as a High Anglican, is at the opposite religious pole from Arthur Vincent. Once again the young man has a lofty idea of his mission but is distracted by petty problems. And both novels have a rather ridiculous sub-plot about the disappearance of a young girl.

Another theme, familiar to readers of Jane Austen and

Trollope, is the clergyman-hero's search for a suitable living. Frank Wentworth wants to get married but cannot afford to do so if he remains a perpetual curate. Unlike the Dissenting minister, he belongs to a 'good' landed family and could, if he chose, get a living from his aunt. But the aunt is Evangelical and Frank is too idealistic to modify his principles, so when she comes to hear him preach at Easter he deliberately makes the service as High as possible:

> At that moment – the worst moment for such a thought – it suddenly flashed over him that, after all, a wreath of spring flowers or a chorister's surplice was scarcely worth suffering martyrdom for. This horrible suggestion, true essence of an unheroic age, which will not suffer a man to be absolutely sure of anything, disturbed his prayer as he knelt down in silence to ask God's blessing .... Not for a dozen worlds would he have sacrificed a lily or a surplice on this particular Easter, when all his wordly hopes hung in the balance. But to think at this crowning moment that a villainous doubt of the benefit of these surplices and lilies should seize his troubled heart! (3)

There are parallels with the curate in *A Son of the Soil* who can find nothing more important to preach about than the twentieth Sunday after Trinity. But Frank also works hard among the poor, and here there is no doubt about the value of what he is doing. 'The bargemen and their wives did not know much about the Christian Year; but they understood the greater matters which lay beneath.' (10)

The same kind of problem is faced by Frank's brother Gerald, who like him is an Anglican clergyman and 'a priest by nature'. He is on the point of going over to Rome, which for him means becoming a Catholic priest – 'If I am not a priest I am nothing'. The problem is that he has a wife and several children, and although she is a silly woman who cannot understand his conscientious difficulties she still has her rights:

> 'You may go to Rome' [Frank tells him] 'and cease to be a priest of the Anglican Church; but you cannot cease to be a man, to bear the weight of your natural duties' ... (16)

Gerald finally realises that it is impossible and when he leaves the Church of England finds himself without a vocation or an income. The suggestion is that 'perhaps he was making a sacrifice of his life for a mistake' (40). It is useless to look for a perfect Church which has all the answers. As in *Salem Chapel*, we are reminded that Carlingford is a very small place and that beyond it is a great mystery:

> The heart of the Curate ached to think how many problems lay in the darkness ... all the inequalities of life, side by side, evermore echoing dumbly the same awful question; and over all shone the calm sky which gave no answer .... 'Can your Church explain why one man is happy and another miserable? – why one has everything and abounds, and the other loses all that is most precious in life? .... Outside lies a world in which every event is an enigma, where nothing that comes offers any explanation of itself; where God does not show himself always kind, but by times awful, terrible – a God who smites and does not spare. It is easy to make a harmonious balance of doctrine; but where is the interpretation of life?' (40)

This was written soon after Maggie's death, when Margaret was preoccupied with the problem of suffering, but from the beginning of the Carlingford series she had been arguing for a non-dogmatic form of Christianity. Differences between the churches no longer seemed important; Frank is a good priest in spite of, not because of, the lilies and surplices. Life, she suggests in the last chapter, is 'not the smooth road it looked, but a rough path enough cut into dangerous ruts, through which generations of men and women followed each other without ever being able to mend the way'.

The Perpetual Curate is a long novel containing several elements which do not always mix. The religious theme is the most important, but there are also a mystery, a love story, and a sub-plot based on the parable of the Prodigal Son. There are two reprobates in the book, graceless middle-aged men like Willie who cause endless trouble to their relations. A much more successful sub-plot concerns the Rector's wife, Mrs Morgan, who has waited ten years to get married and is aware that her bloom has faded. Her disillusionment with her husband, and the tension between them, is beautifully conveyed, and looks forward to the sophisticated comedy of the next Carlingford novel.

Miss Marjoribanks was rediscovered in the 1960s by Q. D. Leavis, who thought it the only completely good Oliphant novel and a stepping-stone between *Emma* and *Middlemarch*. Perhaps the best way to describe this book, written the year after Maggie died, is as a dark comedy. The wit and irony never falter; from the first page to the last it is extremely funny. Yet, as John Blackwood pointed out, it has a certain 'hardness of tone'.[4] Many of the situations it describes are disturbing and painful, and although there is a believable happy ending the author is obviously well aware of the darker aspects of life.

'The story is a story without a plot from its very nature',[5] Margaret told Blackwood, and, a little earlier, 'It is to bring out Miss Marjoribanks that is the aim of the story, and not to attempt any complications of plot.'[5] All the main events are natural and convincing. Lucilla comes home to keep house for her father, an elderly and unsentimental Scot, and sets out to raise the tone of Carlingford with her Thursday evening parties. (There are hints that, had she been a man, she could have been a successful doctor or politician.) Her name is linked with several men's but her 'superior' qualities usually frighten them off. Eventually, at thirty, she marries her cousin Tom Marjoribanks, whom she refused years earlier, and persuades him to buy an estate 'where her influence might be of untold advantage, as Lucilla modestly said, to her fellow creatures' (51).

Lucilla is an unconventional person who skilfully uses conventional language in order to get her way. She claims that she knows nothing about politics at the very time when she is master-minding a by-election in Carlingford. In the first chapter she tells everyone that she intends to be 'a comfort to dear papa' after her mother dies, when she really wants to leave school and have a taste of independence. She puts off marriage for several years, again using her father as an excuse, because she is eager to try out the possibilities of being single.

The novel has been called 'a relentlessly satirical portrait of a female egoist',[7] which, up to a point, is true. But Lucilla's egoism, unlike that of Emma Woodhouse, confers actual benefits on other people, ranging from pleasant parties to comfortable homes and jobs. She does not simply believe herself to be, but really is, superior to most of those around her, if only because everything she does is done well. A much worse form of egoism is studied in Barbara Lake, 'a creature of no earthly good', who makes everyone else suffer when her feelings are hurt. The Lakes are 'a family of artists', regarded with some suspicion by the bourgeoisie of Carlingford, and her sister Rose works seriously at drawing and design. However, Barbara tries to steal one of Lucilla's admirers and, when she fails, spitefully leaves home so that Rose will have to give up her job and keep house. The contrast between the two sisters is much the same as in *The Doctor's Family*, but in this case the more unselfish one is totally defeated:

> Her Career was dear to her heart, and those two tears welled up from the depths; but then there would be nobody else to do it – a consideration which continually filters out the people who are good for anything out of the muddy current of the ordinary world . . . (35)

'Dead selfishness and folly', we are told, are 'the two most invincible forces in the world.' (35) In the end Barbara gets her husband but there is no one to marry Rose and her career is sacrificed, like Margaret's, for her family.

Lucilla is a highly intelligent woman who pours her energy into Thursday evening parties simply because she has nothing more important to do. After ten years of it she becomes bored:

> She had come to an age at which she might have gone into Parliament herself had there been no disqualification of sex, and when it was almost a necessity for her to make some use of her social influence . . . . When a woman has an active mind, and still does not care for parish work, it is a little hard for her to find a 'sphere'. And Lucilla, though she said nothing about a sphere, was still more or less in that condition of mind which has been so often and so fully described to the British public – when the ripe female intelligence, not having the natural resource of a nursery and a husband to manage, turns inwards, and begins to 'make a protest' against the existing order of society, and to call the world to account for giving it no due occupation – and to consume itself . . . (42)

People are beginning to comment on the fact that she is twenty-nine and still single. The author is ambiguous about whether or not this has advantages. Some of the married women whom Lucilla knows envy her, and it is clear that several men privately despise women and make them miserable when they have the power. Lucilla does not attract this type of man because she is so obviously self-sufficient and treats the stronger sex with 'a certain mild pity and charitable contempt' (31). Yet 'no woman feels herself set at her true value' if no one wants to marry her (36). The weakness of her position becomes obvious as soon as her father is no longer there. Dr Marjoribanks, without condescending to complain to anyone, dies suddenly after he has found out that he is ruined, in a very powerful scene:

> Meantime the snow fell heavily outside, and wrapped everything in a soft and secret whiteness. And amid the whiteness and darkness, the lamp burned steadily outside at the garden-gate, which pointed out the Doctor's door . . . . The bell that had roused him when he was young, still hung near him in the silence of his closed-up house when he was old, and still could make him spring up, all self-possessed and ready, when the enemy Death had to be fought with. But that night the snow cushioned the wire outside, and even made white cornices and columns about the steady lamp, and the Doctor slept within, and no one disturbed him; for except Mrs Chiley and a few chronic patients, there was nothing particularly amiss in Carlingford . . . (42)

Reactions to the Doctor's death are studied unsentimentally. He is not a particularly religious man, and it is 'hard to think of him under any other circumstances, or identify him with angels and spirits'. Lucilla is grieved and shocked, but cannot help her thoughts 'wandering to all kinds of profane out-of-doors matters' and is disgusted with herself for her 'inappropriate state of mind' (43).

The author sums up, 'Nobody was made altogether desolate by his death, nor was any heart broken, but they wept for him honestly' (45). Remembering that her own feelings about Maggie's death were not at all ambiguous, one is impressed by her artistic detachment.

Lucilla soon realises that her social importance is gone and that she is 'a penniless single woman with nobody to look to, and nothing to live on' (44). But whatever happens she has 'no intention of sinking into a nobody' (46). She is on the brink of a conventional marriage when Tom reappears and practically forces her to take him. There is, perhaps, an element of wish-fulfilment in the fact that Lucilla marries her cousin and buys their great-great-grandfather's neglected estate. However that may be, the comic love scene is thoroughly satisfying because Margaret wisely did not attempt to write straight romance. Tom, who breaks or loses everything he comes in contact with, represents 'honest love' or male energy which only needs to be directed into the right channel. While he is assuring her that 'you shall do nothing but enjoy yourself and take care of yourself' (51), Lucilla is busy planning a career for both of them. Marriage will not alter the fact that she wants and needs an active life. At the end of the novel she has decided to get Tom into Parliament and to reform the 'village nuisances' herself.

It is hardly possible to overpraise *Miss Marjoribanks*, which grows more impressive every time it is read. Novels about middle-class women leading sheltered lives can become boring; 'witty' novels frequently become trivial. This novel, like Jane Austen's, triumphantly avoids these dangers, and is a worthy climax to the *Chronicles of Carlingford*.

There was, however, one more novel to come. Margaret began writing *Phoebe Junior* 'partly to amuse myself, and on a sudden impulse'[8] in 1872, and it was published in 1876 with the subtitle *A Last Chronicle of Carlingford*. She was under a great deal of pressure at this time, for reasons which will become clear, and the novel is not outstanding. The name was obviously derived from *The Last Chronicle of Barset* and there are other signs that she had been influenced by Trollope; it contains a clergyman with money problems and a sub-plot which fairly blatantly imitates the main plot of *The Warden*.

She was still very interested in the tensions between Church people and Nonconformists. Phoebe Beecham is the granddaughter of Tozer, the grocer who is a leading light of Salem Chapel; her parents have remained Dissenters but become highly respectable. When she visits her grandparents in Carlingford she is rather shocked by their plebeian ways and aware that the gentlefolk will despise her in spite of her ladylike appearance.

Like previous Oliphant novels, *Phoebe* explores the pain of individuals who are very uncertain of their social status.

Like most of the female characters whom Margaret admired Phoebe is a tough young woman, and she resembles Miss Marjoribanks in having an iron will behind a prim and proper facade. She makes friends with the Mays, a large motherless clerical family who have the sense not to be prejudiced against Dissenters. They are explicitly compared to the family of the same name in Charlotte Yonge's *Daisy Chain*, but are not 'a set of prigs like those people' (19). It looks as if Margaret had been irritated by that novel, in which the daughters are expected to sacrifice themselves for Papa as a religious duty. In *Phoebe Junior* Mr May is exposed as an egoist:

> He took it for granted, frankly and as a part of nature, that he himself was the first person to be considered in all matters. So he was, of course – so the father, the breadwinner, the head of the family ought to be; and when he has a wife to keep him upon that pedestal, and to secure that his worship shall be respected, it becomes natural, and the first article of the family creed; but somehow when a man has to set forth and uphold this principle himself, it is less successful . . . . A man who has thus to fight for himself does not appear in an amiable aspect to his family, to whom, as to all young creatures, it seemed natural that *they* should be the first objects . . . (10)

The 'hardness of tone' which had been noticed in *Miss Marjoribanks* has become still more pronounced in *Phoebe*. Some of the characters are good people, including a spinster who devotes herself to her brother's children, taking the opposite attitude to Mr May's. Phoebe herself, though, behaves in a way which most novel-readers would have found unpleasant. Mr May's son is idealistically in love with her but she prefers to marry a rich and stupid man and encourage him to go into Parliament, on the understanding that she will write his speeches. Again, this looks like a wry comment on *The Daisy Chain*, where Flora May is punished for doing the same thing. Phoebe's actions are not what George Eliot would have called 'ideally beautiful', but she does good within her limits and looks likely to be content.

The novel has been admired by some critics but seems to me not completely successful. It is clever and amusing but has no central theme. At any rate, this was the last of a series which '*almost* made me one of the popularities of literature. *Almost*, never quite.'

6 Two Families to Support (1865–75)

There had been a good many changes in Margaret's circle during the two years she had been out of England. Old Mrs Janet Wilson had died in Edinburgh and her daughter Jessie was about to marry a much younger man, James Sime.[1] Frank and Jeanie now had two small daughters, Margaret Oliphant (Madge), born in September 1863, and Janet Mary (Denny), born in February 1865. Margaret may well have gone to Birkenhead to attend the wedding and to see her nieces, but she did not expect them to play a very large part in her life.

She looked up Jane Carlyle, who had been desperately ill and looked like 'a weird shadow, not quite canny'.[2] She also heard from another old friend, Dinah Mulock, who had married the publisher George Lillie Craik. After she had read *Agnes* she sent Margaret a short, pained note, 'I think you will yet be sorry for having written *Agnes*' – the reason being that it 'does not "justify the ways of God to men"'.[3]

Margaret was still feeling too raw to attempt any such thing. She wrote to Mrs Tulloch around this time that while she worked mechanically at translating 'I am going over and over all the details of those four days that made such a terrible change in my life. I begin to understand better the Principal's illness, for now and then my mind fixes on one point till I get almost to feel as if it was I who had sacrificed my child.... I can say this to you, dear, to relieve my heart, but of course at the same time I am going on and making arrangements all the same as if I loved it, as one must do.'[4]

The chief thing she had to arrange was her sons' education. For several months she had been very tempted to send them to Eton or Harrow, preferably Eton, although she did wonder whether 'boys of no particular pretensions and who have their own way to make would be in the right place at this most aristocratic of schools'.[5] Only two years earlier she had gently made fun of English public schools in *A Son of the Soil*, where the Scottish characters had remarked that there were 'schules in Edinburgh far afore anything that's kent in England'.[6] The difference was that in Scotland boys were trained for a profession and expected to be self-reliant at an early age, while the English system trained them for nothing in particular and kept them dependent on their parents until they were well into their twenties. Story, and probably other friends, warned her that she was making a mistake and that they would do better in Edinburgh. However, Margaret went to Windsor and was so pleased with the cheerful little town that she decided to settle there and send Cyril, now aged nine, to Eton as a day-boy.

In the 1860s Eton was rapidly consolidating its position as the 'most aristocratic of schools'. Local boys, to whom it had been open in earlier times, had been squeezed out, and the sons of the old and new ruling classes were crowding in. John Blackwood's son Jack, who was the same age as Cyril, was a pupil. The fees were high and Margaret knew that if she died or stopped earning the boys would have nothing. However, the Carlingford series had been so successful that she thought she could risk it, and she was sure that in the long run it would be a good investment for her children, who were both very bright.

In December the family moved into 6 Clarence Crescent, Windsor, a genteel residential area which was to be their base for the next thirty years. It was a sunny little house with its own small garden and a large piece of ground with 'fine trees and wild nooks and corners' nearby. Most of the neighbours were elderly so the boys had it practically to themselves. The school was a mile away, so Cyril had to walk there early every morning, in his tall hat and long trousers; Cecco having a tutor at home.

In the spring of 1866 Margaret sent the last number of *Miss Marjoribanks* to Blackwood, feeling justifiably that she had done a good piece of work. But the publisher had detected a 'hardness of tone', which he disliked, in the later stages, and eventually he paid her less for it than for *The Perpetual Curate*. Margaret was upset and wished she had made a bargain in advance, knowing that other writers, particularly Dinah, were paid far better than herself. Meanwhile her novel *Madonna Mary* was appearing in *Good Words* with illustrations by Geddie Macpherson. It is a much weaker book than the others she had written recently, and one gets the impression that, as she recovered from the worst of her suffering, her creative power relaxed.

There was no doubt that, after the move to Windsor, she felt better. She sometimes wondered how anyone could have got over two such blows. 'I thought it was for the young people round me, and no doubt it was so, but equally without doubt my own life burst forth again with an obstinate elasticity that I could not keep down.'

Jane Carlyle came to Windsor at the beginning of April and reported that 'Mrs Oliphant seems to me to be eaten up with long visitors'.[7] Principal and Mrs Tulloch were staying, with Sara and Fanny, now in their mid-teens. Jane invited them to a party at her house later in the month, to meet J. A. Froude. They all went to London on 21 April 1866, only to hear as they turned into Cheyne Row that she had died suddenly that afternoon.

This was the first break in Margaret's circle of friends, who, as Jane had realised, were becoming increasingly important to her. The 'innermost chamber of the heart' was empty;[8] she had no husband and no daughter. But she did have many other rewarding relationships. Her closest friends for several years were the Tullochs and the Macphersons, as well as Isabella Blackwood and an Emma FitzMaurice, whom she had known in Ealing. She also became very fond of one of her neighbours, a little woman called Ellen Clifford who lived at 4 Clarence Crescent and who is the 'Aunt Nelly' of the Little Pilgrim stories. 'She was far from being wise or clever, generally reputed rather a silly little woman; but with a heart of gold', Margaret wrote. Apparently she was one of the few people to whom she felt able to talk about Maggie. Nelly's life was spent caring for a senile mother and an invalid brother. One way she kept them amused was by playing cards, and Cecco, aged seven or eight, often went over 'in his little velvet suit, to make the fourth at whist'.

Another great friend whom she met at about this time was her future biographer, Annie Louisa Walker, a distant cousin. Annie had been born in Staffordshire around 1840 and had lived in Canada as a girl. While still in her teens she had had several poems published in newspapers and magazines; one of them, 'Work, for the night is coming', was taken up by Moody and Sankey without her permission and became a famous hymn. Her parents died soon after they came back to England and Annie, who had not met Margaret before, drifted rather helplessly towards her because she was a relation, and because she wanted to write. Margaret was sceptical about her work but recommended it to publishers, and eventually Annie brought out four novels. She also became a kind of housekeeper and secretary after Jane Hockey left to get married in 1866.

Early in 1867 Margaret visited the House of Commons for the Reform Bill debate and met her namesake, Laurence Oliphant (1829–88). He was a long-time contributor to *Blackwood's* and had recently been elected for Stirling as a left-wing Liberal MP. So far as either of them knew, they were not related – Laurence was a Condie Oliphant, from Perthshire – but they were about the same age and had a good deal in common. Both of them were great travellers; Laurence had been a barrister in Ceylon and a war correspondent in Russia and China and written popular books about his adventures. Both, under a witty and sophisticated exterior, were deeply concerned with the problems of leading a more moral and less 'wordly' life. Although few people knew it, Laurence was already contemplating giving up his promising career. 'When it became clear to me', he wrote, 'that, in order to succeed, party must be put before country, and self before everything, and that success could only be purchased at the price of convictions which were expected to change with those of the leader of the party, my thirst to find something that was not a sham or a contradiction in terms increased.'[9]

At the time Laurence told Margaret only that he despised his present way of life. In fact he had come under the influence of an American 'prophet', Thomas Lake Harris, and later in the year he suddenly left England to live in a community calling itself the Brotherhood of the New Life.

Throughout 1867 Margaret worked on a long and poor novel, *Brownlows*, which appeared monthly in *Blackwood's*. She also did a suitably respectful review of *The Early Life of the Prince Consort*, although she had little patience with Queen Victoria's very public mourning for her husband:

> If any of us ordinary people were to treat our friends and visitors and society in general in the same way we should simply put ourselves out of the pale of society, and lose both visitors and friends. I doubt whether nous autres poor women who have had to fight with the world all alone without much

> sympathy, can quite enter into the 'unprecedented' character of the Queen's sufferings. A woman is surely a poor creature if with a large happy affectionate family of children around her, she can't take heart to do her duty whether she likes it or not. *We* have to do it, with very little solace, and I don't see that anybody is particularly sorry for us.[10]

A few months later Blackwood asked her to review the Queen's Highland Journal, hinting that if the Palace liked her work it might be possible to get her a Civil List pension. Margaret was sceptical but agreed, 'on condition that I am not to be asked to tackle the holy Albert again'.[11] Soon after she had written it, in January 1868, she heard that her brother Frank was in great trouble.

At this time Frank Wilson was fifty-two, and for as long as Margaret could remember he had been the most solid and reliable member of her family. He had been working for the Bank of England for over a quarter of a century and had been happily married to Jeanie for fifteen years. Their elder children, Frank and Nelly, were about thirteen and twelve, and the little girls four and three. Margaret tells us that he had been a great Radical in his youth, but seldom bothered to use his vote now he had got one.[12] As a girl she had been devoted to him and he had been kind and concerned when she was in trouble. But over the last few years he had had a nervous illness which made his hands shake badly and this had made it difficult for him to write to her. Perhaps their relationship had never quite recovered from the abrasive few months she had spent in his house in 1860. When she heard about the disaster she went to Birkenhead and found he had left for France, alone.

Exactly what had happened is not clear. In a letter to Blackwood Margaret wrote, 'My brother has been in bad health for a long time, and I fear it has affected his mind, for he has brought himself into a position which is simple ruin as far as one can see for himself and his family'.[13] In any case, his job was lost, and with Jeanie's brother and sister both out of the country there was no one to look after the helpless family but her. She agreed to pay his bills and over the next few months tried to find another job for him. Meanwhile, Jeanie and the little girls went after him to France and Margaret took the other two children back to Windsor.

'I fear I shall have more reason than ever for hard labour', she wrote wearily, '. . . one seems to be always dragged back by the heel when one hoped to have got the better of this world.'[14] Her depression increased later in the spring when she found that *Brownlows* had made a loss. 'My burdens for the moment are almost intolerable for I have two families to support, and the prospect of dropping into the shade is doubly painful.'[15]

However, there was some good news on the way. In March some of the ladies at Windsor Castle arranged a meeting for Margaret with Queen Victoria, who recorded in her journal, 'She is very pleasing, so simple, quiet and intelligent. She said writing came quite naturally to her, and has been doing so for the last 20 years'.[16] Meanwhile, Principal Tulloch, who was one of the Queen's chaplains in Scotland and on very good terms with her, was trying to see if something could be done for Margaret. On 20 June came an announcement from 10 Downing Street, 'The Queen has, on Mr Disraeli's recommendation, granted a pension of the Civil List of £100 a year to Mrs Oliphant'.

After the first shock, her brother's children settled down. Nelly went to her other aunt, Jessie Sime, and Margaret and her sons soon became very fond of young Frank. He was a big strong boy, friendly and a hard worker, 'such a one as is a stand-by and tower of strength in a family'. In a way Margaret was pleased to think that she could give him a better training than his parents could have afforded. She sent him to Eton as a day-boy with Cyril.

As she constantly said, nothing mattered so long as the children were well. Cyril had begun to be noted as one of the outstanding Eton boys – 'the brightest, wittiest, most sparkling little fellow'. He was the captain of the lower school, a good athlete, a brilliant actor, and at barely thirteen caused a sensation by winning the Prince Consort's prize for French. One of his friends was a slightly older boy, Howard Sturgis, the son of an American banker, who often came to the house in Clarence Crescent and was much impressed by Margaret. Although she was only about forty at the time, she seemed to him like an old lady with her white hair and black dress. Like everyone else who met her, he noticed her Scottish accent, dark eyes and enormous 'natural dignity', also that she never spoke about her husband or Maggie:

> She had a friend, a clever agreeable woman, who took her full share in all the innocent enjoyments Mrs Oliphant loved to plan, but who was always big with sighs over her own departed happiness, and the cruelty with which the world had used her; and I remember even as a boy dimly apprehending the contrast between the two women, the greater nobility of Mrs Oliphant's attitude towards the past.[17]

Possibly the friend was Annie, who was well-known in the family for her self-pity. There were plenty of 'innocent enjoyments'. Sara and Fanny Tulloch came for long visits and Margaret organised 'home theatricals' to please them. It was at her house that Sara met Frank Tarver, a language master at Eton, whom she married in 1870. There were boating parties, dances, suppers with 'festive mint sauce'. Margaret appeared to have nothing to do but give her children and their friends a good time. After they were in bed she sat up until two in the morning and wrote.

Her novel *The Minister's Wife* attracted several reviews when it came out in June 1869. It dealt with the religious revival in the West of Scotland in 1830, when various people claimed to have been cured by a miracle. Some of it is interesting, but it was obviously written in haste and is spoiled by a murder plot. The *Daily News* wrote:

> With the exception of George Eliot, there is no female novelist of the day comparable to Mrs Oliphant .... Her genius is her own, her defects are confined mainly to the race of novelists and arise mainly from the necessity of filling three volumes with matter which would be more impressive and effective if confined within narrower limits.
>
> ... We cannot close *The Minister's Wife* without expressing a hope that the writer in any future work will avoid what we are forced to term 'sensational claptrap'. She can describe character so well, her resources are so manifold, her felicities of composition so striking, that she does not require the 'blood and thunder' so essential to the third-rate novelist.[18]

Margaret took this review seriously enough to cut out and keep, but she probably felt that it was not in her power to follow its advice. There was nothing she could do about the three-volume system, and the public had shown that it wanted blood and thunder. As for comparisons with George Eliot, they were ridiculous. But there are signs that she bitterly regretted having to write pot-boilers. In the same month she began to publish a new novel, *The Three Brothers*, in Trollope's magazine *St Paul's*. It contains an unmistakable portrait of herself as Mrs Severn, a widow who supports her children by turning out pictures at high speed. 'Sometimes she pulled at the tether that bound her, with that impulse towards excellence which is in every sensitive nature. But she could not stop long enough in her ordinary work to achieve anything beyond it.'[19] She says:

> 'I don't deceive myself. I get money for my pictures, and that is about what they are worth. But ... don't you think it sometimes makes my heart sick, to feel that, if I could but wait, if I could but take time, I might do work that would be worth doing – real work? .... But I can't take time: there are the children, and daily bread, and – he taunts me that I paint six pictures for his one!'[20]

Another poor novel, *John*, began to appear in *Blackwood's* in November. Yet at the same time she was writing extremely good non-fiction; readers who examine the bound copies of *Blackwood's* between 1867 and 1870 and compare the dreary pages of *Brownlows* and *John* with such essays as 'Elizabeth and Mary', 'Historical Sketches of the Reign of George II', and 'Miss Austen and Miss Mitford', will marvel at the difference. Month after month, as the years went by, she produced book reviews, excellent articles on the English poets, accounts of art exhibitions. She used her knowledge of Europe to make readers acquainted with foreign authors – most often modern French writers, but she also wrote essays on Leopardi, Goethe, Schiller and Turgenev. She had her blind spots, like her indifference to Dickens, but on the whole she is a stimulating critic and a good and amusing biographer. She could handle almost any subject well; her discussion of Bishop Berkeley, for instance, is as clear an account of a complex ideology as anyone could wish to read.[21] In later life she often said that she preferred biography and criticism to fiction.

In the spring of 1870 young Frank Wilson had been at Clarence Crescent for two years. His father had finally got a job, presumably as a clerk, with a railway that was being built in a remote part of Hungary. One evening in April Margaret and a group of friends had come back from an afternoon on the river and were having a late supper when someone handed her a telegram. She was not at all alarmed; telegrams were very common in her circle. For the rest of her life she remembered 'the long table and all the bright faces round it, the pretty summer dishes, salad, and pink salmon, and ornamented sweet things, and many flowers, the men and boys in their flannels, the girls in their light summer dresses'. The telegram said, 'Jeanie is dead, and I am in despair'.

Her first thought was that young Frank, who was at the table, must not be told straight away that his mother was dead. Jeanie had died in her sleep after what was supposed to be a mild attack of fever. She was not much over forty, but Margaret thought she had probably not been strong enough to cope with what happened to her. Soon afterwards Frank arrived at Victoria with the two white-faced little girls, Madge and Denny. He was shaking so convulsively that Margaret thought she would never get him to Windsor, but was less distressed than she had expected. 'Grief is the strangest thing', she wrote later, '. . . Frank, poor fellow, had got over his sorrow on the long journey.'

In a sense, though, Frank never did get over his wife's death. There was probably no reason why he should not have stayed on in Hungary, but it seems not to have occurred to him. He simply came to Margaret 'like a child glad to get home'. He talked about getting a job, and she tried to find him one, but very soon his hands were shaking too much to hold a pen. It was clear that he would never work again:

> Of course I had to face a prospect considerably changed by this great addition to my family [she wrote]. I had been obliged to work pretty hard before to meet all the too great expenses of the house. Now four people were added to it, very small two of them, but the others not inexpensive members of the house. I remember making a kind of pretence to myself that I had to think it over, to make a great decision, to give up what hopes I might have had of doing now my very best,

> and to set myself steadily to make as much money as I could ... I don't think, however, that there was any reality in it. I never did nor could, of course, hesitate for a moment as to what had to be done.

Frank settled down quite comfortably, just as Willie had done after he came back from Etal. He read his paper, took his walk, and sat in his easy-chair for the rest of the day. Like their father, he had little to do with the rest of the family, and he and Margaret had drifted so far apart that they no longer had anything in common. The situation which she had imagined in *The Doctor's Family* had become a real one. She was totally responsible for him and his children.

In the summer of 1870 Laurence Oliphant came to see Margaret at Windsor. For the last two years this sophisticated man of the world had been living in Thomas Lake Harris's community in America, cleaning out stables and carting manure. What he thought of her changed circumstances is not known, but she found him as amusing as ever. The prophet had sent him back to England to earn money and when the Franco–Prussian war broke out in July *The Times* gave him work as a war correspondent.

One of the most extraordinary things about Laurence is how he regularly managed to get important work each time he re-emerged from obscurity. His biographer, Anne Taylor, suggests, convincingly, that he may have been a spy. He certainly knew many people in high places who were prepared to help him despite being baffled by his religious opinions. Margaret, more hard-headed than her namesake, had no doubt that Harris was a charlatan but hoped that Laurence would not find this out. She would rather, she wrote to Blackwood, 'that he went in for any amount of extravagance and enthusiasm than that he fell back into your banal world, and contented himself like other people'. If he found out 'the weakness of his system', she thought, it would kill him.[22]

She herself was distressed about the war. Her neighbour, Mrs Macdonald, whom she considered a remarkable woman, had a daughter married to one of Louis Napoleon's marshals. Margaret was no longer a keen politician (she could hardly have tolerated the extreme right-wing *Blackwood's* if that had been the case) but she knew France well by this time and instinctively sympathised with the losing side. In September she went to St Andrew's for Sara's wedding, and then settled down to writing several unimportant books, novels and a biography of Montalembert, who had died earlier that year. Although he was still happy to take her non-fiction, Blackwood had obviously decided that he could not expect any more good novels, and she therefore had to use what other outlets she could find. Her work went to her old friends, Hurst and Blackett, and also to Chapman and Hall, Tinsley, Chatto and Sampson Low. She agreed to let an evening newspaper, the *Glasgow Star*, publish one of her novels in daily instalments, although she felt this was rather degrading. In the event she was cheated and made nothing out of it.

She had eight people to support, including 'cousin Annie', and as has been seen relationships within the household were strained. In particular she found it hard to relate to Madge and Denny, and perhaps, preoccupied as she was, she did not really try. They were 'very chilly, scared, distrustful little things', she wrote remorsefully later. Probably they were in a state of delayed shock. Over the last few years their home had been broken up; they had been dragged off to France and then to Hungary; their mother had died and they had finally found themselves living with an aunt who was kind but had little time to pet or play with them. Apparently they took after Jeanie's family and were not like the Oliphants in any way. They were such unobtrusive children that many of the accounts of Margaret's life at this time give the impression that they did not exist. The house revolved around the three boys. She had insured her life so that her sons would each have a thousand pounds if she died, and had asked the Principal and Blackwood to be their guardians if that happened. Both of them, she thought, would be 'able to help themselves in the way of scholarships' when they were a little older. Frank was being coached for the Forestry Examination, in the hope that he would get a job in India.

At the end of 1871 Margaret visited France to get materials for the Montalembert biography, taking Cecco, who was almost twelve. He was a bright little boy, already very interested in working out family trees. The country was freezing cold and still devastated by the war. She spent a dreary fortnight at the Chateau de La Roche en Bressy, knowing she had little in common with the Montalembert family who seemed to think that she was a lady of leisure and could spend as much time on her work as she pleased. She consoled herself by reading the first number of *Middlemarch* – 'These superior heroines are very awful people, and of course poor Miss Brooke has got to have her heart broken'.[23]

On the way back they stopped in Paris and met Laurence Oliphant, who was now the chief correspondent for *The Times*, and his mother. Margaret took a drive with them to see what the capital looked like after the cruel suppression of the Commune in May. The streets were filthy, heaped with slush and mud; the cabs moved at a footpace and several buildings were half burned down. Lady Oliphant was looking after some of the French children who had lost their mothers. Both she and Laurence were summoned back to America by Harris in the next eighteen months.

Back in England, Margaret began to look around for a larger house for her family, and in May 1872 they moved to 8–9 Clarence Crescent, two doors away. It was an expense which she could only just afford. A little earlier, she had written to John Blackwood:

> As you have been my very kind friend always, let me tell you once more exactly what my position is. My money is almost always spent before I get it, or received only just in time for pressing necessities, so that the pleasant sensation of feeling even three months clear before me is one which very rarely occurs to me. I have four people, an entire family, three of them requiring education, absolutely on my hands to provide for, with fifty pounds a year from another relative to help me in doing so – and nothing more. My only chance of ever escaping from this burden is to train and push on my nephew into a position in which he can take this weight upon himself. This process of course involves a great additional expense, and I cannot let my own boys suffer for what I am obliged to do for him. For the next three years, during which I shall have all three at work, I can look forward to nothing but a fight *à outrance* for money, however it is to be honestly come by. I don't care how much or how hard I work, and fortunately my sanguine temperament and excellent health save me from the gnawing of anxiety which would kill many people. At the end of these three years Frank, I hope, will have a capital position, and be able to relieve me to a considerable extent, and Tiddy

> will have reached the age to which scholarships are possible, and according to all human probability will be able to do much of what remains to his education for himself. Now, perhaps, it would be wiser, with this tremendous struggle before me, to retire from my pretty house and pleasant surroundings and go to some cheap village where I could live at less expense. I hold myself ready to do this should the necessity absolutely arise; but you will easily understand that while still in the full tide of middle life I shrink from such a sacrifice.... What I am doing is not done without much and serious thought, nor am I insensible to the fact, perhaps the hardest of all, that I must resign myself to do second-class work all my life from lack of time to do myself full justice. I make this sacrifice, however, with my eyes open, not deceiving myself on the subject. One of my boys, perhaps, may take up my imperfection and make it into something worthy to live.[24]

It should be remembered that Jeanie's surviving brother and sister, Daniel Wilson and Jessie Sime, were just as closely related to the Wilson children as she was. Probably it was Daniel who gave her the fifty pounds a year; Jessie, a polite and pious lady, did the absolute minimum. She had reluctantly taken the eldest girl, Nelly, but made it clear that she expected her to get a job as soon as possible. The full burden of providing for the other three fell on Margaret, who was perhaps more hard-pressed then than at any other time in her life. She was producing at least two long books a year and an article for *Blackwood's* most months. It was said, although it was not true, that she had once written an entire number of the *Magazine*. Although she had domestic help (the little girls were mainly looked after by the Swiss maid, Lina) she was never shielded from family life in the way that a middle-class male breadwinner expected to be. John Blackwood, for instance, wrote after a few days' holiday with his own son that it had been a pleasure to get to know the boy and 'I quite understand how all the servants and every one are so fond of him'.[25] Margaret, by contrast, always had a great deal to do with the children and expected to be on call for most of the day. Writing had to be done at odd times, and at night. Fortunately she needed very little sleep and was hardly ever ill.

She felt that she could not keep going at all if she had to scrape and pinch, so she spent money lavishly when she had it.

She gave the children presents, took holidays whenever possible and had a constant stream of guests in the house. The result was that she was always in debt and always promising to write a new book or article to wipe the debt out. Occasionally there were awful moments when it looked as if her work was not wanted. One of the worst was at the end of 1872, when she found that she suddenly needed a large sum. She went to London to see George Smith, Charlotte Brontë's publisher, with the MS of a novel, but had no luck. 'The consequence was that I seemed to be at a dead standstill.'

She went home and felt slightly dazed as she crossed the threshold of the house, where everything was going on as usual, 'every corner full and warm as if it had a steady income and secure revenue at its back'. She had never told her brother or the children about her problems and did not do so now, but the night was one of dreadful worry. Next morning a man from the *Graphic*, a new weekly paper, came to see her. He told her that they needed a serial straight away and would pay her £1300.

The novel she gave them was *Innocent*, which she began to write at once. As its name suggests, it was a murder mystery, and not surprisingly in the circumstances it was not very good. She hardly bothered to disguise her contempt for the subject-matter, saying at one point where we visit the heroine in prison, 'I will confess to the gentle reader that I never was in a prison, and I do not know how it looked'.[26] So long as her work was getting printed, she could afford to take it lightly:

> Thank Heaven, I don't remember much one year what I wrote the year before [she wrote to Blackwood in May 1873] . . . how could I write another word more if my conscience was oppressed with a recollection of all the rubbish I have poured upon the world? . . . . Please don't let anybody upbraid me with writing too much until the year 1876, if we live to see it, by which time I hope the bulk of the schooling will be over, and I will not mind it.[27]

She did, however, manage during this time to write one good novel. After a break of four years, Blackwood agreed to serialise *The Story of Valentine and his Brother*, which appeared in the *Magazine* throughout 1874. She took more pains with it than usual, even destroying a chapter which did not satisfy her, and the result was that, although it is not about anything very important, *Valentine* is extremely readable and well written; only the love scenes drag.

By 1874 things seemed to be getting better. She went to Florence at Easter to prepare a book on the great men of the city for Macmillan. The result was *The Makers of Florence* (1876), one of her most popular works. She had a great deal to do with Macmillan from then on, negotiating mainly with Dinah's husband, George Lillie Craik. She liked the idea of writing travel books, 'this is my only way of giving my boys foreign trips'.[28] The three of them were all doing well. In the summer she was photographed on the steps of the Windsor house with Cyril, Cecco, and her nephew Frank. Cyril was about to join the sixth form, and was coming 'first in every examination, as a matter of course, and almost without effort'.[29] A. C. Benson, who was then at Eton, described him as:

> a small, lightly-built, curly haired boy, handsome, attractive-looking, stepping rather jauntily and with an air of entirely unembarrassed amusement – indeed a charming-looking creature, with an expression at once sensitive, impressionable and whimsical.... He had great personal attractions and charm of manner; it seemed as though any success might be awaiting him.

Cecco at fourteen was 'a very quiet boy, with a highly animated and I thought roguish expression, with bright black beady eyes, very friendly and amiable, but decidedly silent'. He was known to have unusual interests, like heraldry and genealogy. Benson has also left his impression of Margaret herself:

> She was comely, and would indeed have been beautiful, if it had not been for her mouth, which had something roughly shaped and abrupt about it, the upper lip projecting sharply over the lower. About the whole face there was a look of reserve, even of endurance, more of repression than of suppression, as if a naturally expansive and genial nature had been thwarted and baffled.[30]

He tells us that she was on the best of terms with her sons, but was rather quiet in company. Mrs Story put it more sharply,

'When she pleased she could be very agreeable, but she did not always so please, and when indifferent to her company, she was very silent and took no part in general conversation'.[31]

She tells us that when Margaret was staying with them at Rosneath she would ask the servants for an extra pair of candles each night, and that they were always burned out in the morning. Her light could still be seen when the rest of the household was getting up and she came down a few hours later 'serene and smiling'. John Blackwood's daughter noticed the same thing when she visited them, 'She worked early and she worked late, and yet there was no time in the day when she could not be seen'.[32]

'The little house in Clarence Crescent', wrote Howard Sturgis, 'overflowed with her courtiers.' There were flowers in every room and several pet dogs, and her friends were constantly coming to stay. A letter of 1873 mentions a sick friend who was taking up all her spare moments. Who it was is not known, but she was worried about her two closest women friends during these years. Robert Macpherson died in 1873 and Geddie, who had four children, was left to pay off his debts. In constant pain from rheumatism and heart disease, she supported herself by English lessons, drawing and literary work, 'an accomplished and cultivated woman through all her toils'.[33] The Tulloch family were going through a bad time too. The Principal had a second nervous breakdown in 1869, and another four years later, and in 1871 Mrs Tulloch had a serious illness which she never really got over. She went on looking after her husband and children, but her health was shattered. They often came to Windsor to see their married daughter Sara and the younger girl, Fanny, lived for long stretches of time in Margaret's house.

When the photograph was taken it looked as if her responsibilities were getting lighter. 'Next year', she wrote to Blackwood, 'I expect everything to be changed.' Frank was going to India, Cyril to Oxford and the two little girls to a school in Germany. Her brother talked about going off by himself after his children had left. Margaret decided to let the house, as she was still spending far too much, and move into a lodging for 'six months' utter retrenchment'.[34] In the event, things did not work out quite like that.

Early in 1875 Margaret became bored with the work she was

doing on the Florence book and impulsively began a novel about a feckless elderly man; the two frightened, unattractive children whom he has produced late in life; and the woman who somewhat resentfully looks after them. *The Curate in Charge*, written in February and March, developed into one of her most interesting books.

Frank took a first class at Cooper's Hill engineering college, and asked to be sent to the Punjab. His aunt was determined to give him a good time before he went. There was a tradition, in a Scottish family she knew, that on the night before a boy left home the whole party had a bottle of champagne in which to drink his health. (This is described at the beginning of *Kirsteen.*) She wanted Frank to have the equivalent of a bottle of champagne. She had arranged to take all three boys to Switzerland for the summer, and in the middle of July she went to London with them to meet Isabella Blackwood and see the sights.

She was still not sure what to do about Frank's father; it was obvious to everyone but himself that he was not strong enough to live on his own. They had a few pleasant days in London. The boys went to the Eton and Harrow match at Lord's, all wearing little blue bows; the fifteen-year-old Cecco straining to keep up with the two bigger ones. Next day a telegram came saying that the elder Frank was very ill.

They went back to Windsor to find him semi-conscious. At first it seemed that he might live for another year or two, and Margaret told her sons that it would not be possible for him to go to strangers now. They agreed; Cyril cheerfully, Cecco with an effort, for he was a reserved boy who had never really liked having his home invaded by Wilsons. But after a few days Frank died in his sleep. At fifty-nine he had 'withered away to the barest skeleton of living'. They had got on each other's nerves in the last few years but Margaret, remembering the old days in Liverpool when she had read her novels to him and their mother, was much more upset than she had expected. 'However', she wrote to Blackwood from a darkened house, '(and that is saddest of all), there is no feeling possible but that it is best that his shattered life should have ended now, while still his children are with him, and all the last pious offices can be paid him by his son's hands.'[35]

Cyril left Eton soon afterwards. He had come third in the final examinations, and his tutor told her that although he did not 'plod' he was quite capable of getting an Oxford fellowship. He and Frank escorted the little girls to Mademoiselle Schumacher's school in Arolsen, arranging to meet Margaret, Cecco and Miss Clifford in Switzerland. There is no doubt that Margaret believed she was doing the best thing for her nieces. Madge was coming up to twelve, Denny ten, and there were very few good schools for girls in England at the time. But one cannot imagine her sending any of her own children abroad. Possibly it was a relief to get rid of these unresponsive little girls who had never shown her any affection. They had not seemed very upset by their father's death, and they left England apparently with no emotion.

Margaret and her party reached Interlaken in mid-August and the boys joined them. Suddenly an anguished letter arrived from the two little girls. As soon as they were left in Germany they had become terribly distressed. 'Oh, come and take us home', Madge wrote, or words to that effect, 'oh, come, come and take us home. We will be as good as angels if you will only come and take us home.' Margaret was astonished and moved. She still believed that it was better for them to be educated abroad, but she sent them a basket of toys and cakes and tells us that they soon got over their home-sickness. It was a turning-point in their relationship. From then on, she wrote – and everything confirms it – they were 'my true children, the unquestioned daughters of the house'.

In Interlaken they had met Anne Thackeray, the novelist's elder daughter and herself quite a well-known writer. Unmarried at thirty-eight, she lived with her sister Harriet Marian (Minnie) and Minnie's husband Leslie Stephen. Anne struck most people as a 'wild, amusing, creative and muddle-headed creature of impulse';[36] she was always coming out with howlers such as, 'There are forty millions of unmarried women in London alone'.[37] Beneath the comic exterior, she was one of the kindest and least smug of Victorian literary women. She had adopted two baby cousins whose mother had died and had felt responsible for her younger sister since they were children. She and Margaret became great friends and forty years later Anne recalled, 'She was one of those people whose presence is even more than a *pleasure*; hers was a stimulus; she was kindly, sympathetic, and yet answering with that chord of intelligent antagonism which is so suggestive and makes for such good talk'.[38]

From Interlaken they went on to Grindelwald, where they

were joined by Mr and Mrs Leslie Stephen and their little girl Laura. Minnie was expecting another baby in the winter. Margaret and Anne sat on the porch under the clematis talking and writing, and Leslie Stephen took the boys on the mountains. He and Margaret got on well, despite their religious differences, and, with some encouragement from his wife and her sister, he invited her to do a serial for the *Cornhill Magazine* of which he was editor.

She and the boys came back to England in September. Cyril moved into Balliol on 15 October, and Frank sailed from Portsmouth on the twenty-fourth. Margaret could not help feeling rather terrified at launching them into the world, especially as it was likely to be many years before she saw her nephew again. She hoped, though, that from then on things would improve.

'With that year began a new life', she wrote, 'one of which I cannot speak much.'

7 The Woman Question: Some Novels of the 1870s

For almost as long as Margaret had been writing books, there had been public and private discussions about what was then called 'the woman question'. During the third quarter of the nineteenth century women's suffrage societies were founded; female ratepayers got the vote in local elections; John Stuart Mill published *The Subjection of Women*; there was a Married Women's Property Act; Girton College and the Girls' Public Day School Trust opened and Florence Nightingale and George Eliot became famous in their different spheres. (Margaret wrote afterwards that the question of whether women could or could not be great writers had been solved by George Eliot 'in a way most flattering to all who were and are fighting the question of equality between the two halves of mankind'.[1]) Until recently we have forgotten how fiercely this question was debated. It could no longer be assumed that a woman's place was in the home and that virtually all of them would get married. Suddenly everyone was aware of issues like the vote, higher education for girls, and what was to be done with old maids.

It is usual for people who know only a small amount about Margaret Oliphant to call her an anti-feminist, and perhaps write her off. 'Cousin Annie', who edited her *Autobiography*, laid her wide open to this charge by quoting a letter which refers to Mill's 'mad notion of the franchise for women'.[2] This was *à propos* of an article, 'The Great Unrepresented', which appeared in *Blackwood's* in September 1866. Incidentally, this article did not say that women who wanted the vote should not have it, only that she did not want it herself. There had been two earlier articles, 'The Laws Concerning Women' (April 1856) and 'The Condition of Women' (February 1858), which were on the whole critical of the women's rights movement. However, her views had always been more complicated than simple antifeminism, and a few years after the article on Mill they changed. Her considered opinion, written in the 1890s, was that his work, 'though it brought him no credit', helped to produce 'those great and beneficial alterations and new stipulations in law which have made the position of women so much more independent and worthy'.[3]

While she had never believed that women were inferior, she did believe, at least at first, that they had a different sphere from men. 'I don't agree with the working-woman idea very much', says a character in *Lucy Crofton* (1860), 'I don't think any lady does an unbecoming office when she sweeps her own hearth and serves her own table'.[4] Like many women in the later twentieth century she reacted against feminism because it appeared to undervalue the work which women were already doing. As a devoted mother (who particularly valued little girls), she found it hard to believe in women who disliked children. 'It is the want of natural duties which makes women – perhaps ambitious, perhaps clever – possibly something higher than both – chafe at the narrow round in which they are supposed to be held', she wrote in *Orphans* (1858).[5]

Some women sought an escape from this 'narrow round' through romantic and sexual fantasies. Margaret had noticed this tendency in the work of Charlotte Brontë and came back to it in 'Novels', an article published in *Blackwood's* in September 1867. 'Women driven wild with love for the man who leads them on to desperation before he accords that word of encouragement which carries them into the seventh heaven . . . who give and receive burning kisses and frantic embraces, and live in a voluptuous dream, either waiting for or brooding over the inevitable lover – such are the heroines who have been imported into modern fiction.' This type of novel seems to have been just as popular in the 1860s as it is now. Looking at some of Ouida's and Rhoda Broughton's works she picked out the sentence, 'My hair fell in its splendid ruddy billows over his great shoulder', for well-deserved ridicule.[6] Modern novels, she remarked, were full of heroines who were interested only in men and 'throw their glorious hair over the breast of any chance companion . . . . What need has a woman for a soul when she has upon her head a mass of wavy gold?'

The growing tendency to treat women as sex objects repelled her, and this particular article is dismissive about women's rights. At the time she still believed that women who drew attention to themselves, whether by demanding the vote or writing torrid romantic fiction, made the whole of their sex look ridiculous. Her views altered over the next few years, during which time she realised that she agreed with most of the feminists' aims. She believed in a Married Women's Property Act, a mother's right to the custody of her children, women doctors, and university education for girls. When *Blackwood's*, in 1876, published a story, '1895: The Lady Candidate', which made fun of women who wanted to go into Parliament, she wrote to the editor:

> This sort of glib nonsense has by degrees brought me round to the conviction that however indifferent I may be personally to political privileges the system which supposes me incapable of forming a reasonable opinion on public matters is very far from a perfect one . . . and as all women are not girls of twenty, and some of us are reasonable beings, it is worth while considering I think whether perpetual impertinence of this kind may not have an effect quite the reverse of that which I suppose its originators intend. I am almost sorry to say that I don't feel myself much sillier than the majority of men I meet.[7]

By 1880 she was prepared to say in public, 'I think it is highly absurd that I should not have a vote, if I want one'.[8]

Early in 1882, while writing the *Literary History of England*, Margaret managed with some difficulty to find a copy of Mary Wollstonecraft's *Vindication of the Rights of Woman*, which had long been out of print. As a reputed atheist and a woman who had lived with men outside marriage, she might have been expected to affront some of Margaret's deepest prejudices, but in fact she found the *Vindication* very readable and thoroughly sympathised with the Mary whose father drank and who had done 'literary drudgery' to support her sister. She suggested that the demand for women's rights had 'risen almost invariably from women compelled by hard stress of circumstances to despise the men about them'.[9]

In some of the novels written in the later 1870s, before she had read Mary Wollstonecraft, she began to look seriously at the question of work for women, particularly those with dependants. Earlier novels had shown women who were stronger than men and shouldered their burdens, but, apart from Menie in *The Quiet Heart*, most of them operate inside the home. *The Curate in Charge* (1876) considers other possibilities. It is, incidentally, a much better novel than most of those written around this time.

As in *The Doctor's Family*, the main theme is 'women who have other people to carry on their shoulders' (18). Mr St John at sixty is still a country curate because he has never pushed himself forward. His unworldliness is really, the author suggests, a refined form of selfishness, as he ignores his responsibility for his children. Hester, his first wife, has had to stay single until she is forty:

> It had been tacitly understood all along that she was never to leave her father, and as he was very kind in manner, Hester accepted the lot with enthusiasm, and thought it was her own choice ... What was to become of her when her father left her, Hester never asked herself, and neither did the old man ... [She] lived contented in the old rotten tumble-down vicarage, doing the same thing every day at the same hour year after year, serving her father and the parish, attending all the church services, visiting the schools and the sick people. I hope good women who live in this dutiful routine get to like it, and find a happiness in the thought of so much humble handmaiden's work performed so steadily; but to the profane and the busy it seems hard thus to wear away a life ... (2)

Mr St John passively accepts the situation and does not marry her until her father dies. Hester looks after him efficiently and has two daughters, Cicely and Mab, who are very bright and energetic. Their mother sometimes regrets 'that they were not boys: but then she would think of her husband and the regret was never expressed' (2). These early chapters introduce the theme of ineffectual men and strong women, who are a little contemptuous of them but still feel obliged to take care of them.

After Hester dies Mr St John drifts into marriage with the governess, a feeble ladylike person who is desperate for a home. We are cautioned against thinking that marriage is necessarily the best solution to her problems. 'She might have been living now, a respectable single woman', the girls' aunt tells them, instead of which she dies after giving birth to twin boys. 'Yes, she did die of it. You don't understand these things – you are only children.' (7) The little boys are sickly, unappealing and afraid of their sisters, who have all the trouble of looking after them. Almost certainly they are based on Margaret's nieces, for whom she had such ambiguous feelings at the time, but it is quite consistent with the theme of the novel that they should be male.

The question is whether the girls are going to live like their mother and stepmother or have the chance of something better. Mr St John takes it for granted that they will do the first – 'A good girl', he says, 'is always happy at home.' (6) Mab and Cicely, 'the artist and the housekeeper', represent two aspects of Margaret's personality. Mab only wants to paint (and can earn money by doing so) while Cicely is the one who copes with babies and tradesmen. Through her the author presents the worm's-eye-view of the woman who, like Martha in the parable, feels slightly hostile to the 'higher' life because if she does not do the dirty work no one else will. At this point Mr St John's job is taken from him and given to the young fellow of an Oxford college, who does not need it. As in *The Rector*, we are invited to consider the relationship between the world of learning – represented by Oxford dons, celibate in those days, who 'don't care for common troubles' (15) – and the claims of ordinary life. Roger is a dilettante who collects precious china and yet feels dissatisfied in the midst of plenty. A man cannot live for art 'when he is merely a critic, commentator and amateur – not a worker in the same' (8). Moreover, he is a clergyman, and feels that he ought to be doing something to justify his existence. The result is that he takes the job, though without wanting to deprive the curate, and the old man dies of delayed shock leaving the girls with their living to earn.

Cicely, who has emerged as the person who holds the family together, decides not to let her brothers go into an orphanage and to get work as the parish schoolmistress to support them. Here we come up against a Victorian taboo; a lady could be a governess, if it was absolutely necessary, but not a schoolmistress. Her friends tell her that it will 'take away from her her rank as a gentlewoman' and drop her, so she seems likely to have a hard life with little personal satisfaction. The author knows that readers will expect her to escape from it by getting married, but this, she thinks, is a 'contemptible expedient':

> That Cicely's brave undertaking ought to come to some great result in itself, that she ought to be able to make her way nobly, as her purpose was, working with her hands for the children that were not hers ... having that success in her work which is the most pleasant of all recompenses ... this, no doubt, would be the highest and best ... (19)

In the end Roger falls in love with her because he is eager to come out of his ivory tower. 'Make me somebody in life', he asks her, 'not a mere spectator.' (20) However, the novel avoids a conventional ending. It seems very likely that Cicely will marry him, but she still has not made up her mind.

Diana Trelawney also centres on a woman who works. This novel has a curious history. It was not published until 1892, but had been written by June 1877 and sent to John Blackwood; after his death in 1879 both Margaret and the publishers forgot about it for years. But it faithfully reflects her preoccupations in the 1870s. Diana is an attractive woman of thirty who has been a schoolmistress but unexpectedly inherits an estate. Like many Oliphant heroines, she is a thoroughly good administrator, whose work is 'important and valuable and necessary, not the things done for the mere sake of occupation which are the lot of so many women' (3). She resembles her creator in having hangers-on, in the shape of Mrs Norton and her niece Sophy, 'peevish, humble-minded, weakly little gentlewomen'. Even while she sponges on Diana Mrs Norton feels superior to her – 'she, a lady of private means, not requiring to work for her living' (2). Sophy is a mindless girl 'ready to accept any love-making that should come her way'.

Although the plot – in which a man is manoeuvred into marrying Sophy when he prefers Diana – seems incredible, this is still a witty and well-written novel. Diana, like her namesakes in Scott and Meredith, is a rather remarkable person whereas Sophy is a nonentity – 'the most charming blank sheet of paper on which a man could desire to inscribe his name'. She and her aunt make spiteful remarks about Diana whom they instinctively see as a rival:

> 'Gentlemen don't care for such clever women. They like someone to look up to them, not a person who is always

> standing on her opinion .... It is not just an equal he wants. He wants a clinging, sweet, dependent creature . . .' (11)

Margaret was always bored by heroines 'of the all-that-is-good-and-lovely kind',[10] and Sophy is a caricature of the perfect Victorian young lady, who behaves in the appropriate way for a heroine but is actually mean and spoiled. Diana is aware of what is happening but does not mind enough to interfere. Like Margaret, she is not surprised when other people behave badly, and does not see romantic love as the centre of her life. 'I have got a trade, an occupation', she says. 'Women with that are better not to marry.'[11]

Within the Precincts (1879) looks at women workers from a different angle. Lottie, the heroine, has a beautiful singing voice but thinks it is unwomanly to perform in public. 'She was ready to have worked her fingers to the bone, indoors, in the privacy of the family, for her father and brother ... but to work publicly for her living, what was that but to proclaim to all the world that they were incapable?' (3) However, her father, brother and fiancé all want to make money out of her. 'The desire of women for work', the author warns, 'is apt to be supported from an undesirable side.' (32) Given that men have no feelings of reverence or respect for women, the best thing Lottie can do is to cultivate her talent. She has to suffer disillusionment and unhappiness, but she may become an artist.

1. Mrs. Wilson and Margaret, after her marriage

2. Kellie Castle

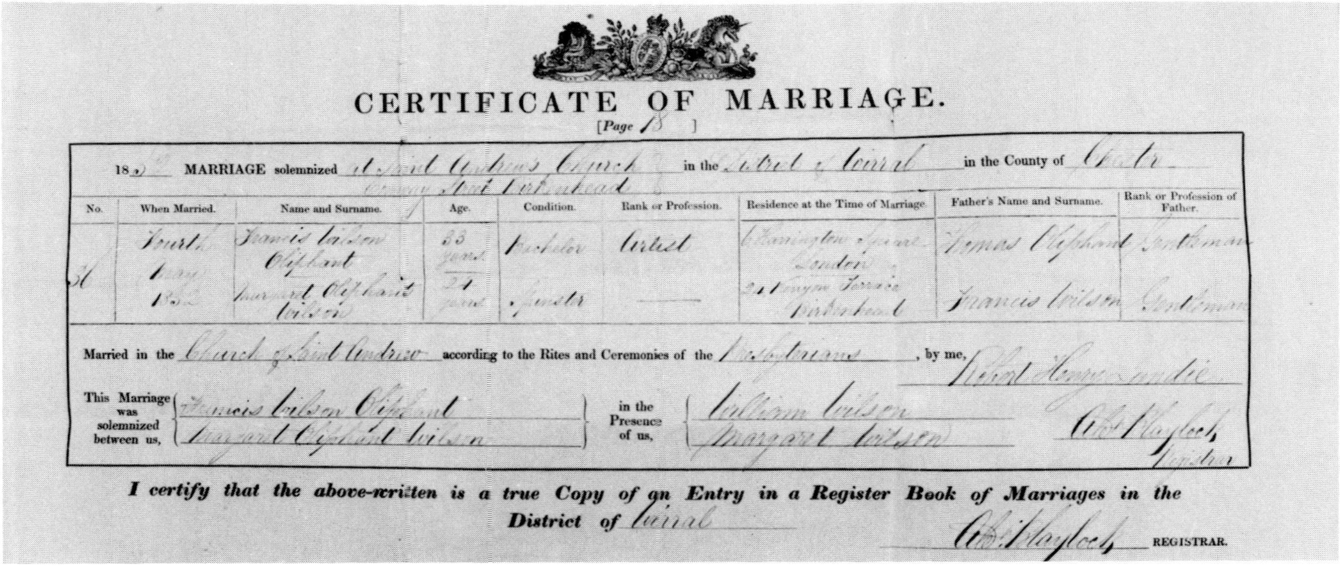

CERTIFICATE OF MARRIAGE.

[Page 18]

18 52 MARRIAGE solemnized at Saint Andrew's Church Conway Street Birkenhead in the District of Wirral in the County of Chester

No.	When Married.	Name and Surname.	Age.	Condition.	Rank or Profession.	Residence at the Time of Marriage.	Father's Name and Surname.	Rank or Profession of Father.
36	Fourth May 1852	Francis Wilson Oliphant	33 years	Bachelor	Artist	Kennington Square London	Thomas Oliphant	Gentleman
		Margaret Oliphant Wilson	24 years	Spinster	—	24 Conyers Terrace Birkenhead	Francis Wilson	Gentleman

Married in the Church of Saint Andrew according to the Rites and Ceremonies of the Presbyterians, by me, Robert Henry Lundie

This Marriage was solemnized between us, Francis Wilson Oliphant, Margaret Oliphant Wilson

in the Presence of us, William Wilson, Margaret Wilson

Robt Haylock, Registrar

I certify that the above-written is a true Copy of an Entry in a Register Book of Marriages in the District of Wirral

Robt Haylock REGISTRAR.

3. Marriage certificate of Margaret and Frank Oliphant. Both fathers are incorrectly described.

4. Margaret as a young woman, about 1860 (from *The Bookman* 1897)

5. 'Come home to be a burden.' Geddie Macpherson's illustration for Margaret's novel, *Madonna Mary*

6. Robert Herbert Story in 1860 (from *Memoir of Robert Herbert Story* by his daughters)

7. Principal Tulloch

8. Cecco, Margaret, Cyril and Frank Wilson, 1874

9. Margaret in 1883

10. Denny's drawing of Margaret, 1895

11. John Blackwood, Margaret's publisher

8 Prodigal Sons (1875–84)

With her family scattered far and wide, the house seemed unnaturally quiet. Only Cecco, who was still at Eton, remained with his mother, and she was a little worried that he was 'too fond of home, and prefers my society to that of other boys, which I don't think quite good for him'.[1] The plan of moving into a cheap lodging was never carried out.

There was one tragedy in her circle in November 1875. After the holiday in Switzerland she had asked Anne Thackeray to visit her and Anne had agreed to come for one night, although she was worried about leaving her sister just then. The next day she was summoned back to London by telegram; Minnie Stephen had had a stillborn baby prematurely and died. Margaret had asked a few people to dinner to meet her, 'and you may imagine the ghastly effect of a vacant place so caused'.[2] Anne, who flouted all convention two years later by marrying her cousin Richmond Ritchie, seventeen years her junior, became a lifelong friend.

It has been said that when Margaret came back from Switzerland 'she might yet have become the outstanding woman writer of the century'.[3] As she realised, the strange new quiet ought to have made it much easier for her to work. But although her brother and most of the children were no longer with her, she still had to pay fees for the four of them who were being educated. As always, she was desperate for a steady income. Around the end of 1875 she tried to interest Blackwood in a 'book cyclopaedia', or companion to English Literature, which she pointed out had never been done before. 'I should be so thankful to have this kind of solid underground work going on which would not require the constant reproduction of one's name to the weariness of the world.'[4] Nothing came of this, but over the next few years she was very busy with a new series, Blackwood's *Foreign Classics for English Readers*, of which she was the general editor. She wrote three volumes herself, on Dante, Molière and Cervantes ('I don't know a word of Spanish, but I must do this'[5]) and recruited several of her friends, like the Principal and Anne Thackeray, to write others. One gets the impression that she wasted a good deal of time and did not make much money after all.

With one exception, she produced no good novel in the next five years. *Carita*, the novel she had promised Leslie Stephen, began in the *Cornhill* in June 1876 and provided 'the bulk of a year's income'. It was followed by several more pot-boilers – *Young Musgrave, Mrs Arthur, The Primrose Path, The Greatest Heiress in England, He that will not when he may, Harry Joscelyn, In Trust*.[6] She must have been aware that many people who had admired her Carlingford novels now thought she was played out. John Blackwood, in particular, had long since ceased to think of her as a serious artist. When she offered him a novel in mid-1878 he asked her if she really thought it was 'likely to make a marked success':

> I don't suppose that at fifty one is likely to begin a new career [she replied] ... and of course I can have no desire to thrust myself upon you if you do not find my books answer.[7]

Frank wrote that he had settled happily in India, but she began to suspect after a year that Cyril was wasting time at Oxford. One of his letters home, in November 1876, suggests that they had had words about this:

> I write just a line in a great hurry to apologise most fully and honestly for the ill-temper I displayed in my answer to your perfectly just remonstrance. I can only say that it might have taken a milder form.[8]

Later in the month he told her he was working hard but 'gradually giving up all hopes of my first'.[9] In fact he got a second, to his mother's bitter disappointment. In the spring he got into some sort of trouble and was sent home for a few weeks.

On 19 June 1877, Margaret gave an open-air party on the island of Runnymede to celebrate the twenty-fifth anniversary of her connection with *Blackwood's*. 'One could hardly realise how long it was', wrote John Blackwood's daughter, 'when we saw Mrs Oliphant that day looking so well and handsome in her gown of grey silk and her white lace bonnet, completing the pleasing picture she made with her delicate colouring and beautiful white hair'.[10] Cyril proposed Blackwood's health and the party was a great success. 'How I envy you!' Dinah Craik wrote afterwards. 'Your son's person and manner are charming, and his speech was perfect.'[11] A. W. Kinglake, the historian of the Crimean war, who was one of her warmest admirers, also wrote to thank her and congratulate her on her sons – 'both such nice young fellows'.[12]

At this point she was not seriously worried about either of them, although she wrote to Macmillan from St Andrew's that summer that it was a 'struggle to get the boys to do a little work notwithstanding the attractions of golf'.[13] Cyril became twenty-one in November, and she wrote to John Blackwood:

> He is a very good sweet-hearted boy, and very tender to me, but I can't help feeling doubtful whether he has enough of the sterner stuff in him to get success .... I am going to enter him directly at the Inner Temple. If all these boys of ours had but ten thousand a year what delightful fellows they would be! I fear that is what our modern education trains them for, more than anything else.[14]

On 24 May 1878 Geddie Macpherson died suddenly in Rome. Ever since Robert's death she had been supporting herself and her younger children by various odd jobs – 'now and then nearly dying, but always struggling up to work again'.[15] She had just finished writing a memoir of her aunt, Anna Jameson, which Margaret edited and saw through the press. Reviewing it herself, she feared that the 'modest merits' of these two women would quickly be forgotten.[16]

All this time she was writing affectionate letters to the two little girls. They kept asking to come home, but she explained that there were no good girls' schools in England and 'I want you to be very well educated and perhaps if you are clever to go to Cambridge like the young men. They have no college for ladies at Oxford yet but there are two at Cambridge'.[17] Occasionally they came back for holidays and there were more discussions with the Wilson family about their future. Their elder sister Nelly was still in the charge of Jessie Sime, who had made it clear that she did not want her. She had grown up to be very eccentric and failed to find work as a governess. Margaret would have preferred that she and Jessie should support her between them, but this suggestion was coldly received. However, her brother Frank sent her a generous slice of his income, and Margaret had her at Windsor more than half the time and bought nearly all her clothes. Eventually she settled in Toronto with her uncle Daniel Wilson.

Annie Walker was another semi-permanent guest. She had tried to support herself by teaching and writing, but disliked one and was unsuccessful at the other, and she appreciated the many luxuries which she got at Clarence Crescent. Margaret was quite willing to keep her on as a secretary and lady-housekeeper, but she noted wryly that she might not be alive for ever.

In August 1878 she and Cecco, with the Tullochs, the Tarvers, and their children, spent a few weeks at Dunkirk. It was an expensive trip, but she convinced herself that she could pay for it by writing articles. One reason for coming abroad was the health of Mrs Tulloch, who was never free from asthma. She looked 'dreadfully thin and worn ... it is incredible how so little flesh and blood should be expected to keep in the soul'.[18] With another of her close friends dead so recently, Margaret was considerably frightened. It also struck her at about this time that Cecco was behaving a little oddly. At eighteen he was extremely silent, stayed by himself as much as possible and ignored the Tulloch girls, whom he did not like.

Cyril had gone to Ballater in Aberdeenshire to work with his tutor and some other young men. 'Do my dearest boy write regularly twice a week at least', she begged him. '. . . I am so far off from you and have no longer the alternative of telegraphing if I get very anxious. And you know I cannot help a panic taking hold of me now and then.'[19] Later in the month she wrote, 'I have been a fortnight here and I have only had two letters from you ... I think you might have treated me a little better ... I have hurriedly finished my paper for next month, which is not very good but will do I suppose for padding as well as most magazine literature'.[20] After Cyril had been silent for eleven days, she burst out:

> I had hoped after all that has passed that you would have thought it worth your while to keep me in mind and do what you could to soothe and calm my anxieties but instead of this you have left a longer gap than ever before.

A letter had come at last, 'but not the less have I felt the indifference to my feelings which makes you so careless about writing. I wish I could be as careless as you, and cease to calculate upon you as any element in happiness . . . . I hope your work is *really* going on as it ought, but your means and your time wouldn't seem to me quite to justify repeated visits to Ballater or any where else, incurring new expenses . . . . Recollect for heaven's sake that neither you nor I can afford any playing with your time, and that there has been folly enough in your career hitherto. If I do you injustice it is your own fault in leaving me without information.'[21]

On this occasion, it seems, Cyril soothed her down. From Dunkirk, the party went on briefly to the Low Countries and Paris, coming home in September. It had been an unsatisfying holiday. As usual, she had spent more than she had intended; she had bought some old Flanders lace which she knew she could not afford and Blackwood had refused to take several of the papers which were to have paid for the trip. Back in Windsor, she arranged to let her house and take one in Oxford for the first half of 1879, as Cecco was about to join his brother at Balliol and she wanted to be near them.

That autumn she sent Blackwood the manuscript of *A Beleaguered City*, which eventually became one of her most famous novels. She had spent much more time on it than she usually did, knowing it to be better than average, but he did not take it.

In February she moved into 4 Crick Road, Oxford, a tall house (which is still standing) in a pleasant tree-lined avenue. Her arrival caused a small flutter, and Masters, Principals and professors all visited and asked her to dinner parties. Probably she met Mrs Humphry Ward, who was living round the corner with her husband and young family and was secretary to the newly-formed Somerville College. She had not yet begun to publish novels but when she did, a few years later, Margaret was astounded by her success. Her belief that Oxford dons were out of touch with human problems was confirmed when she heard that some of them had been making unpleasant remarks. 'My name seems to be sufficient warrant for all manner of accusations of incorrectness, from all the whippersnappers of young scholars.'[22]

Cyril's final examinations were due in May, and she was intensely worried. She asked Blackwood to introduce her to the

Foreign Secretary, Lord Salisbury, with the view of getting him a place in the Foreign Office. His sons had been at Eton with hers but 'there seems no chance of getting at a Minister without introductions'.[23] In the past she had never asked for favours, but she was becoming desperate.

She stayed in Oxford until June and met Turgenev, who was taking an honorary degree; then the family went home to await Cyril's results. As she had feared, he got another second:

> He has been very unwell during this last most important year which is some sort of excuse [she wrote to Blackwood] but idleness is at the bottom of it. I am putting all sorts of irons in the fire for him now – the Duke of Richmond for one and I hope Lord Salisbury too. If he should get an offer either of a school inspectorship or a public office appointment he would take it – though I still think the bar would be the thing most suited to him – but two or three years more of study and fees, and an uncertain prospect at the end, appals me.[24]

In the end it was decided that Cyril should read for the bar, living partly at home and partly in London where he worked at a barrister's chambers.

That spring Madge and Denny came home for good. They were now in their mid-teens and fiercely devoted to each other. They wrote letters in a secret code when they were apart and resisted any attempt to split them up, or to make them live anywhere but with Margaret. Although there had been some talk of them being governesses, Margaret hated the idea. Over the next few years she tried to prepare them for a career in which they could earn money while living at home. She paid for Madge to take lessons from a leading wood-engraver, and Denny went for a while to a boarding-school in Windsor and then studied art.

On 29 October 1879 John Blackwood, whose health had been breaking up for some time, died at Strathtyrum. Most of his work had already passed to his nephew William, who became the next editor of the *Magazine*. Margaret had known John for over a quarter of a century and had always valued his comments on her work. She wrote affectionately to Isabella – 'Who is there now for whose opinion one will care as one did for his?'[25] – without knowing that a greater blow was on the way.

At the end of October her nephew Frank Wilson, who was now twenty-five, had been working at Rupar as an assistant engineer on the Sirhind canal. He was a robust young man, and had already survived one bout of fever, but around this time he went down with typhoid and died the day after Blackwood. Communications with India were so slow that Margaret did not even know he was ill until the last week in November. She waited for a week in terrible suspense, only to hear, a month after it had happened, that he was dead.

It was a total shock. Frank had been the only child whom she had not worried about. She spent a miserable Christmas with her three nieces, 'now deprived of the last prop that absolutely belonged to them'.[26] The young people, who had not seen Frank for four years, recovered quite quickly, but it was much less easy for her.

More than ever, at the end of this 'dark and heavy year',[27] she was thinking about the mystery of death. She wrote a ghost story, 'Earthbound', which was the first to be subtitled 'a story of the Seen and the Unseen'.[28] Coincidentally, her novel about the relationship between living and dead, *A Beleaguered City*, came out at the same time. She got an enthusiastic letter from a young fellow-contributor to the *Cornhill*, Robert Louis Stevenson:

> I look in vain for anything like it since the *Pilgrim's Progress* – or before. How it might read to posterity, is a thing neither I nor you can tell: but to your contemporaries, as to some others, it will be truly good news.
> . . . I have thought often, how many arrows an author shoots in the air – I daresay, so have you. In the *Beleaguered City*, you have lodged some three or four in my heart. I have cried heartily; I feel the better for my tears; and I want to thank you. Let that excuse this otherwise inexcusable letter.[29]

It is always worth remembering how closely the Victorians were acquainted with death. Many of them who, like Margaret, could not take the old religion for granted but still needed some kind of consolation welcomed the *Beleaguered City*, and several of them then and later thought it her finest book. Although it had seemed unlikely that she could begin a new career in her fifties, this did happen to some extent over the next few years. The novel was followed by several supernatural stories which, she said, were 'not like any others. I can produce them only when they come to me',[30] and these stories were widely admired.

Cyril spent the New Year at Daventry in the home of Sir Rainald Knightly, the father of a friend. 'Think a little of the brother you have lost', Margaret wrote, 'and of the aspect which life takes in the light of such an event.'[31] A few days later she asked him to 'try to secure Sir Rainald's influence with Lord Salisbury, if he knows him well enough, or cares enough for you to exercise it on your behalf. In old times men of position used to ask a youth in whom they took any interest, or his parents, whether they could not help him on. I suppose competitive examinations have made an end of that admirable custom.'[32]

'I am very anxious as the years go on', she wrote to William Blackwood in February 1880, 'to get regular work which I can arrange beforehand and which will bring in regular payment.'[33] If he heard of an editorship or similar post, would he think of her? Blackwood did not respond, but at this time Macmillan offered her a thousand pounds – a year's income – to write a literary history of England between 1790 and 1825. Margaret took more time than usual over this book, which was published in 1882, and it is one of her best works of non-fiction. It enabled her to write at length about some of her favourite authors – Cowper, Burns, Scott, Coleridge, Wordsworth – and to discover more about half-forgotten figures like Mary Wollstonecraft. Twentieth-century readers may feel that some writers get too much space and others, like Blake, too little, but they can still enjoy and learn from it.

At the end of the year George Eliot died. Margaret had never met her, although she had once been in John Blackwood's London house when the older novelist, just after finishing *Daniel Deronda*, had stopped briefly at the door. Her death was followed by Thomas Carlyle's in February 1881. 'Alas, here are two who were living authors so short a time ago both gone and open to the dispassionate examination of history.'[34]

In April she took a brief holiday in Venice, where she met Henry James, with the idea of getting material for another travel book. Later in the year she saw a good deal of Laurence Oliphant, who was back in England, and his wife Alice, a charming and idealistic woman much younger than himself. It was not a normal marriage in any sense of the word. Both of them were still dominated by Harris, who made them spend most of their time apart. When Laurence returned to the States Alice took a cottage in Windsor and the two women became very close friends. Alice left England early in 1882, the last time Margaret was to see her. She lost another great friend at about the same time when Miss Clifford (Aunt Nelly) died in her sleep at the end of February, aged fifty-eight. It was a shock to her neighbours in the Crescent, but Margaret soon began to feel that it had not been a bad way to die:

> [She] had known all the round of sorrows that fill a woman's life, without knowing any of its warmer blessings. She had nursed the sick, she had entertained the weary, she had consoled the dying. She had gone about the world, which had no prize or recompense for her, with a smile.

So Margaret wrote a few weeks later in 'A Little Pilgrim', another supernatural story which attempted 'to follow my dear little friend into the unseen'.[35] It was popular on both sides of the Atlantic, selling twenty thousand copies when it came out in volume form, and over the next few years she wrote some more stories with Nelly as the central figure. They added to her growing reputation as a novelist of the 'seen and unseen'.

With one exception, the Little Pilgrim stories are uninteresting and badly written. But at much the same time Margaret was entering on a marvellous creative period. Throughout 1881 she worked on one of her best novels, *The Ladies Lindores*, and at the end of the year she wrote her most famous short story, 'The Open Door'. Perhaps her work was again becoming a refuge from personal unhappiness, for by the early eighties she was desperately worried about her sons.

Margaret had always thought that Cyril was a brilliant boy. 'If Tiddy is spared and turns out according to his promise, he will be somebody, or I deceive myself',[36] she had written proudly when he was only about five. Other doting mothers have thought the same, perhaps, but at least three of Cyril's schoolmates recorded their impression that he seemed to be born to succeed. At Eton he took one prize after another. He was a fine athlete, an excellent amateur actor with a good singing voice, and a strikingly handsome young man. He made friends easily with both sexes – too easily, according to Margaret. Cecco, Mrs Story said, was 'as plain as his brother was good-looking',[37] but she also thought him the more intelligent of the two. He was certainly a better writer than Cyril and in the long run a harder worker. But he spent much more time on his private interests, like heraldry and genealogy, than on the work he was supposed to be doing. He liked to be left alone to read and had a sharp temper which was causing concern to Margaret as early as 1878.

But different though they were, there was still a certain family resemblance. They could not remember their father and had had no chance to model themselves on men who worked for a living. Margaret had thought it wrong to worry them with her financial problems, so they had grown up used to having everything they wanted and assuming that, like their Eton friends, they would find suitable jobs when the time came. But by 1882 Cyril was twenty-five and still earning nothing, and his mother was becoming frantic. She asked Blackwood if he could employ one of her boys – 'as the best Cyril is likely to be is a briefless barrister'[38] – but he did not respond. Later in the year she began a novel, *The Wizard's Son*, which gives a painfully clear picture of their deteriorating relationship.

The central characters are Mrs Methven, a widow, and her son Walter, who lives at home and amuses himself with 'a little cricket ... a little lawn-tennis, a little flirtation', while she struggles to find a job for him:

> She was stricken with shame to think of all the fine things that had been predicted of Walter in his boyish days, and that not one of them had come true. People had ceased now to speak of the great things that Walter would do. They asked, '*What* was he going to do?' in an entirely altered tone, and this went to her heart. Her pride suffered the most terrible blow. She could not bear the thought; and though she maintained a calm face to the world, and represented herself as entirely satisfied, Walter knew otherwise, and had gradually replaced his old careless affection for his mother by an embittered opposition and resistance to her, which made both their lives wretched enough. How it was that he did not make an effort to escape from her continual remonstrances, her appeals and entreaties, her censure and criticism, it is very difficult to tell. To have gone away, and torn her heart with anxiety, but emancipated himself from a yoke which it was against the dignity of his

> manhood to bear, would have been much more natural. But he had no money, and he had not the energy to seize upon any way of providing for himself.... Notwithstanding the many scenes which took place in the seclusion of that poor little house, when the mother, what with love, shame, mortification, and impatience, would all but rave in impotent passion, appealing to him, to the pride, the ambition, the principle, which so far as could be seen the young man did not possess, Walter held upon his way with an obstinate pertinacity, and did nothing.[39]

If *The Wizard's Son* had all been as good as its first few chapters, it would have been an outstanding novel. But Margaret probably found it too painful to develop the situation, and brought in an unconvincing supernatural plot. Anything which Cyril may have said or written in his own defence has not survived. He would probably have retorted that he would have been happy to take a job if one had been offered. To quote again from *The Wizard's Son*, the family 'preserved a show of happiness and tender union long after the reality was gone'.[40]

Meanwhile, Cecco was idling away his time at Oxford, and in his final examinations in 1882 he got only a Fourth. A letter from his mother written at about this time shows that she was equally annoyed with both of them:

> I have to be in town tomorrow occupied with painful business with my bankers and others, and not well knowing how it is all to end God help me. I am very tired of it all, and sick of my life, but I must struggle on till an end comes somehow or other. God grant that your brother and you be somehow stirred up to come to my aid and prevent my old age, if I live to old age, from the dreary drudgery of failure and downfall.[41]

There were some tragic deaths around this time among the families she knew. John Blackwood's son, Jack, died in May 1882, aged twenty-five, and at the beginning of 1883 Sara Tarver most unexpectedly lost her ten-year-old son Wladimir. Margaret had delivered the child herself and had felt for many years that Sara was almost like a daughter of her own. She spent a great deal of time trying to console her, noting rather sadly that Sara thought no one else had ever been so miserable. But now, twenty years after the death of Maggie, she felt that perhaps she if anyone was qualified to 'justify the ways of God to men', and in one of the Little Pilgrim stories she tried to do so.

Cyril was alarmingly ill that spring – apparently with kidney trouble – but by April he seemed better and was, at last, offered a job. It was as a private secretary to Sir Arthur Gordon, who was going out to Ceylon as Governor in 1884. In the summer Cecco went to Göttingen to study German, hoping this would help him to get a post at the British Museum. Margaret joined him at Heidelberg later that year. She finished *The Wizard's Son* – giving it a happy ending, now that she was feeling more optimistic about Cyril – and wrote one of her best ghost stories, 'Old Lady Mary'. While she was there she got an extraordinary piece of news; Annie Walker, now in her forties, was about to marry an elderly widower, Harry Coghill, who had ten thousand a year. Margaret was amused to think that her poor relation should suddenly have been raised to such a lofty position. 'Well! let us console ourselves that the price of all that is not a pleasant one to pay.'[42]

She returned to England just before Christmas. Annie's wedding took place in London on 29 January, and Cyril left for Ceylon the next day. Almost immediately afterwards Margaret left for Italy to do some more work on the Venice book. Her house was let – she was to get into the habit of doing this so that she could travel – and she planned to spend several months on the Continent with Cecco, meanwhile asking the Speaker of the House of Commons to recommend him for a job. They had a pleasant time, seeing a great deal of George MacDonald, whose talent Margaret had recognised years before. She was in Grindelwald when a telegram came from Cyril announcing that he was on his way home. It turned out that he had had several attacks of fever in Ceylon, and the doctor had warned him that the climate would kill him. He had kept the news from his mother to avoid upsetting her.

Margaret rushed back to England and was in time to meet his ship. He looked fairly well, but she decided to take him to St Andrew's to convalesce. He and Cecco played golf every day while Margaret had long talks with her old friends the Tullochs. The Principal was working on a book, *Movements of Religious Thought*, which was dedicated to her. Over the last twenty years she had grown very fond of the little town. But for the first few weeks there she was utterly miserable about the boys, who, at twenty-four and twenty-seven, were still without jobs.

One evening she was too restless to stay at home and followed them out to the golf club. She tried to glimpse them through the windows, but could not. It was almost dark, with only one band of light on the horizon, and she wandered across the links towards the sea in a terrible state of distress. Suddenly, as she wrote afterwards, 'there came upon me a great quiet and calm'.[43] To her complete surprise, the pain had gone, and she asked herself whether this was 'the peace that passeth all understanding'. This was probably the closest she ever got to a spiritual experience, and it impressed her deeply.

Yet, as she went back to the house, she realised that nothing had changed. It looked as if her sons would be dependent on her for the rest of her life.

9 The Seen and Unseen

It has been said that Margaret Oliphant was basically a realistic writer, and the fact that she wrote several supernatural stories does not contradict this. By any standard, they are rather unusual works. Some are extremely fine, others not, but all show an awareness that the universe operates according to certain laws which are not normally changed. All of them have a serious purpose, which is to measure the great gap between the 'seen' world around us and the 'unseen', where the dead have gone.

Not surprisingly, this had preoccupied her ever since Maggie died. She had written at the time, 'I try to realise heaven to myself, and I cannot do it. The more I think of it, the less I am able to feel that those who have left us can start up at once into a heartless beatitude without caring for our sorrow. Do they sleep until the great day? Or does time so cease for them that it seems but a matter of hours and minutes till we meet again?' After fifteen years, she could write about it more calmly, but she was still speculating about the relationship between seen and unseen. She did not, like some of the bereaved, try to find comfort in spiritualism; it seemed degrading to suggest that the departed spirit would communicate 'with its nearest and dearest through the legs of a table'.[1] But although she did not claim to have had any personal contact with the dead, she clung to the hope that it was not impossible.

For a few years after 1878, and at intervals for the rest of her life, she wrote several long and short stories exploring this theme. The first and best-known was the short novel *A Beleaguered City* (1880), which she once called 'the one little thing among my productions that is worth remembering'. At least one of her contemporaries, and probably more, thought it was 'her *magnum opus* . . . completely separated by all who are competent from the remainder of her books',[2] and modern critics have spoken of its 'sublimity' and 'imperishable beauty'.[3] Whether or not one agrees, it is certainly much better than most of the novels she had written in the 1870s.

The story is told by various citizens of Semur, a small French cathedral town which the author had visited in 1871. The chief narrator is the mayor, Martin Dupin, who represents what could be called the plain man's point of view. He is decent, bourgeois, determined to uphold Republican institutions – 'so long as I retain my position at the head of the community, it is my duty to see that all have their due' (2). This means resisting the clerical party who want to give the Church undue privileges and who are on the whole right-wing in politics. Margaret used her now extensive knowledge of France to explore the place of religion in a democratic state.

Martin is an agnostic; his wife, 'whose prejudices I respect', is a believer, though with some reservations. She is called Agnès, like the heroine of Margaret's autobiographical novel, and is still mourning the death of their only daughter. We are constantly reminded that women are the more devout sex, perhaps because they have more to put up with:

> The *bon Dieu* – if, indeed, that great being is as represented to us by the Church – must naturally care as much for one-half of his creatures as for the other, though they have not the same weight in the world . . . . (1)

At the beginning of the story the town is sunk in materialism. Several people openly say that the only god they respect is money, a creed which is 'against the dignity of human nature, if nothing more' (1). But then comes a series of extraordinary happenings. In the middle of summer, the town grows cold and dark; then a placard appears on the cathedral ordering the people of Semur to 'yield their places, which they had not filled aright, to those who knew the meaning of life, being dead' (2). The priest is as bewildered as everyone else and, in a sense, the revelation has nothing to do with him. 'Here there were no doctrines, nothing but that pregnant phrase, *la vraie signification de la vie*.'(2)

After this the citizens are compelled by an unseen force to leave the town – 'softly, firmly, irresistibly pushed out'. Resistance is pointless:

> I rushed forward with all my force and flung myself against the gate. To what use? it was so closed as no mortal could open it.

The gate embodies the ruthless separation between dead and living, and it soon becomes clear that the city has been occupied by the spirits of the dead. Some people, mostly women, can actually see them; Agnès has a brief glimpse of her child which reconciles her to her loss. Others can see nothing and are left wondering why they have not been chosen. But the immediate problem, as Martin soon realises, is what to do with this crowd of helpless people:

> It was I to whom everyone would look – for lodging, for direction – everything that human creatures want. It was my business to forget myself, though I also had been driven from my home and my city . . . (3)

While he and his wife struggle to keep the community together (there is a particular stress on the need to look after children) some people get drunk, others complain bitterly and a few religious enthusiasts say that they have seen angels with peacocks' wings, a claim we are not expected to take seriously. Human beings have a strong tendency to trivialise religion, but the real argument for a God is independent of miracles; it is that people instinctively call on him when they are in trouble:

> 'O God', I cried, 'whom I know not, am not I to thee as my little Jean is to me, a child and less than a child? Do not abandon me in this darkness. Would I abandon him were he ever so disobedient? (3)

It is remarkable how often the author stresses that women have a better grasp of reality than men because they are more closely in touch with basic human needs. When the time comes for a messenger to return to Semur they have no part in the decision-making process:

> To sit there silent [Martin reflects], to wait till we had spoken, to be bound by what we decided, and to have no voice – yes, that was hard. They thought they knew better than we did:

> but they were silent, devouring us with their eager eyes. I love one woman more than all the world; I count her the best thing that God has made; yet would I not be as Agnès for all that life could give me. It was her part to be silent, and she was so, like the angel she is, while even Jacques Richard had the right to speak ... (4)

Consciously or otherwise, this echoes a point often made by the suffrage societies; even the best women had no right to vote while the worst men often had. Martin is pushed back through the gate by the people, who swear they will behave better in future but are happy to let him risk his life. But he finds no one there; the dead are not able to communicate with the living, or only at rare times. There is only a hint that someone has visited the room where his daughter's picture is kept:

> The veil was boldly folded away; the face of the child looked at me across her mother's bed, and upon the frame of the picture was laid a branch of olive, with silvery leaves ... (6)

The suggestion that the dead have not completely died was enough to make the book popular with religious Victorians. Yet the really impressive thing about *A Beleaguered City* is the way in which it avoids a conventional ending. People return to their homes and are deeply affected for a while, but this soon passes away. In the last chapter, Martin tells us:

> The wonderful manifestation which interrupted our existence has passed absolutely as if it had never been. We had not been twelve hours in our houses ere we had forgotten, or practically forgotten, our expulsion from them. Even myself, to whom everything was so vividly brought home, I have to enter my wife's room to put aside the curtain from little Marie's picture, and to see and touch the olive branch which is there, before I can recall to myself anything that resembles the feeling with which I re-entered that sanctuary . . . . Everything is as it was; and I cannot persuade myself that, for a time, I and mine were shut out, and our places taken by those who neither eat nor drink, and whose life is invisible to our eyes. Everything, I say, is as it was – everything goes on as if it would endure for ever. We know this cannot be, yet it does not move us. Why, then,

> should the other move us? A little time, we are aware, and we, too, shall be as they are – as shadows, and unseen. But neither has the one changed us, and neither does the other. There was, for some time, a greater respect shown to religion in Semur, and a more devout attendance at the sacred functions; but I regret to say this did not continue. Even in my own case – I say it with sorrow – it did not continue.

If there is another plane of reality, it cannot be expressed in pious clichés or contained within the formulas of any church. God does not require, as Agnés says rather heretically, 'that all should be alike' (8). The real contrast is not between believers and non-believers but between those who live for the moment and those who have some idea of '*la vraie signification de la vie*'. As so often in Margaret's work, this is expressed through a willingness to accept responsibility.

'The Open Door', first published in *Blackwood's* in January 1882, is generally recognised as one of Margaret Oliphant's finest works, and has often been reprinted.[4] Colonel Mortimer, the narrator, rents an old house near Edinburgh on his return from India, where several of his children have died. His only surviving son, Roland, becomes ill because he is sure that he can hear a wretched creature in the grounds on winter nights imploring to be 'let in'. The mystery centres on a ruined building which includes an open door:

> Probably it had been a servants' entrance, a back-door, or opening into what are called 'the offices' in Scotland. No offices remained to be entered – pantry and kitchen had all been swept out of being; but there stood the doorway open and vacant, free to all the winds, to the rabbits, and every wild creature. It struck my eye, the first time I went to Brentwood, like a melancholy comment upon a life that was over. A door that led to nothing – closed once perhaps with anxious care, bolted and guarded, now void of any meaning.

The Colonel is careful to stress his matter-of-fact approach. 'Of course I do not believe in ghosts; but I don't deny, any more than other people, that there are stories which I cannot pretend to understand'. However, he becomes convinced that if he does not do something to help the creature, Roland will die.

With a series of witnesses, he keeps watch near the door for several nights. They see nothing, but distinctly feel the presence of someone 'pacing up and down before a closed door', and hear him crying, 'Oh, mother, let me in!' The local doctor is a sceptic who insists it is a delusion – 'some trick of the echoes or the winds, some phonetic disturbance'. The Colonel is a reasonable man but feels that he cannot analyse the phenomenon in cold blood when his child's life is at stake, and also that the doctor is wilfully denying plain facts. This was the author's way of saying that rationalists ignored too much of human experience.

Eventually they bring in the Church of Scotland minister, who has 'no cut-and-dry beliefs on the subject', but as an elderly man is 'less liable to be frightened than those that are further off the world unseen'. He turns out to be the one person who can control the situation, because of his firm grasp of human values. 'His whole being seemed absorbed in anxiety and tenderness' when he confronts the wandering spirit, 'whom he knew under these conditions, just as he had known him in the flesh, having no doubt of his identity'. He recognises it as a weak young man, significantly named Willie, who 'had come home thus a day or two after his mother died – who was no more than the housekeeper in the old house – and distracted with the news, had thrown himself down at the door and called upon her to let him in'. The minister makes it clear that God will never reject a prodigal child, any more than a parent would:

> 'She's no here. You'll find her with the Lord. Go there and seek her, not here. Do you hear me, lad? go after her there. He'll let you in, though it's late. Man, take heart! if you will lie and sob and greet, let it be at heaven's gate, and no your poor mother's ruined door'.

Like the window in *Wuthering Heights*, the door is a meeting-place between seen and unseen worlds. Margaret did not admire Emily Brontë but the phrase 'let me in', spoken by Catherine Earnshaw's ghost, may have lodged in her mind. She did admire Holman Hunt's painting, 'The Light of the World', where Christ is knocking at a door overgrown with weeds. But after we have identified possible influences we are left with an impressive short story which is highly thought of by almost everyone who reads it. Part of the reason is that it achieves its effects, like *A Beleaguered City*, through suggestion rather than direct statement.

In the end the basic problem is resolved; the spirit, if that is what it was, has gone, and Roland gets better. It is strongly hinted that if any force can break through the barriers of time and death it is human need. But although the author may feel sure that 'the loving-kindness of God' played a part in the mystery, she does not rule out other explanations. The doctor thinks it was 'ventriloquism, or reverberation', or perhaps a tramp hiding in the ruins. Even the minister is 'sometimes not very sure what he believes'. There is no dogmatism of the kind that repels us in so many Victorian religious writers, but there is one teasing little problem. During their night vigil the watchers have seen a juniper bush growing near the door, although they cannot agree whether it was on the left or the right. In daylight it is not there. Believing as she did that there were many things in heaven and earth that were inexplicable, Margaret did not feel it necessary to tell her readers what happened to the juniper bush.

'Old Lady Mary', which first appeared exactly two years after 'The Open Door',[5] is an equally striking story. Lady Mary, in her eighties, enjoys playing the part of a grand old lady who might even live to be a hundred. She has outlived powerful emotions but still enjoys the minor pleasures and comforts; her life goes 'on velvet'. She is kind to everybody, with the sort of kindness that costs nothing; in particular, she neglects to make any provision for the young cousin who lives with her and who will have nothing when she dies. After she has been told repeatedly that she ought to make a will she writes one out herself and playfully hides it in a secret drawer.

But when she finally dies unexpectedly no human creature knows anything about the will, and it takes her some time to realise that she has jeopardised the girl's future. In the after-life (of which we are told no details) she who has always been treated with great respect begins to realise that something is demanded of her:

> She felt sure that someone had called her by her name, 'Mary'. Now all who could call her by her Christian name were dead

> years ago – therefore it must be a dream. However, in a short time it was repeated – 'Mary, Mary! get up; there is a great deal to do' . . . (3)

This begins the process in which she is stripped of artificial dignity and told that 'you are going to think about your life'. Conscience-stricken, she gets permission to return to earth and try to put things right. But the place which once knew her knows her no more; nobody is aware of her presence and physical reality is too strong for her when she tries to open the drawer:

> She went to the little Italian cabinet which stood against the wall, feeling now at least that she could do as she would – that here there was no blank of human unconsciousness to stand in her way. But she was met by something that baffled and vexed her once more. She felt the polished surface of the wood under her hand . . . yet the smooth surface resisted her touch . . . though she thus saw it and felt, she could not with all her endeavours find the handle of the drawer . . . (6)

Her desperate efforts to communicate with the girl, who also loves her and wants to make contact, produce at most a 'jar and tingle in the inanimate world' (9). We are told in parenthesis that the will does eventually get found, but that is not the main point. When Mary finally gives up, 'her face, which had been so easy, was worn with trouble . . . pity and knowledge were in the lines which time had not made' (15). She has learned to judge herself and take responsibility for others; in that sense, as Keats said, the world is 'a vale of soul-making'.

The Little Pilgrim stories were inspired, as we have seen, by the death of Ellen Clifford in 1882.[6] Like *A Beleaguered City* – although they are much weaker – they appealed to a wide audience because most Victorians were fairly familiar with death and wanted to believe that it was not the end of consciousness. Some simple people imagined that Margaret was writing with special knowledge when she described Nelly's experiences in heaven, but she was only drawing on a stock of vague general ideas. Heaven is seen in traditional terms as a country of blue hills, green turf, and beautiful cities where one is reunited with loved ones. She meets Maggie, who tells her that God knows what he is doing when he separates families, 'He loves them more than we do. When he keeps us from them, it is for love'.[7]

In a later story, the Pilgrim revisits earth and sees the death of a child and the parents' grief; this was inspired by the death of the Tarvers' little boy.[8] Her companion tells her that it was done for the child's own sake – 'the secret was between the child and the Father'. This was the philosophy which Margaret had worked out for herself in the dreadful early months of 1864. She was not to know that Maggie, and countless other children, would not have died if medical science had not been so primitive, and perhaps it was the best argument that she could produce. But in the circumstances any kind of argument sounds unconvincing, and with one exception the Little Pilgrim stories are propaganda of a fairly crude kind.

The exception is 'The Land of Darkness', written at the end of 1886.[9] Although few have heard of it, it is one of the most striking modern pieces of writing about hell. There are a few echoes of Dante, but the inferno of this story has much more in common with the twentieth-century hells mapped out by Kafka, Orwell, Sartre and Beckett. It is an urban hell; in the beginning the anonymous narrator finds himself in a crowded street full of shops. The noise is constant and maddening; traffic dashes along with 'no sort of regulation' and the pedestrians force each other off the pavement. This is the first indication that no one here considers others, or even pretends to do so.

The narrator, of course, is not a perfect character, but it still takes him some time to realise that moral standards no longer exist. Any reference to law, justice or compassion evokes shrieks of laughter. Fights break out in the streets and the injured and crippled are uncared-for. His encounters with his fellow-victims strike a very different note from the pious conversations in heaven:

> I was drawn after a while from the fierce and burning sense of my own grievances by a querulous voice quite close to me. 'This is my corner', it said. 'I've sat here for years, and I have a right to it. And here you come, you big ruffian, because you know I haven't got the strength to push you away.'

Everyone (including the sick, whose suffering does not make them attractive) is so possessed by a 'sense of my own grievances' that there can be no solidarity between them. When the narrator protests that 'it is a shame to let a fellow-creature suffer if we can prevent it' he is told in no uncertain terms that his views are out of date:

> 'Why shouldn't he suffer?' said my companion. We passed as he spoke some other squalid, wretched creatures shuffling among the crowd, whom he kicked with his foot, calling forth a yell of pain and curses. This he regarded with a supreme contemptuous calm which stupefied me. Nor did any of the passers-by show the slightest inclination to take the part of the sufferers. They laughed, or shouted out a gibe, or what was still more wonderful, went on with a complete unaffected indifference.

The feeling here is the same as in Margaret Oliphant's realistic novels, and we can sense the shock of a person who had been brought up with clear ideas of good and evil when she found them openly rejected. In this context, hell is other people. God is not responsible – for, as we discover, people can escape if they really want to – nor is this the old-fashioned hell in which a special class of devils administer tortures. Instead, their misery causes them to torment each other. The narrator wanders into a kind of operating theatre where a man is being vivisected before an admiring audience. Again, everyone laughs when he is outraged and, as in *Nineteen Eighty-Four*, the victim turns on the man who is trying to protect him. He escapes and finds himself in a different species of hell.

In contrast to the anarchy of the first city, everything is highly organised. The handicapped are cleared off the streets so that the sight of them will not offend more fortunate people, and the narrator no longer feels any sympathy because 'the spirit of the place is in you'. He is arrested by two men in uniform, his name taken, and then he is left in a numbered room, bare except for a list of regulations. He soon begins to suffer from what we would now call sensory deprivation, and from the feeling that he is being watched. Walking about the streets is equally depressing because he is in 'a wilderness of men, who were as though they did not see me, passing without even a look of human fellowship, each absorbed in his own concerns'. Hell does not necessarily involve physical pain; the misery is that it is a life devoid of meaning and without caring relationships.

The same problem recurs when he finds another place which is given up to mindless pleasure and throws himself into it. But after a while the music and dancing become intolerable; hedonism is no answer. Even pain is preferable if it has a definite object, and at the end of the story one of his companions has decided to risk 'the most awful and the most dangerous journey' to get out of hell. But the narrator himself is not ready to do this. Like Pozzo in *Waiting for Godot*, he rushes 'on, on, across the waste! On to the cities of the night! On', in an obviously futile attempt to escape from himself.

In Christian terms, Margaret was saying that there was no such thing as eternal damnation and that there was always a way back to God, even after death. This idea, denounced in Calvinist Scotland when she was a girl, had recently become more acceptable. But she was also giving expression to many distinctively modern nightmares. The growth of cities, the breakdown of a single moral standard, the appearance of the 'cash nexus' as the sole relationship between people had created new forms of consciousness, which is why her work so much resembles that of later writers who had never read her. There are the twentieth-century fears of a totalitarian state where one is constantly watched and liable to arbitrary arrest, of boredom, and of rejection if one is weak or physically imperfect. Hell is envisaged as a gloomy plain where nothing grows, and a series of cities characterised by incessant noise, casual violence and unfriendly crowds. Finally, when the narrator stumbles into a vast workshop, there is the fear of the coming machine age. 'They were terrible, these things which lived yet did not live, which were his slaves and moved at his will.' She foresaw that they would become even more powerful in future, even expressing the fear that man might eventually blow up the world. However, we are told that this will not happen because God – or, if one prefers the word, goodness – is too strong.

Margaret left some other, on the whole less successful stories about the supernatural. *The Wizard's Son*, the novel about Cyril which had begun so well, turned into a story about the young man's struggle with the powers of evil, and the realistic and non-realistic elements do not mix. There were also some shorter pieces,

'Earthbound', 'The Portrait', 'A Visitor and his Opinions', and 'The Land of Suspense', a pathetic story based on Cyril's life. Finally there was 'The Library Window', written in 1895, which is a small masterpiece, and will be discussed in its place.

10 Never Penetrating Beyond the Threshold (1884–90)

In the autumn of 1884 Margaret came home from St Andrew's to resume the long struggle to find work for her sons. She was in a calmer frame of mind after her semi-mystical experience. 'I have really enjoyed it', she wrote to Annie Coghill, 'strolling out upon the sands by myself with great peacefulness and refreshment of soul',[1] and she now believed that Cecco, at least, had begun to pull himself together.

She often wondered why the children she had brought up were so different from herself. The boys had neither her generous nature nor her remarkable talents, and the girls, whom she often called her daughters, were conventional compared with her. Madge, the elder by eighteen months, was the more dominant character; Denny was shy and retiring, a 'little Puritan', her aunt called her, because she took no interest in clothes. Both of them were devoted to her and she had a much easier relationship with them than she had with her sons. Cyril had been friendly with them from the time they moved in, but not Cecco. 'They often suffer from the idea that you don't care for them', Margaret told him, 'and find them in the way.'[2]

It was necessary to worry about their future as well as the boys'. A 'singular and scarcely recognised revolution', Margaret noted a few years later, had 'taken place in the position and aspirations of women during the last generation', with 'hosts of young and ardent minds' now struggling 'for their own career and destiny'.[3] She wanted them to be self-supporting, but she did not put the same kind of pressure on them that she did on their cousins. Instead of pushing them out into a safe job like teaching, she paid for them to have a long and expensive art training, although there could be no certainty that they would do well. And she was anxious that they should have their full share of pleasure. They came on foreign holidays with her and paid long visits to Annie, in her new home in Staffordshire, and to Emma FitzMaurice at Ealing. She hoped they would both get married in the next few years, and in fact Denny became engaged to a German officer around the time of Annie's wedding, when she was not quite nineteen. But this was soon broken off.

Meanwhile, she had four young people totally dependent on her, and these were not the only claims. At the beginning of 1885 she was thinking a good deal about Willie. He had now been living in Rome, where he called himself an artist, for nearly a quarter of a century. Margaret had probably sent him money regularly, but they had not met for years because of her horror of going to Rome. She had heard that he was dying 'of a most painful and dreadful malady which has necessitated repeated and very costly as well as painful operations'.[4] He was very much in her mind when she began, in February, to write some fragments of autobiography in the old book where she had recorded her despair after Maggie's death:

> Twenty-one years have passed since I wrote what is on the opposite page. I have just been reading it all with tears; sorry, very sorry, for that poor soul who has lived through so much since. Twenty-one years is a little lifetime. It is curious to think that I was not very young, nearly thirty-six, at that time, and that I am not very old, nearly fifty-seven, now .... Since the time when that most unexpected, most terrible blow overtook me in Rome – where her father had died four years before – I have had trials which, I say it with full knowledge of all the ways of mental suffering, have been harder than sorrow. I have lived a laborious life, incessant work, incessant anxiety – and yet so strange, so capricious is this human being, that I would not say I have had an unhappy life .... Sometimes I am miserable .... and yet there are times when my heart jumps up in the old unreasonable way, and I am – yes, happy.

She put down some reminiscences of her childhood in Lasswade and of Willie – 'the handsomest, brightest of us all'. She seems to have had some idea of leaving a full-length autobiography to be published after her death, but it made little progress. Only a few pages had been written when Willie died in Rome on 23 May.

Another sad memory was of her nephew Frank, who, she now saw, had been the best of the three boys. There was nothing good to be said about Cyril but Cecco was now seriously trying to find work. His great ambition was to be a herald, but failing this he tried unsuccessfully that summer to get a post in the College of Antiquaries. He had also begun to publish articles, usually on little-known subjects like early Scottish literature. He was 'a mine of learning in various recondite ways',[5] but unfortunately, as she knew, he was unlikely to earn a living by academic writing. She was disappointed when Leslie Stephen, whom she had considered a friend, declined to give him work on the *Dictionary of National Biography*. Possibly that explains a rather barbed reference to him in a letter to Macmillan that autumn: 'The only way your good thoughts could come to practical benefit would be to find me something like an editorship such as his friends have more than once found for Leslie Stephen – but then he is a man'.[6]

In January 1886 she heard that Alice Oliphant had died in Syria, and on 13 February came another great loss. Principal Tulloch's friends had long been worried about his recurrent depressive illness. His last and worst attack, in 1881, had prevented him from working for most of a year. Margaret had written to him sympathetically at the time, but she could not refrain from saying:

> But think, please, if it had been me who had been ill, what would have become of me? – no income going on whether one could work or not – no wife to take care of me. You are far better off than I am in these respects, and, to tell the truth, I am often tired to death of work and care.[7]

More recently he had been distressed because the Liberal party, which he belonged to, had been associated with a movement to disestablish the Church of Scotland. When Margaret last saw him, at St Andrew's in the autumn of 1885, she thought he looked ill. In the new year he went with Fanny to Torquay, but declined much faster than had been expected, and his wife, almost worn to a shadow by asthma, reached him only a few days before he died.

Margaret wrote, in *Blackwood's*, 'the fall is like that of a great tree'.[8] The Principal had been very popular in Scotland and had become one of the leading figures in a church which at one time had thought him too liberal. Mrs Tulloch, quiet and uncomplaining, stopped at Windsor on her way back. Queen Victoria called on her personally to express her sympathy, and on 20 February Margaret was summoned to the castle. She and the Queen had a friendly talk – 'It alters one's idea of her', Margaret wrote a little ironically, 'when she is very pleasant to oneself'.[9] Later an orderly came to Clarence Crescent and presented her with some copies of the Queen's books.

Very soon after Tulloch's death she realised that their friends were expecting her to write his biography. She was not keen – 'Literature, I fear, is becoming a profession on which only people with private fortunes can embark. It will be a great sacrifice to friendship for a busy woman like myself'.[10] But eventually she agreed, probably not wanting to hurt the widow's feelings, and arranged to give part of her payment to a fund for his unmarried daughters. The rest of the year was worrying, with an uncongenial book to write, a visit to Germany which turned out badly and the usual struggle to find work for the boys. 'Tiddy's future weighs more on me than yours', she wrote to Cecco, 'for you I feel persuaded will fit into your place somewhere, but whether he will ever do anything is so very doubtful.'[11]

However, in the same year she wrote two of her best short stories, 'Queen Eleanor and Fair Rosamond' and the supernatural 'Land of Darkness'. She also arranged with Blackwood that she should do a monthly review of new books for the *Magazine*. The first, under the general name of 'The Old Saloon', appeared in January 1887.

She had arranged to go north in February to see Mrs Tulloch, but early in the month everything else was driven out of her head by a panic about Cecco. He had had a cough for some time, and since Christmas had been getting very thin. The doctor told her, 'quite calmly', that it could turn into tuberculosis, and she immediately assumed that if she did not get him at once to a warm climate he would die. 'My mind jumps at everything that is worst and most dreadful',[12] she wrote to Annie. Her letters to her publishers at this time, pleading for an advance, show that she had completely lost her usual calm. She had no money to go abroad just then, so it was arranged that in future her

Civil List pension should be paid directly to her bankers instead of to her. Eventually she got Cecco to Pau, where she hoped he would spend his days playing golf. Fresh air and sunshine were the only medicine that had been prescribed.

The next few weeks were a terribly worrying time for her, and it is not surprising that *Joyce*, the novel she was writing for the *Magazine*, was not very good. On 27 March Mrs Tulloch died in St Andrew's. Although Margaret had felt that she would not want to survive her husband, it was another break with the past. Cyril, who had known her for most of his life, was more upset than Margaret had expected. He wrote to Blackwood that he was concerned about the effect on his mother, 'whose oldest and dearest surviving friend is so suddenly taken away'.[13] Possibly he had more affection for her than she believed, but when they were together, he did not show it.

Cecco seemed perfectly well when they came back to England in May. He had been nominated for a post at the British Museum, subject to passing an examination, but the medical officer told Margaret privately that, whether he passed or not, he was not going to let him live in London for years. With his future in jeopardy, it was doubly important to find something for Cyril:

> I have wearied Heaven, or rather the Education Department, with my prayers on Cyril's account for years past [she wrote to Blackwood in August from the Lake District, where the family had gone for Cecco to convalesce] .... I am ready to humble myself to any one and have done so in all quarters with no result. People say to me that of *course* other people will take pleasure in helping me, and that my name will be enough etc. But I have not hitherto found the smallest advantage in anything I have tried .... He is not energetic, but he would work in the routine of an office .... My great anxiety is settling my sons, for which I have struggled ineffectually trying every possible thing I could think of for years. I felt so sure of the Inspectorship or other appointment in the Education Department for Cyril that it did not seem necessary he should go into any of the competitions for the public offices while he was young enough to try.[14]

She bombarded all the influential people she knew with letters, and also wrote to Cyril himself:

> But oh Tiddy dear take care of yourself at this most critical moment. Don't let any one have it in their power to say that you are unworthy. I hope you have written before this, if not please do so – please do so – it is such a thing to me to hear from you, and so little trouble on your part. You might surely write on Sunday afternoon when you can do nothing else.[15]

Cyril used the back of this letter to note down the score of a game of cards.

In the autumn, for a while, things looked hopeful. The Queen, whom Margaret had contacted, let it be known that she would like Cyril to get into the Education Department, and Cecco passed the British Museum examination 'brilliantly'. While waiting for the result he happened to see a 'quiet and orderly' procession of unemployed men going up Bond Street, and made some sneering remarks about them in a letter to Blackwood:

> There are dangers to be dreaded by a man with a new hat, the thing of all others which seems to excite the greatest fury among them, and mine is not yet a month old .... Many people think that the unemployed are not bad fellows on the whole, as long as you don't ask them to work, but they are certainly an abominable nuisance.[16]

Cecco was rapidly turning into a fairly unpleasant young snob. While Margaret protested ritually from time to time that she did not agree with the violent right-wing politics of *Blackwood's*, he fully shared them. He was certainly incapable of seeing the connection between the unemployed and himself. For, in spite of his good result, he did not get the appointment; the Civil Service commissioners deciding that his health was unreliable. Cyril also failed to get a job. At the same time Blackwood told Margaret that his readers disliked *Joyce* and that she was to wind it up as soon as possible. At her age, the outlook was frightening.

On Christmas night, 1887, she wrote a long entry in her pocket diary. Cyril was ill, 'not without fault of his own', and she was writing a short story, 'Mr Sandford', 'in a sort of cheerful despair'. She had not told her family how she felt 'for why trouble the children ... who can do nothing', but it had to find expression somehow:

> All the things I seem to want are material things. I want money. I want work – work that will pay enough to keep the house going which there is no other one to provide for but me. I don't know how to stop, to change to make another way of living, everything is so perplexed and hard. When I try another plan it is always more expense – and here are all these helpless people, boys who ought to be earning their own living, girls who can't but will somehow if I am out of the way, servants, dependants, all accustomed to have everything that is wanted and only me to supply all, and I will be sixty in a few months, and my work is failing, whether my strength is or not . . . . And it does not seem God's will for me that I should ever have any very unusual success – I suppose I did in the Carlingford days, but never had any such praise as Trollope and many others. He and Black would have three times as much as I, Mrs Craik a great deal more, George Eliot of course ten times, and Miss Braddon's books go on selling as well as ever they say – Queer! I don't understand it – not in all these cases at least. And now I suspect the stream is ebbing away from me altogether, and yet I have nothing before me but to work till I die.[17]

'Mr Sandford' is based on her own situation at the time, as well as the dreadful episode in 1872 when she had feared that no one would publish her work. The central character is an elderly artist with four grown-up children – two boys and two girls – who is left without an income when the public grows tired of his work. In the end both he and his family realise that 'they never had been but outsiders, flattered by the cards of a countess, but never really penetrating beyond the threshold'.[18] The story is a masterpiece but, for obvious reasons, she did not acknowledge it for several years.

Most people would have been surprised to hear that Margaret was anything but a successful woman. She was still flooding the market with books, at the rate of at least two per year, and her articles appeared regularly in *Blackwood's* and other magazines. Yet she was always short of money and always borrowing it from her publishers on the strength of future work. She got no income from the books she had already written because she normally had to part with the copyright when the contracts were drawn up. Not unnaturally she had some sympathy with the newly-formed Society of Authors, writing to Blackwood in 1887 that 'as a matter of fact while writers barely manage to live, almost all publishing firms thrive exceedingly. There are of course very good reasons for this but still you can scarcely wonder that the original producer chafes at it'.[19] And although her work was widely published in the United States that brought in no money either, in the absence of an international copyright agreement.[20]

She had plenty of regular readers – including Queen Victoria, Gladstone and Charles Darwin – but she knew that hardly anyone now believed she was a great novelist. With her work coming out so fast – she had written nearly eighty novels now – critics could hardly be expected to take the trouble to distinguish the good from the bad. It was easier to say that she was a delightful story-teller, or to write her off completely.

Her output in 1888 was typically mixed in quality. In June she finished the *Memoir of the Life of John Tulloch*, which for some reason had been the most difficult and troublesome of all her books. In the summer she wrote a good short novel, *Lady Car* (a sequel to *The Ladies Lindores*) and then a poor one, *Sons and Daughters*. She was in St Andrew's in the early autumn, and began to plan a Scottish novel, based on a true story which had been told to her by an eccentric friend, Christina Rogerson.[21] As she worked on it at home in Windsor she became convinced that 'for once in a way',[22] it was good. This was *Kirsteen*, perhaps the best of all her novels, and when Macmillan published it two years later it had a considerable success.

Meanwhile she was in her usual state of worry about the children. Cecco had never shaken off his cough and had to be sent abroad every winter. He continued very silent, and ignored her hints that he should mix with other young people of his age, including girls. Cyril seemed perfectly content to be doing nothing. He had got some work on a fashionable paper, the *Court and Society Review*, but it had collapsed by the autumn of 1888. A. C. Benson has left an impression of him at about this time:

> He lived at home an idle and self-indulgent life, doing a little writing when it pleased him; and no more melancholy decadence than that of the vivid and sparkling Eton-boy into the elderly and deprecating loafer, dawdling about Eton and Windsor, could well be imagined.[23]

If Cyril really looked elderly in his early thirties he must have been going downhill very fast. According to another account he 'fell into vicious ways and a habit of drinking',[24] which made him ill. There are also hints, in *The Wizard's Son* and elsewhere, that he had got sexually involved with unsuitable women, and that his mother had found out.

One wonders whether it was really impossible for these four highly-educated young people to have found regular work. Both the boys, for instance, spoke fluent French and could probably have become language teachers like Sara Tarver's husband. But apparently neither they nor Margaret considered it, always hoping that they would get less demanding and more prestigious jobs. She was also quite happy to keep the girls at home until they got married, although they were now in their mid-twenties and there was no sign of it.

She was anxious to take Cecco to the South of France for a few months at the beginning of 1889. To finance the trip, she advertised for two young ladies to come with them as paying guests. Cyril came as well, perhaps because she was afraid of what he might do if she left him behind. They had got as far as Paris when he collapsed in the railway station with a violent fit. He was unconscious for hours, and she thought twice that he had died. He was carried to the nearest hotel, where Margaret and Cecco stayed with him while the rest of the party went on to Beaulieu. The place was noisy and uncomfortable. After a day or two he seemed better, but Margaret was distressed at having left the girls for whom she was responsible and at the 'dreadful addition to my carefully calculated expenses'.[25] She found herself stranded in France with hardly any money and had to appeal to Blackwood for help.

'Poor Tiddy, when he is ill he always comes back to his child-like ways',[26] she wrote to Denny, whom she had left in Paris to work in a studio. She told Cecco that she hoped it might be 'a turning point and the beginning of a fundamental change'.[27] As soon as he was well enough, he came on to Beaulieu, where they had taken a rambling old house overlooking the bay, and Margaret encouraged him to work on a book for her Foreign Classics series, *Alfred de Musset*. There is no reason to think that Cyril was particularly well qualified to write it, and although it had been promised fully eight years before, he had kept putting it off. Meanwhile she began work on a biography of Laurence Oliphant, who had died at Christmas. The warm climate – with roses, oranges and violets growing in the garden – gave them a pleasant holiday, but she still worried about getting a steady income. Back in England, she suggested that she should hire pillows to the Scottish railways for overnight travellers, but the directors were not interested.

Soon after their return J. M. Barrie, then in his twenties and best known as a journalist, came to see her. Margaret, who hated personal publicity, was rather nervous lest he should put her in a newspaper, but it did not happen, and he became a great admirer of hers:

> Mrs Oliphant was herself the fine Scots gentlewoman she drew so incomparably in her books [Barrie wrote] .... most sympathetic when she unbent and a ramrod if she chose .... She could be almost fearsomely correct, and in the middle of it become audacious (for there was a dash of the Bohemian about her); her likes and dislikes were intense; in talk she was extremely witty without trying to be so (she was often, I think, amused and surprised to hear what she had just said) ... and, more noticeable perhaps than anything else, she was of an intellect so alert that one wondered she ever fell asleep.[28]

In July the Queen's librarian, Richard Holmes, whom Margaret had known for some time, offered Cecco a small piece of work. It was as a temporary assistant in the library at Windsor Castle, cataloguing the books on heraldry and family history for a salary of ten pounds a month. It was never a full time job, but he continued to work there for the next five years. Cyril got no work, and was ill again. In the autumn Margaret suggested to Macmillan that she should write them another travel book, this time about Jerusalem, which she hoped would be 'a very great success'.[29]

Her plan was to take the boys and Madge to Palestine and Egypt in the spring of 1890, while Denny remained in Paris. Macmillan agreed to pay her £1200, and the party set off in mid-March. 'Burn a candle for us, that we may have a good voyage',[30] Margaret wrote to Annie Coghill. By the end of the month they were at Port Said, whence Madge wrote to her sister:

> Oh dear, oh dear, if it were not for the boys or if they were like other people, what a happy little party we should be, as

> it is one or generally both are perpetually rude to Aunt. Sometimes I think the one the worst and sometimes the other.[31]

Margaret herself probably hardly noticed this any more, and her letters from Jerusalem were written in the highest spirits. The city was thronged with Easter pilgrims, including Russian peasants who kissed the stones of the Via Dolorosa. 'The country is very desolate, stony, and grey',[32] she noted, and the heat like summer, but she was enthusiastic about the holy places, the dark-eyed children, the wild anemones and cyclamen and the swallows which flew in and out of the churches. They went on to the Lake of Galilee and Haifa, where they put flowers on the grave of Alice Oliphant. Coming down Mount Carmel, which was brilliant with wild hollyhock, she had a rather unpleasant accident. The three young people were on horseback but Margaret, whose rheumatism had been giving her trouble lately, had to be carried in a chair by the Druse guides. Near the bottom of the mountain the shaft broke and 'pitched me from the shoulders of my astonished bearers on to the grassy though stony soil below'.[33] She assured the Druses, who were very upset, that she was not hurt. But Madge was glad for her sake when the sight-seeing was over:

> What with all of both the boys' vagaries she has too much of it .... Cecco is really dreadful sometimes, in fact it is a perpetual strain if he is in a good way to keep him so, or if not to smooth him down again, he does not usually condescend to take much notice of me. On the other hand Tiddy hardly ever answers Aunt Maggie what I would call properly, even if in a perfectly good temper ... and is always with me, so that is the way we pair.[34]

They got back late in May; Margaret having spent too much, as usual, but otherwise happy to have made the journey. Soon afterwards, though, Cecco became worse and was sent to Switzerland. His temper did not improve; he sent an angry letter to his mother complaining of her 'very querulous' attitude and saying that he was 'extremely unwilling to return. However, I shall probably do so, and we must get on as well as we can'.[35] Cyril seemed run down too, but she was much less worried about him. He and Madge spent most evenings at the piano, playing and singing.

During the summer Margaret got through 'mountains of work' which she said were 'the best help I could have'.[36] Cecco came home, but was advised to go abroad again at the beginning of November. On the fourth, Cyril came into the drawing-room and said he felt very unwell.

He stayed in bed for a few days in an exhausted condition, saying that he had not enough energy to feel pain. After two days he was feverish, and the doctor said he had congestion of the lungs. On the eighth he seemed better and looked at a review of his book on De Musset, which had just come out. But that evening he grew much worse and began to have hallucinations of seeing his name written in the air. For about an hour he gasped for breath, the phlegm rattling in his throat. After midnight he was calmer, and they thought he was rallying. He embraced his mother, held out his hand to Cecco and then turned on one side 'like a child going to sleep'[37] and died.

11 The Great Novels

In May 1880, Margaret published an article, 'The Grievances of Women',[1] in which, for the first time, she publicly expressed sympathy with the women's rights campaigners. She admitted that she wished the subject had never been raised. It was and always had been painful to her to see the contemptuous way in which women were treated, and this had been worse since there had begun to be talk about allowing them votes. But she was less worried about the vote than about the normal male attitude that women were an inferior species:

> Most of us of a reasonable age prefer to keep our sense of injury, our consciousness of injustice, dormant, but it exists in all classes. It has been handed down to us from our mothers, it descends from us to our daughters. We know that we have a great many things to suffer, from which our partners in the work of life are exempt, and we know also that neither for these extra pangs do we receive sympathy, nor for our work do we receive the credit which is our due. But whenever such questions are brought under public discussion we are bewildered to find how little these inequalities in our lot are comprehended, and how doubly injurious is the estimate formed of us by our husbands, our brothers, and our sons.

She pointed out that women worked at least as hard as men and that they brought children into the world at the risk of their lives, yet it was usual to pretend that they were parasites on their menfolk, and women who had not been able to get a man were despised. 'The chief grievance to women', she wrote, 'is the perpetual contempt, the slur upon them in all respects, the injurious accusation, so entirely beyond all possibility of proof that denial means nothing .... For the sentiment of men towards women is thoroughly ungenerous from beginning to end, from the highest to the lowest. I have thought in my day that this was an old-fashioned notion belonging to earlier conditions of society, and that the hereditary consciousness of it which descended to me, as to all women, was to be disproved by experience. But experience does not disprove it.'

If there is one theme running through her novels of the 1880s, it may be called 'the grievances of women'. During this decade, although she went on writing pot-boilers as usual, she produced her best short stories, supernatural and otherwise, and several novels which seem to me her finest work. They have had even less critical attention than the *Chronicles of Carlingford* or the *Beleaguered City*, but they are all remarkable, though sometimes flawed, books. They are about alienation between husbands and wives, parents and children, and about women, sometimes weak and sometimes strong, with heavy burdens to bear. She was increasingly unwilling to write love stories with happy endings, and her attitude to male pretensions had become, if possible, sharper than before. Incidentally, these novels disprove her own claim (in the *Autobiography*) that she was unable to create convincing characters.

The Ladies Lindores (1883), though a long novel with several plots, is basically about 'human torture, human cruelty' (18). The 'ladies' are a mother and two sisters, Caroline and Edith. The father, Lord Lindores, has got his peerage unexpectedly and is determined that his daughters should increase the power of his family by making 'good' marriages. Their brother is 'his father's heir, very clearly alive to the advantage of having, when his time came, no provision for his sister hanging like a millstone round his neck' (6). The gentle Caroline is made to marry Pat Torrance, a violent man 'without an intellectual taste or higher instinct' (5), because he is rich and has a house full of art objects which he doesn't know how to appreciate, and wants a lady of culture and title to go with it. The author points out that, unlovely though he is, the girls think him a great prize because he is 'so to speak an appointment, a post for life which would remove all anxiety about their future comfort from their own minds and those of their parents' (15). There is an ironic picture of the marriage market, run from London, where the girls are expected to strain every nerve to get a husband. Contrasted to the deferential English are the solid and sensible Scots, one of whom says, 'It's grand to be an auld maid' (8). It is certainly better to be an old maid then to endure a marriage like Caroline's, 'Poor Lady Car! with nothing but a little discussion about Wordsworth or Shelley to stand in place of happiness to her heart' (22).

The suggestion is that Caroline is over-civilised and therefore unable to protect herself against the brutal world in which she finds herself. Her sister Edith (though a much less convincing character) refuses to be bullied. Margaret had obviously been thinking a great deal about the question of obedience – the chief virtue recommended to women in her youth – and had concluded that it was actually an evil. There is general misery when the women in Lord Lindores' family, with their more humane values, give in to him; Caroline's mother is unable to protect her daughter and realises that her husband is a tyrant, 'judging for them, deciding for them, crushing their private wishes' (6):

> 'This is the curse of our life' [she says]. 'I can do nothing; I cannot go against your father, Edith, and yet I am neither a fool nor a child. God help us women! we have to stand by, whatever wrong is done, and submit – submit!' (34)

If they are crushed for too long, their emotions will take unacceptable forms. Everyone who has read the novel has been startled by the scene in which Caroline, 'who had been so dutiful all her life', cries out that she is glad her husband is dead:

> 'to think I shall never be subject to all *that* any more – that he can never come in here again – that I am free – that I can be alone ... I don't know how I have borne it. I don't know how I can have lived, disgusted, loathing myself. No, no; sometime else I shall be sorry when I have time to think, when I can forget what it is that has happened to me – but in the meantime I am too happy.'

Her mother, who tries always to feel the right thing, cannot bear this. Nor does the author totally exclude compassion for Torrance. But the point is that Caroline's situation has made her cruel, and should never have been allowed to happen. 'She had come out of death into life. Was it wrong to be glad? That it was a shame and outrage upon nature was no fault of poor Carry.' (29)

Once she is free, Caroline insists on taking control of her own life and marries an old lover, one of those weak men so common in Oliphant novels. By the end she has 'gone far away from her mother', and Lady Lindores, disillusioned in her husband and son, experiences 'that other personal sense which comes to most – that with all the relationships of life still round her, mother and wife, she, for all solace and support, was like most of us virtually alone' (34). This sense is very strong in the later novels. Most people, especially women, have to accept that life is not perfect and, most painful of all, that their daughters will probably have to go through the same unhappiness as themselves.

Although there is a marriage in the last chapter, perceptive readers would have been aware that this was not meant to be a happy ending. In the sequel, *Lady Car* (1889), Caroline realises that her new husband is a dilettante and is alienated from her son. She dies in a state of utter disenchantment, 'What could she do more, that gentle, shipwrecked creature, unable to contend with the wild seas and billows that went over her head? What had she ever been able to do?' (15)

Lady Caroline is a memorable picture of a woman too sensitive to cope with the normal strain of living; most Oliphant heroines are tougher. *Sir Tom* (1884) – the sequel to an undistinguished novel, *The Greatest Heiress in England* – again raises the question of obedience. Lucy is the wife of Sir Thomas Randolph, who is much older and a reformed rake. It is not a passionate marriage (indeed Lucy has no idea what passion means); Sir Tom, though genuinely fond of her, has married her partly because she has a great deal of money. He is incredulous when she feels it her duty to give part of this money away, against his wishes. 'A man may have the most liberal principles about women, and yet feel a natural indignation when his own wife shows signs of desiring to act for herself .... He thought her a sort of child-wife, whom a little scolding or a kiss would altogether sway.' (6)

The novel owes something to Henry James, whose *Portrait of a Lady* Margaret had reviewed in *Blackwood's* in March 1882. As in James, little happens; it is primarily a study of emotions. The innocent Lucy begins to feel threatened by the sophisticated people around her, who look down on the 'ordinary housekeeping woman'. She is sharply told that she is not to be too absorbed in her child but should be attending to her husband's career. There is a Jamesian contrast between straightforward Anglo-

Saxons and those who have lived on the Continent and acquired a hard polish. When two figures from her husband's past, a fascinating Contessa and a teenage girl, move in, Lucy does not know how to communicate with them. They assume that women's lives revolve around men and that marriage is a business operation, while her suggestion that they could work for their living seems ridiculous. Gradually both she and the reader become convinced that the Contessa is Sir Tom's mistress and the girl is his child:

> For a long time after the sounds of various persons coming upstairs had died away, Lucy lay silent waiting for her husband's appearance, but at last, unable to bear the vague wretchedness of her thoughts any longer, got up and put on a dressing-gown and stole out into the dark gallery to go to the nursery to look at her boy asleep, which was her best anodyne. The lights were all extinguished except the faint ray which came from the nursery door, and Lucy went softly towards that, anxious to disturb little Tom by no sound. As she did so a door suddenly opened, sending a glare of light into the dark corridor. It was the door of the Contessa's room, and with the light came Sir Tom, the Contessa herself appearing after him on the threshold. She was still in her dinner dress, and her appearance remained long impressed upon Lucy's imagination like a photograph without colour, in shadow and light. She gave Sir Tom a little packet, apparently of letters, and then she held out both hands to him, which he took in his. (38)

This kind of writing is powerful because it suggests far more than it states. Lucy is aware of a threat to her marriage, but it is too shadowy to be grasped. The light/darkness imagery, at which Margaret excelled, here takes the form of a black-and-white photograph which gives an over-simple image; the scene, which is actually quite innocent, appears menacing. Lucy is 'aged and changed' (32) by a situation 'utterly beyond all rules known to her' (25), but she feels it would be degrading to compete with another woman and prefers to withdraw. The couple are reconciled after the dangerous illness of their child, but we are left with a strong impression that women cannot win. If they are domestic and virtuous like Lucy men will laugh at them; yet while men run after the other kind of woman they discuss her in a fairly brutal way, and her reign is over once she begins to grow old.

As in *Mansfield Park*, the author is amused by the heroine's limitations, even while she sympathises with her, and the 'bad' characters are drawn with zest. But she does not moralise, like Jane Austen in the latter novel, and these characters are not punished. Perhaps the real point is that the worldly and the simple are actually incapable of communicating.

'If Mrs Oliphant had devoted two years instead of six months to *A Country Gentleman and his Family*', wrote one critic, 'we should not now be sighing over the oblivion of her fame'.[2] This novel, published in 1886, shows her at her best and worst. There is a melodramatic sub-plot, but if this were cut away, which could easily be done, we would see that the main story is outstandingly impressive. Critics have long agreed that *Daniel Deronda* is a great book, in spite of having two plots, one of which is unsuccessful, so there is no reason why we should not concentrate on the good main part of *A Country Gentleman*.

The anti-hero, Theodore Warrender, is a subtle, frighteningly convincing portrait of an intolerant personality. A 'fastidious, hot-headed, impatient young man', he is expected to do brilliantly at Oxford but will not take his tutor's advice. 'He had a fancy for out-of-the-way studies, for authors who don't pay, for eccentricities in literature, in short, for having his own way and reading what he chose.' (1, 1) As a result, he gets a bad degree (like Margaret's son Cecco a year or two earlier), and withdraws from academic life, bitter that his talents are not appreciated. The remainder of the story shows him repeating the same behaviour pattern in human relationships.

When Theo's father dies he inherits his country estate, The Warren, and immediately begins to treat everyone around him in a high-handed way. The author (who appears in the novel as Mrs Warrender, a much more lively and unconventional person than her children) realises that he is too 'intolerant of the usual conditions of humanity' (2, 17) to be normally happy. He decides that he wants to marry an older woman, recently widowed after an unhappy marriage, who has a very close relationship with her small son. As usual, he gets his way, battering down her feeling that she is injuring her child:

> Presently the manner in which the child calculated upon her, ignoring every personal claim of hers, awoke a little spark in Lady Markland's breast. A little while ago she would herself have said . . . that she had no life but in him, that for her there was no future save Geoff's future. Even now it seemed guilt in her that she should have calculations of her own (2, 11).

The situation soon becomes intolerable because the impish little boy grates on his stepfather's nerves. Characteristically, although he knows he is behaving badly, Theo feels that 'it was he who was the injured person', and that he is 'not capable of doing himself justice' (3, 18) when the child is around. He insists that his wife should part with Geoff and leaves home when she refuses. The novel ends abruptly, with very little information about what will happen next.

A Country Gentleman is a profound study of complex emotions, and of 'the wounds which people closely connected in life so often give to each other' (1, 17). Frances, Theo's wife, eventually finds it impossible to live with him because he makes demands which no normal human being can satisfy:

> To continue perfect in his eyes, after their marriage, she would have needed always to agree with him, to think his thoughts. He exacted this accord with all the susceptibility of a fastidious nature, which would be content with no forced agreement, and divined in a moment when an effort was required to conform her opinions to his . . . . What he wanted was the perfect agreement of a nature which arrived at the same conclusions as his by the same means, which responded before he spoke, which was always ready to anticipate, to give him the exquisite satisfaction of feeling he was right by a perpetual seconding of all his decisions and anticipating of his thoughts. Had he married a young creature like Chatty, ready to take the impress of his more active mind, he might have found other drawbacks in her to irritate his *amour propre*, and probably would have despised her judgment in consequence of her perpetual agreement with him. But the fact was that he was jealous of his wife, not in the ordinary vulgar way, for which there was no ground of possibility, but for every year of additional age, and every experience, and all the life she had led apart from him. He could not endure to think that she had

> formed the most of her ideas before she knew him; the thought of her past was horrible to him. A suspicion that she was thinking of that, that her mind was going back to something which he did not know, awoke a sort of madness in his brain. All this she knew by painful intuition now .... She was aware of the forced control he kept over himself, not to burst forth upon her, and she would have fled morally, and brought herself round to his ideas, and sworn eternal faith to him, if it would have done any good. But she knew very well that his uneasy nature would not be satisfied with that ... (3, 13)

Eventually she asserts her rights and throws off 'the yoke which he had made so heavy' (3, 18), but on one level she still wants him and is appalled when she realises he is not coming back. Clearly the author believed that romantic and sexual feelings did exist in women, but were not the most important part of their lives. The mother–child relationship, though, is central, and is more satisfying than anything else they are likely to get. Indeed she hints in the last paragraph that the only truly happy people are the insensitive and complacent.

The novel has much wit, but a cold bleak atmosphere. Both the houses where the action takes place are repellent in different ways. Lady Markland's home, which mirrors her desolate life with hcr first husband, has a 'nakcdncss which madc thc spectator shiver':

> The wood round it had been wantonly and wastefully cut, and it stood almost unsheltered upon its little eminence, with only a few seedling trees, weedy and long, like boys who had outgrown their strength, struggling about the heights. The house itself was thus left bare to all the winds. (1, 5)

By contrast, The Warren is smothered in trees, 'damp and warm and full of the mould of ages', and the Warrender girls are dull limited people whose ideal is to 'keep the linen in order, and make your own underclothing, and sit round the fire at home' (1, 2). Their mother cannot grieve for her dead husband and feels 'swallowed up in the dull current of the family life' (1, 4). On the whole, this is a disturbing book, and it must have taken all the banalities of the sub-plot (which has a fallen woman, a blameless heroine, and an interrupted wedding) to reassure its readers that they were getting nothing out of the ordinary way.

There is a sequel, *A House Divided Against Itself* (1886), but it is nothing like as good as *A Country Gentleman*, and the two books have no real relationship.[3]

All the foregoing novels had shown Margaret's awareness of the fact that marriage can bring its own problems for women. At around the same time she began to consider the case for celibacy – that the women who did not marry had more energy free for work. It was a topical subject in the 1880s, with the surplus of women increasing steadily and more and more middle-class girls getting jobs. Lucy in *Sir Tom* had already pointed out that 'there are so many things that girls can do – there are things open to them that never used to be' (25). Certain kinds of work were still considered unfit for ladies, but might well be preferable to the ordinary life of the better-off woman, which, she had remarked in the same novel, was 'stagnation more or less gracefully veiled' (13).

Her spinsters do not remain unmarried because they are incapable of affection. Catherine Vernon in *Hester* (1883) breaks her heart, like Mrs Methven in *The Wizard's Son*, because the boy she has brought up dislikes and resents her. She is a 'dry tree', but also a high achiever who runs the family bank and generously supports a crowd of ungrateful relatives. Her young cousin Hester also wants to do 'work of which something good might come' (8), and Catherine tells her that she has it in her to become 'an excellent man of business; but it can't be' (45). It is impossible, in normal circumstances, for a girl to have a profession because society will not permit it.

Joyce (1888) is an unsuccessful novel but raises some interesting questions and shows how her mind was working at this time. Joyce is a teacher who loves her work and, most unusually, wants to go on with it after marriage. Her fiancé does not welcome this:

> He felt profoundly that to be able to keep his wife at home, and retain her altogether like a garden enclosed for his private enjoyment, was a supreme luxury ... but he doubted greatly whether it would be possible to bring Joyce to perceive that this was the more excellent way, and that it would be meet

> for her to give up her work and devote herself entirely to her husband. He comprehended something of her pride, her high independence, and even indulgently allowed for the presence in her of a great deal of that ambition which is more appropriate to a man than a woman; therefore he was prepared to yield the question in respect to the work ... (14)

When she is suddenly raised to the rank of a lady Joyce does not know which class she belongs to or what sort of man she should marry. In the end she marries no one but settles on a distant Scottish island where she teaches the people the arts of civilisation.

A year or so later Margaret came back to this question in a far more impressive novel. *Kirsteen* (1890) is arguably her masterpiece, although the same claim has been made for *Miss Marjoribanks* and *A Beleaguered City*. Set in Scotland in the early nineteenth century, it draws on her own memories of a primitive community in which the coach was the main form of transport, most women lived and died where they were born and places like London seemed unimaginably far away.

The Douglases, like the Oliphants, are a poor, proud family, believing devoutly in their ancient name which now means very little. Their father is a violent man (who has probably murdered slaves in the West Indies); their mother an invalid sunk in self-pity. The boys are sent off one after another to India, not to be seen again for years, while the girls, 'just as precious a gift from their Maker as their brothers' (6), are abused for being female and treated as household drudges. Kirsteen is the only one who has the courage to break away from home, although she does not do this until after her father has made it impossible for her to stay there and retain her self-respect. Against all the traditions of her family, she goes to remote London and becomes a 'mantua-maker', insisting that she wants to work and not to be 'a cumberer of the ground' (22). Like her creator, she works not only because it is necessary to support herself and others but because she actually likes it. 'She was delighted with the beautiful materials ... she applied herself to the invention of pretty confections and modifications of the fashions with much of the genuine enjoyment which attends an artist in all crafts.' (23) At first she is affected by the snobbish belief that trade is degrading and thinks she is marking time until she gets married. But she realises that work is to be the centre of her life when her fiancé dies, like Frank Wilson, in India. She becomes famous for her good workmanship and buys back the alienated lands of her family, who return the gift by despising her:

> Kirsteen was glad to accept the position of inferiority thus allotted to her on all sides. She was neither mother nor wife, nor ever would be so. The others took a higher position than hers. (35)

Ironically, the old house of Douglas is redeemed by a daughter, not a son.

It is clear from the beginning that Kirsteen has much purer and simpler standards than most of those around her. She is 'a help to every one that bore her name' (22), whether they deserve it or not, and is totally committed to one man, although it turns out to be 'for death instead of for life' (15). We are left in no doubt that she has lost something precious:

> 'I am young, and we're a long-lived race – I will maybe live to be a hundred. No bairn will ever be at my breast – no man will ever take my hand.' (33)

However, since it is necessary, she is quite strong enough to survive alone and to make a success of her life. Her three sisters, although they 'fulfil every duty of woman' (46) by getting husbands, are far inferior. One of them boasts that she 'never goes a step without my man' (37), the second pretends to be weaker than she is to flatter a potential husband, and the youngest is ready to let herself be seduced out of sheer frustration. Kirsteen, who has a 'one-ideaed soul' (39), is baffled by her perversity, but still feels that she cannot 'forsake her little sister even though the circumstances were such as she did not understand' (40).

Loyalty to one's family is, for Margaret as for more conventional Victorians, a supreme virtue. But she is wryly aware that few members of this family value Kirsteen as she deserves. The strong and responsible are exploited, at all stages of life, by the weak and selfish. Yet although she is a 'dry tree', and has to endure spiteful remarks, by the end of the novel the elderly Miss Douglas has emerged as a distinguished woman:

> She drove the finest horses in the town, and gave dinners in which judges delighted and where the best talkers were glad to come. Her hospitality was almost boundless, her large house running over with hordes of nephews and nieces, her advice, which meant her help, continually demanded from one side or other of a large and widely extended family. No one could be more cheerful, more full of interest in all that went on. Her figure had expanded a little like her fortune, but she was the best dressed woman in Edinburgh, always clothed in rich dark-coloured silks and satins, with lace which a queen might have envied. (46)

Like Catherine in *Hester*, and like Margaret Oliphant, she is a lavish spender, the mainstay of a tribe of friends and relations, a woman who has a blank in the 'innermost room' but has undeniably made a success of her life.

Kirsteen is a novel which can be appreciated on many levels. It is enthralling as a story and much of it is, like *Miss Marjoribanks*, grimly funny. 'A wife cannot throw up her situation with the certainty of finding another at a moment's notice as a good housekeeper can do – even if she has spirit enough to entertain such an idea. And poor Mrs Douglas had no spirit, no health, little brains to begin with and none left now, after thirty years of domestic tyranny and a "bairn-time" of fourteen children. What could such a poor soul do but fall into invalidism?' (1) But there is also a note of piercing sadness. The novel is full of images of candles in the darkness, threatening to flicker out and so 'foreshadow the extinction of the race' (5). Margaret's emotions about the decline of her own family are hinted at in the many references to 'the auld name, that was once so great' (46). But that did not alter the responsibility of the individual to struggle.

The Marriage of Elinor (1892) is one of her most accomplished novels, and the last of the really fine ones. It is not likely to appeal to readers in the same way as strongly dramatic novels like *The Ladies Lindores* and *Kirsteen*. There is not very much action; the plot (which involves a robbery and a trial) is only tenuously connected with the real theme. Its strength is in the way it explores and illuminates a painful situation.

Elinor insists on marrying a rakish man about town, against

everyone's advice. 'I don't see you putting up with things, making the best of everything, submitting to have your sense of right and wrong outraged perhaps', her friend John tells her. 'Some women would not be much disturbed by that. They would put off the responsibility and feel it their duty to accept whatever was put before them. But you – it would be a different matter with you.' (5)

The breakdown of the relationship is not shown directly. Instead, and this is really unusual, the author concentrates on the unhappiness of Elinor and her mother when they are separated, physically and emotionally, by her marriage. She refers (Chapter 22) to the relief she felt when her own mother died, and this novel reworks the theme of *The Quiet Heart* through a much more mature sensibility. Mrs Dennistoun, who is used to 'a very quiet, orderly life' (13), is offended by her son-in-law's drinking and failure to find work. But she is aware that a mother-in-law is usually blamed for everything that goes wrong and tries hard 'not to interfere with the life of her child.' (18) The emotions of the older woman, a figure whom most novelists would have found completely uninteresting, have seldom been explored with so much sympathy.

Elinor's husband sponges on her mother, without bothering to conceal his contempt for her, and the marriage collapses when he has an affair while Elinor is pregnant ('a state of health that of itself disgusts a man' (26)). She goes home with the baby, and we realise to our surprise that the author is saying that the mother–child relationship is more basic than that between husband and wife. 'It was not a happy thing', she admits, 'that Elinor should have made shipwreck of her life, should have left her husband and sought refuge in her mother's house. But how could it be otherwise than happy that Elinor was there?' (24) The little household of two women and a child turns out to be surprisingly stable.

There is no second romance for Elinor, as the reader might have expected. John thinks he is in love with her, but is clearly the kind of man who gets involved in impossible relationships because he prefers not to marry anyone. Nor is she ever really reconciled with her husband Phil. She continues to 'live her own life' for as long as possible, but after her son has grown up and her husband has become 'an old fogey' they share a house and 'presented at last the appearance of a united family' (48). It is the kind of open ending, neither 'happy' nor tragic, at which Margaret excelled.

The suggestion is that the two halves of humanity have basically different values and interests. Sexual passion is not really important for women except for a relatively short time, and on the other hand men cannot understand women's feelings for their children. In the same way, no communication is possible between Elinor's friends with their slightly prim middle-class values and the aristocratic set which surrounds Phil. The author certainly has more sympathy for the first group than the second, but she does not judge either. 'A woman who has known life learns to understand and forgive a good many things.' (22)

12 The Great Short Stories

Few, if any, of Margaret's full-length novels can be called absolutely perfect. But some of her short stories are as good as any in the English language, if only because she did not have to pad them out. Those remaining uncollected at her death were published with an introduction by J. M. Barrie in *A Widow's Tale* (1898). Several of the stories in this volume deal with the impact of male sexuality on women, who usually learn to make a life for themselves and their children without men. 'A Story of a Wedding-Tour' is about a bride who runs away from her husband, who appreciates her as a sex-object but is 'indifferent to herself'. 'He took it for granted that, being his wife, she would naturally be pleased with what pleased him, and his mind went no further than this.' When she leaves him, she suddenly becomes a new person:

> It was not ... Janey, the little governess-pupil; it was not young Mrs Rosendale.... Who was it? Janey? Janey herself, the real woman, whom nobody had ever seen before ... (1)

Ironically, the woman who is best remembered as a Victorian prude probably wrote better than any Englishwoman of her century about sex as an irresistible force, swamping the decencies and conventionalities, and apparently did so without offending anyone. 'A Widow's Tale' and 'Queen Eleanor and Fair Rosamond' are both about fairly sheltered middle-class ladies to whom it comes as a painful shock. Nelly Brunton, in the first story, stops pretending to be heartbroken by her husband's death because the life-force is too strong for her. Although she has children, they are too small to be 'companions for a woman in the full tide and height of her life' (9). There is general horror when she takes away a younger girl's lover:

> That she, poor Jack's widow, hardly out of her weeds ...

> should have interfered with May's love affair, should have taken her place, and carried on something which she could not herself deny to be very like a flirtation with her young cousin's admirer! How terrible, how treacherous, how shocking it was! At the bottom of her heart there remained that dreadful little guilty sense that there was pleasure in it ... (4)

But Nelly wishes to keep her flirtations within the limits which society tolerates and is deeply upset when the man makes it clear that he only wants an affair. She realises that he is 'a coarse-minded man', who cares little for her and nothing for her children, but feels she has to marry him (the marriage quickly breaks down, of course) to save her reputation:

> A woman who has had poor Nelly's experiences seldom retains a girl's dream of superlative womanhood, of the crown and the sceptre. But to endure to be spoken to like this – to feel the question to be not one between two lovers, but between a man who was not 'an infernal cad' and a woman who was not 'a fool' . . . was almost more than flesh and blood could bear. (8)

We hear the same disillusioned note in 'Queen Eleanor and Fair Rosamond', written in 1886, a Victorian version of the legend of Queen Eleanor who tracked down her husband's mistress with a bowl of poison. Eleanor Lycett-Landon is the middle-aged wife of a Liverpool businessman who has raised a large family with no signs of trouble. What is wrong with the Lycett-Landon marriage ('Lycett' presumably equals 'licit') is that no passion is left in it and the husband and wife have no real need of each other:

> It was rather a relief to them all when the father went away again. They did not say so indeed in so many words, still keeping up the amiable domestic fiction that the house was not at all itself when papa was away. But as a matter of fact there could be little doubt that the atmosphere was clear after he had gone.... There was nothing impassioned in their affection for their father, and Mrs Lycett-Landon was happy with her children, and quite satisfied that her husband should do what he thought best ... (3)

Gradually it dawns on the unsuspecting wife that something is not normal, and she follows her husband to the suburban love-nest which he shares with a young girl whom he has married bigamously. 'It seems as if they must break out – as if common life and duty become insupportable', says a friend (8). Her feelings, when she finally knows the truth, are not conventional:

> This modern Eleanor, who had fallen so innocently into Rosamond's bower, had no thought of vengeance in her heart. She had no wish to kill or injure the unhappy girl who had come between her and her husband. What good would that do? Were Rosamond made an end of in a moment, how would it change the fact? (7)

She is able to 'put away' her husband without too much regret; her main worry is how to minimise the scandal and particularly how to break the news to her grown-up children. The girl (and the girl's mother) are victims, like her, of the man's need to break out. He is not romanticised, degenerating at the end into an 'elderly, stout ... oh so commonplace!' man. But neither is he totally condemned, for it seems that both sexes have to behave according to their nature and that the values of men and women are really incompatible. Women are preoccupied with caring for their families while men are absorbed in 'more important things' (2) like business and, occasionally, sex. Eleanor is left to bring up the children alone, which she does successfully, while her husband can give no explanation of 'the strange passion which made him, at fifty, depart from all the traditions of his virtuous life'.

J. M. Barrie called this story 'as terrible and grim a picture of a man tired of fifty years of respectability as was ever written', a feeling which modern readers will probably share. 'Mrs Oliphant wrote so many short stories that she forgot their names and what they were about', he commented, 'but readers, I think, will not soon forget this one; and if not this, when shall their hearts grow cold and their admiration wane for the wonderful woman of whom it is but the thousandth part?'[1]

'Mademoiselle', for once, shows sex as a beneficial force. It was rather unusual for Margaret to write a convincing love story, but this one does work because the heroine is not a conventional type. Claire, a French governess of thirty-five, is both disillusioned and experienced. She has got over the Jane Eyre-like stage of passionate rebellion against fate and accepts that her employers see her as a creature without personal feelings. She does not expect her life to change, except for the worse; she is unlikely to find work as she gets older and has only the dreary prospect of saving enough money to pay 'for the expenses of a last illness (if not too long), and of her burial after, which was a great relief to think of' (1).

The story is about her slow emergence from a state of virtual death into life. Thirty-five is not old for an unmarried woman – the author points out – but society considers her 'at least ten years in advance of her male contemporaries' (5). Her employer's cousin, who has not noticed her when she appears to be a 'sensible person of middle age', falls in love with her when he accidentally sees her in her dressing-gown and with loose hair, a fact which is conveyed without fuss. Claire resists him because she is reluctant to believe that anything good can happen to her and because she fears being called a designing woman who has trapped a younger man.

The reactions of her employers, insular and insensitive, are very funny. They assure her that she is getting old (while her lover, at the same age, is still young) and ought to protect herself by getting married, but are outraged when she proposes to marry into their family. Claire finally sees that there is no point in worrying about their feelings and decides to do what is obviously in her interests:

> 'Would it not be better' [Charles asks her mother] 'for Claire to be the mistress of her own house, and that a good one, to have her own life, and that a prosperous one, even though weighted with a husband, than to live and work as she is doing now?'
>
> 'Perhaps I should think the husband the best part of it', said Madame Castel. (8)

It is a satisfyingly happy ending, but not too sweet to be believable. The reader knows that only a piece of luck has saved Claire from a terribly monotonous life, and that for most women there is no other way out. Although Margaret had suggested, in *Kirsteen*, that a profession could be a worthy alternative to marriage, 'Mademoiselle' reminds us of the darker side of employment, in particular the fear of old age.

Old age is the theme of what is perhaps her finest short story, 'Mr Sandford'.[2] Margaret wrote it, as has been said, at the end of 1887, when she was getting towards her sixtieth birthday and very worried about her large and expensive family. Mr Sandford is a well-known artist, 'approaching sixty, but in perfect health ... a successful man, who had attained at a comparative early age the heights of his profession'. He has a comfortable lifestyle, a loving wife, and several children who 'took a great deal out of the family stores without bringing anything in' (1). Suddenly he makes the shocking discovery that people are no longer buying his pictures and that in a few months' time he will have nothing:

> So much in the bank, and after that nothing; and all the liberal life going on; the servants who could not be sent off at a moment's notice; the house, which could not be abandoned; the family all so cheerful in their false security, who had no presentiment of evil. (4)

The parallels with the author's life are obvious, but in 'Mr Sandford' she produced a story of much wider significance. It is a meditation on the rôle of the artist in a society where art is treated as a commodity, on ageing, and on the anguish of a breadwinner thrown on the scrapheap before his time. In an age of mass unemployment, it does not seem at all dated, apart from the fact that for Margaret's generation unemployment meant either dependence on relatives, or destitution.

Mr Sandford has made his reputation with the kind of pictures Frank Oliphant had painted, large historical set-pieces with titles like 'The Black Prince at Limoges'. But the public has grown tired of them and the younger generation think of him as an 'old fogey'. The author does not make the familiar complaint that public taste has grown worse since her youth. Mr Sandford tries to paint a picture in the new Impressionist style as a joke, to prove 'how easy the trick was', but realises that it demands a kind of skill he hasn't got. There is even a hint that at times he has worked less for the love of art than for an income:

> There was very little fault to be found with the picture ...

> except, perhaps, that, had not this been Mr Sandford's profession, there was no occasion for its existence at all ... (2)

On the whole, Mr Sandford has done and is still doing good work, although, like Margaret, he has never 'made a hit'. It is nobody's fault that his pictures are no longer wanted; it is in the nature of things. But he cannot afford to concentrate on his own hurt feelings because the really urgent problem is how to provide for his family. He realises that, as his life is heavily insured, the best thing for them would be for him to die. They would get a small income – 'much better to have than a man who could earn nothing' (6) – and his sons would be forced to make an effort. When he is fatally injured in an accident, perhaps because he has not tried to save himself, his only feeling is of overwhelming relief.

The ending is in the author's best ironic vein. It is clear that although Mr Sandford's family did not want him to die this has, in fact, benefited them. His widow feels that she only wants to die too, 'but she was a very natural woman', and in time she gets used to her new life. 'Everything was miserable enough indeed, but there was no humiliation in the breaking up of the establishment.' The pictures begin to sell once more, 'for a Sandford was now a thing with a settled value, it being sure that no new flood of them would ever come into the market'. There is enough money for the family to live on in a modest way. 'But it is not to everyone that it is given to die at the right moment', Margaret concluded, rather ominously, 'as Mr Sandford had the happiness to do.'

13 On the Ebb Tide (1890–97)

After Cyril had been buried, in Eton cemetery, Margaret's one thought was to get her only surviving child out of England before the winter. Within a week she, Cecco and Denny were at Davos in the Swiss Alps, arriving on what would have been Cyril's thirty-fourth birthday.

At first she told herself and others that she consented to what God had done. Life with Cyril had been growing impossible. 'For years I have been thinking and thinking in anguish', she wrote privately, 'what will he do when I die. And now this question is solved. I have been powerless to do anything for him, to bind up his young life, to accept the thousand and thousand disappointments and thoughts of what might have been. It is only nature that cries out, not my judgment.'[1] But of course she could not keep this up. She constantly thought about the delightful child he had been and asked herself what had gone wrong, and if it was her fault. 'I only want my boy – my heart cries out for him and will not be silenced',[2] she wrote to Madge, who had stayed in England. A month later she told her that she did not believe she would live very long:

> Don't distress yourself.... I am perfectly well, and people don't die because they wish it, or because they think it's the best thing. I will wait patiently the Lord's will, but I don't feel as if I could ever have the heart to fight or struggle for the daily bread again, whereas you three might be comfortable enough, with your several earnings, and what I should be able to leave behind. Do you remember or did you ever read 'Mr Sandford'?[3]

Probably Madge protested violently, and Margaret's heart sank when she realised how much the girls and Cecco still depended on her. She hoped they would all marry 'and so be weaned from me',[4] but, meanwhile, it seemed necessary for her to go on living.

She found the place very dreary, with nothing to be seen but pine trees, snow, and a dazzling blue sky. Several people there were obviously dying of tuberculosis, but the Swiss doctor assured her that Cecco would get better. She took a short walk in the snow every day and spent most of the rest of the time working. Anne Ritchie had sent her Scott's *Journal*, composed in his last years when he was writing virtually full-time to pay off his debts. Although she believed Scott to be a much greater writer than herself she felt a deep affinity with him. She was producing a volume every sixteen days, a feat which most people considered impossible. 'And I am sixty-two, older than Sir Walter was when he died. I am a wonder to myself, a sort of machine . . . always fit for work whatever has happened to me.'[5]

As a matter of fact she was not quite as strong as she thought and early in 1891 she collapsed with severe internal pain. They moved on to the milder climate of San Remo and in May returned to Windsor. Since she shrank from going back to Clarence Crescent, they rented a smaller house, 33 Park Street. There was only one room available for a study, and Cecco had it, Margaret doing her work at the drawing-room table.

In a fairly short time she had taken up the threads of her life again, producing books and, more rarely, articles at her usual appalling speed. She now found biography and criticism much easier work than fiction, and only one of the novels written after Cyril's death – *Old Mr Tredgold* – has much value. She wrote discriminating but friendly reviews of younger writers like Stevenson, Barrie and Kipling. She was not so impressed by Thomas Hardy, but, reviewing *Tess* early in 1892, gave her opinion, though with some reservations, that it was a work of genius.

This review was written in the South of France, where she had gone for the winter with Cecco and Madge. Denny was still studying art in Paris. The sisters wrote to each other regularly and Madge's letters make it clear that she was anxious not to go on being a burden on her aunt. She noticed how worried Margaret was about Cecco, who was still very thin and had frequent tantrums, and how their friends sponged on her, staying at the villa for weeks without paying their share of the rent. She encouraged Denny, who was never very sure of herself, to work at her painting – 'Succeed we both *must*, *must*'.[6] But it may have occurred to her that the boys, with much more in their favour, had not succeeded. Apparently she had told Margaret a few months after Cyril's death that she wanted to get paying work quickly, but Margaret had assured her there was no hurry:

> Are you to qualify yourself for the highest work, which is better paid, which you can have at home and do at leisure with credit and profit, or are you to snatch at the immediate profit and give up that? .... It is a kind of choice which almost any artist is compelled to make. Your uncle Frank had to choose between painting, on which all his mind was set, and his painted glass, which meant his living, and he was obliged to choose the last .... I have had to do something of the same kind, and if I were dead it would be a choice you would be obliged to make .... But as long as I am here at your back I grudge it for you.[7]

They went back, reluctantly, to Clarence Crescent in July. That autumn Cecco was in St Andrew's for the golf; Madge went with him, and it was probably there that she met William Valentine, the junior partner in the firm of Spalding and Valentine, jute cloth manufacturers of Dundee. Apparently he made it clear very soon that he wanted to marry her and after she had returned to England he wrote frequently and came south more than once to see her.

Madge was flattered, but definitely not in love. Mr Valentine was fourteen years older than herself, and admitted that he knew hardly anything about art or literature. On the other hand he was a kindly man, and she was twenty-nine and must have felt the tremendous pressure on young women of her generation to get married. She thought it over during the early months of 1893, while she worked at her engraving in London, staying with Margaret's friend Emma FitzMaurice whom she privately considered a bore. If she had been more successful in her career, or met someone she liked better, that might have turned the scale, but finally, in the spring, she agreed.

Margaret had watched this going on with mixed feelings. She had hoped and even prayed for years that the girls would get married, but she could not take to Mr Valentine or he to her. She allowed herself to say privately that it showed 'the foolishness of giving expensive training to young women'.[8] In June she took Madge to see her future home at Elmwood, Lochee, a 'nice solid Scotch stone house'[9] less than half a mile from the factory, but found the whole set-up rather too bourgeois for her taste. 'Quite between ourselves', Madge wrote to Denny, 'I think everything is made more difficult by Aunt Maggie who is so totally out of her element.'[10] But now that it was settled, she threw herself into the arrangements for the wedding, which took place in Windsor on 26 July. Cecco looked unwell that day, and very soon afterwards he collapsed.

Margaret spent the summer and autumn in a dreadful state of worry, trying with hardly any success to find something that he could eat. Meanwhile, Madge sent her a series of desperate appeals. Although she had a certain amount of prestige in Dundee, as the niece of a famous novelist, she felt it was 'a hole the very end of all things', and missed the 'general atmosphere of culture' and the 'old happy hard-working life'.[11] She kept begging her to come for a long visit:

> You are the person I love best by far in this world – Willie might not like hearing that but I cannot help it, it is so. So terribly so, he comes a long way behind.[12]

Margaret wrote to her almost daily but did not go to her. Quite apart from her fear of leaving Cecco, she did not want Madge to be put in the position which she had been in after her own marriage. 'I wish I could carry her burdens', she wrote to Denny, 'but I can't – at least I must not increase them.'[13] A slightly later letter, of 15 October, says:

> I go to Church on the first Sunday of the month, but I fear I remain where I am now on the others, hearing the bells, and by and by reading the service, and thinking of my boys – one of whom we know not where he is or how employed in the great and terrible Unseen, and the other whose every change of countenance I watch so anxiously – and of my girls, one breasting the waves of life already for her own hand. You are the only little sheltered one my little Den, and your shelter so precarious, nothing but this poor worn life of mine.[14]

She went with Cecco to the Riviera that winter, as usual, but by the summer had admitted that he 'will never I fear now be strong'.[15] It is remarkable how everyone, including the doctors, refused to admit the obvious fact that Cecco had tuberculosis. Over the last few years they had been constantly together; Margaret fretting over every small change in his condition. He worked part-time in the Royal Library and collaborated with his mother on an unsatisfying book, *The Victorian Age of English Literature*. He was neither as prolific nor as popular a writer as she was, but he published several articles and a travel book about Palestine, and in 1894 was planning another about the Riviera. He had very few friends and people often felt oppressed when they were with him. Madge had commented before her marriage on the 'mysterious weight of Cecco ... he seems with his curious temper, poor boy, to drag all of us down'.[16] Howard Sturgis, who had recently moved back to Windsor, found a 'curious air of age about him'. He was only thirty-four,

> but I used to feel as if his mother and I were people of ordinary middle age and normal condition of life, who had somehow to moderate and hush our talk when he was by, as one does for a much older person who must not be disturbed or worried.[17]

Madge was expecting her first child that autumn and Margaret went to Scotland to be with her, though feeling 'torn in pieces between the two'.[18] The baby, a girl, was born on 9 September, and Margaret was delighted to find that she seemed determined to struggle for life. She was named Margaret Oliphant Harris Valentine. A week later she returned home and found Cecco ill with an inflamed throat and tongue. As usual, he seemed to get better and worse for a fortnight. On 1 October 1894 she was so alarmed that she called the doctor, who said he was suffering from exhaustion. Late that night they had almost given up hope. At half past eleven, he rallied. Margaret tried desperately to warm his hands, which were already cold. 'The doctor left expressing hopes, but had not been gone ten minutes when he sank again all at once, and peacefully like a child breathed out his last breath.'[19]

Some hours later, Margaret wrote another long entry in the notebook which had not been touched since a few months after Cyril died. After forty years in which she had thought of herself primarily as a mother, she had no living child. It was true that Madge and Denny were like daughters to her, but the two boys for whom she had made so many plans and sacrifices were gone. 'They say I have been foolish in my treatment of them', she wrote, ' – one cruel man the other day told me I had ruined my family by my indulgence and extravagance – I do not honestly before God think so.' It was not her fault that their father had died, and she still could not think it had been wrong to give them all the good things she could afford. And yet, in the end, she had been able to do nothing for them:

> What a struggle I have had, what endless work and striving, and all ending in these two graves – if I had broken down as so many women might in that sad time in Rome after my husband died before Cecco was born, how very very little difference would it have made. The children would have sunk too, with nobody to take care of them, and it would all have ended so much sooner. . . . Let nobody think that the few books I will leave behind me count for anything. I have no such thought. The world would have been none the poorer and my children little the worse if I had dropped by the side of their father's grave.

However, she could not bear to think that Cecco might as well have died at birth. Both she and Annie, who came to her at once, comforted themselves by creating a saint-like image of him which he certainly had not deserved. Equally intolerable was the thought that it had been a 'horrible accident'. 'Let me feel', she wrote, that 'it was the will of God.'[20]

In spite of everything she still felt as strong as ever, although Annie thought her 'only the white shadow of what she had been'. Mental anguish did not even give her a headache. The immediate need, after the first few days, was to finish an article and to go to Madge, who was very unwell. Taking Denny and Fanny Tulloch, who had attached herself to the household around this time, they went to Scotland for a few weeks and then brought Madge and the baby to London. Both girls did everything they could to support her, and Madge stopped complaining of her marriage at about this time. Perhaps the baby, to whom she was devoted, helped to reconcile her to it. The three women were unconsciously repeating a pattern which Margaret had established soon after her own marriage – women and children forming a little world which as far as possible excluded men. Madge must also have become aware that Margaret could not take much more. There was no denying that her husband and her aunt were incompatible, but from then on she wrote her cheerful letters most days and came for long visits whenever she could.

The companionship of her nieces and the baby undoubtedly helped Margaret to get through the next few months. She also read and wrote compulsively – 'these two things keep me going, since go I must'.[21] One of the first pieces of work she did was a paper for *Blackwood's*, 'Fancies of a Believer', in which she tried, yet again, to justify the ways of God:

> I can only claim to be one of the people whose nature it is to believe rather than doubt, and to whom, where all is mysterious, the way which I have been taught to believe is God's way of accounting for the universe seems more reasonable and less difficult (where all is difficult) than any other way.

It was natural, she admitted, that the bereaved should resent God even while they still needed him, and that they should feel totally depressed by the absence of any contact with the dead. 'We try to think that perhaps they whom we have lost are still near us, but feel in our very souls how far, how distant, how absent they are. Rachel weeping for her children, and will not be comforted because they are not; no words more true have been found out through all these centuries.'[22]

Just before Cecco's death, Blackwood had asked her to write the official history of the publishing house. She liked the idea, feeling that it would 'involve a most important piece of the recent history of literature',[23] and now he offered to pay her five hundred pounds a year while the work lasted. She decided to take two years over it (she had two other books on hand, but that was no problem) and she seems to have made up her mind at about this time that she wanted to live for those two years and no more. Her connection with the Blackwoods had begun when she received the proofs of *Katie Stewart* on her wedding day, and had lasted over forty years; she now felt that it would be appropriate to 'wind up the long laborious record'[24] with this history.

She also began work again on her autobiography, with the idea of leaving a little more money for Denny. She was worried about her younger niece, who at thirty was still unmarried and had failed to get her pictures exhibited. 'I think it is very bad for her living continually under my shadow', she wrote to Annie. 'She gets more undecided, more hesitating and less confidence in herself every day.'[25] Soon afterwards Denny legally changed her name to Oliphant, and when Margaret made a will she left everything to 'my adopted daughter'.[26]

In February 1895, four months after Cecco had died, Denny made a pencil drawing of her aunt which is now in the Scottish National Portrait Gallery. The determined set of the mouth shows that, at sixty-six, she was in no danger of losing her intellectual grasp. But although she had not changed very much in the previous twenty years, she now looked her full age. 'The wit had all gone out of her eyes, though not quite from her talk', wrote J. M. Barrie, '. . . what had started to be the old laugh often ended pitifully. The two sons who had been so much to her were gone, and for the rest of her days she never forgot it, I think, for the length of a smile. She was less the novelist now than a pathetic figure in a novel.'[27]

Novel-writing had become very hard work now. She finished a book about Rome, thinking for a time that she would like to go back as 'so much happened to me there',[28] and went through several boxes of the Blackwoods' letters from the early part of the century. Back at Windsor, working on her *Autobiography* in the bitterly cold early months of 1895, she had a strange feeling that if she were to push her way into Nelly Clifford's deserted house she would find Cecco, as a boy, playing whist with the three old people. 'I wonder sometimes if what has been ever dies! . . . . I have so often felt, with a bewildered dizziness, as if that might be.' She had sometimes had the same sensation when she passed her own old house on the way to King's Cross, and felt that if she only had the courage to knock on the door and go straight in she would find Frank and the children there.

In October she took Denny to Paris for some more art training, feeling concerned that she had 'a very dull limited life with me'.[29] It was over thirty years since she had come here with the little boys after Maggie had died. Later that month she began to plan her last great supernatural story, 'The Library Window'.[30]

This was probably based on a visit to St Andrew's half a

century before, and the narrator, an unworldly girl who prefers books to society, is evidently the teenage Margaret Wilson. But there is no trace of self-pity, although we know that she was intensely miserable that autumn as the anniversaries of the boys' birthdays came round, and the story is a flawless piece of work. On the first reading, the subject-matter may seem trivial. The girl becomes fascinated by a window across the street, where she thinks she can see a man writing, as in the legend about Sir Walter Scott. Like the open door in the story of that name, the window is a meeting-place between the known world – which the author describes with her usual wit and realism – and the unseen. Sometimes it is blank; at other times it gives a clear view of the writer's study – 'full of quietness, not disturbed by anything' – which, when she tries to get inside it, is not there. It turns out that the man was a scholar, who 'liked his books more than any lady's love', and has been dead for years. There is no explanation of the mystery. No doubt Margaret had in mind the text about seeing 'through a glass darkly'; the story is full of images of light and its opposite – 'the evening in June in Scotland', when 'it is daylight, yet it is not day'. People are constantly straining their eyes to see something which is not there or ignoring it when it is visible. It is very largely about human efforts to see into the unseen. But there is also a suggestion that the writer 'had to take up some other kind of work for his living, and then when his leisure time came, gave it all up to something he really loved'. The study which she glimpses through the library window represents the world of scholarship and serious creative writing, which she could enter only at odd times.

Simultaneously, she was working on an article which in the long run did more harm to her reputation than anything else she wrote. 'The Library Window' is half-forgotten but 'The Anti-Marriage League',[31] her attack on *Jude the Obscure* and other 'sex-question' novels, is well-known to Hardy students, and has created the impression that she was an outraged Victorian matron. As a matter of fact Margaret was quite capable of writing about sexual questions without prudery. She had just told Madge that she had enjoyed *Trilby* – 'but I am afraid your husband would think it wicked'.[32] She had stood by her friend Christina Rogerson when her morals were attacked. But she detested the growing tendency, in the 1890s, 'to place what is called the Sex-question above all others as the theme of fiction'.[33] In an earlier review of *Tess*, she had said that she preferred 'a world which is round and contains everything, not "the relations between the sexes" alone'.[34] Above all she was repelled by novels which separated 'the Sex-question' from children and responsibility. 'The children', she insisted, 'are a most serious part of the question of the abolition of marriage.'[35]

Traditional morality was coming under attack. Grant Allen's *The Woman Who Did*, a novel about a woman who rejects marriage, had just gone into its twentieth edition. Hardy's *Tess* and the recently-published *Jude* had sold far better than his earlier novels because they had the reputation of being scandalous. Margaret felt that something was seriously wrong when the public which frequently ignored good work bought books for this kind of reason. 'I have been thinking over Hardy's book', she wrote to Blackwood from Paris, 'and I don't feel sure that it might not be my duty to treat it and a few others of the same kind seriously putting my name to the article.... The evil is very great. I only doubt if my voice is authoritative enough to denounce it.'[36]

The article, published in January 1896, is good slashing stuff, although at times she allowed her dislike of Hardy's 'grossness' to overpower her. She admitted that Hardy was a genius, and praised some things in the novel, but she gave it as her considered opinion that no writer of his stature had ever before produced so indecent a book. When it appeared it caused a mild sensation. Other people had been upset, in the past, by Margaret's 'dangerous facility of sarcasm and stinging speech', and Hardy, who had not liked her when they met, was bitterly hurt:

> Talk of shamelessness [he wrote]: that a woman who purely for money's sake has for the last 30 years flooded the magazines and starved out scores of better workers, should try to write down rival novelists whose books sell better than her own, caps all the shamelessness of Arabella, to my mind.[37]

Madge's second child, William, was born on 22 December, and Margaret went to Dundee in the New Year to see him. She spent about a month there in a rented house, probably to keep out of Mr Valentine's way. On this, which turned out to be her last visit to Scotland, she wrote a short story, 'The Heirs of Kellie', which is based on the history of her family. It is uneven, but the opening, at least, shows that she had lost none of her skill. Sir Walter Oliphant of Kellie Castle, at the beginning of the seventeenth century, is looking back on a long and eventful life and trying to decide who is to inherit his lands. His 'natural heirs' are gone – his sons are dead, like Margaret's – but he has a young sister, Jean, and a cousin, Peter Oliphant, who wants to marry her. In the end, though, he overlooks them and leaves the castle to Lord Oliphant, the head of the family, who fills it with bloodthirsty young men. Contrasted with them is the sober, responsible Peter, despised by his cousins for being an ordinary yeoman, who takes the difficult decision not to fight for his rights. Jean is a young girl burning with indignation against the law 'that takes your natural heritage out of your hands, because, at God's will, not your own, you are a lass born instead of a man'. She has romantic ideas about raising her kinsmen to fight for her, but Peter argues – using the family motto, 'À tout pourvoir', as his justification – that this would not be worth the loss of life:

> 'But for the lads that would follow me, and rise at your name – the fishers at St Monance, the small farmers intill Carnbee – every man with his little gear that he has gathered out of the heavy ploughland or the stormy sea – do ye mind that every one would be putten to the horn, their sma' tenements levelled with the earth, and their bairns scattered to the winds?.... To provide for all, that's what it means – no to devote them to death and ruin for our service . . .' (5)

This is all the more difficult because he knows he would have been a good head of the family, while those who take his inheritance are not worthy of it. Peter and Jean 'subdue their pride to the acceptance of their fate', and withdraw to the small farm of Over-Kellie, 'The family kept their homely life unbroken there for many generations, keeping up the old name and kindly tradition long after the Lords Oliphant . . . were, like the Flowers of the Forest, a' wede away' (8). Margaret must have seen this as an emblem of her own life and the disappearance of almost everything she had valued. The Oliphants were losers. But she had done her best to 'provide for all', and could at least, like her ancestor, accept her fate with dignity. And she still hoped that 'at the end of the dim valley' there 'begins to glow over the dark braes the rising of a better sun'.

For some time now Margaret's friends had been urging her to leave Clarence Crescent, where everything reminded her of the boys. In April 1896 she moved, with Denny and Fanny Tulloch, into The Hermitage, a small furnished house (which was all that she could now afford) on Wimbledon Common. It was shabby but comfortable, with a great deal of space and fresh air – 'just on the edge of the fine and fashionable but quite out of it unfortunately'.[38]

After the short burst of creativity at the turn of the year, she went on working systematically at the *Annals of a Publishing House*. Boxes of old letters kept coming from Blackwood, some of them referring to herself as a young author. As she finished the first volume and went into the second she began to fear that, after all, she might not die when it was done. She felt as strong as ever, and it was horrible to think that at her age she might have to go back to touting for work. But in the summer she had a renewed attack of internal pain which stopped her working for a fortnight, and reported in October that 'I have worked a hole in my right forefinger – with the pen, I suppose! – and can't get it to heal'.[39] Soon afterwards the publisher J. M. Dent called to suggest that she should write a book about Siena:

> She was a lady under middle height, with a beautiful low broad forehead, and very dark keen eyes which held you strongly. You felt somehow that no suffering would break her spirit, and that her body must obey to the last ounce of its strength her indomitable will. This I felt although I did not know her story until afterwards.[40]

Annie Coghill was shocked when Margaret told her that she was proposing to go to Siena to gather materials. She had had several attacks of pain which forced her to write on the sofa, and two of her oldest friends, Emma FitzMaurice and Isabella Blackwood, had died within a month of each other in the winter of 1896–7. Margaret said smilingly that there was never anything the matter with her. She felt she had no choice but to do the book, since no other was lined up, and St Catherine, the patron of Siena, was the kind of woman who had always interested her. But work was becoming much more difficult. She was well aware that she was behind the fashion and that any reputation she might have had was declining fast. In the spring of 1897 'Mr Sandford' was reissued as one of two stories in a small volume, *The Ways of Life*. Margaret wrote a preface, called 'On the Ebb Tide', in which she admitted that it had been

> produced under the influence of that strange discovery which a man makes when he finds himself carried away by the retiring waters, no longer coming in upon the top of the wave, but going out. This does not necessarily mean the decline of life, the approach of age, or any natural crisis, but something more poignant – the wonderful and overwhelming revelation which one time or other comes to most people, that their career, whatever it may have been, has come to a stop; that such successes as they may have achieved are over, and that henceforward they must accustom themselves to the thought of going out with the tide.[41]

Before starting for Siena she wrote Blackwood a long article, ''Tis Sixty Years Since', surveying most of the important social changes since 1837. Queen Victoria's diamond jubilee was approaching, and she thought so much rubbish would be written on the subject that a more serious article might not be out of place. There was a long list of major events to record – railways, the penny post, telegrams, the growth of the British Empire and of foreign travel, chloroform and antiseptics which had transformed medicine, daily newspapers, a national education system and the mass production of books. She left England on 10 April, soon after her sixty-ninth birthday, and came back at the end of the month feeling ready to start on the Siena book.

Madge, who was expecting her third baby that summer, had come to the Hermitage for a long visit bringing little Margaret and William. Margaret thoroughly enjoyed the company of the children, who called her Granny, and for a while seemed better. She went to a pleasant party in town and 'apparently moved about with less fatigue than she often did'. But the attacks of pain soon returned. Early in June several doctors confirmed that, as she suspected, it was the beginning of the end.

Her reaction, like Mr Sandford's, was one of intense relief. She was lifted on to the sofa daily and spent most of her time reading or – in the sleepless nights – thinking. She was practically unable to eat, but had no pain. 'I am only waiting', she told her friends, 'and I hope I shall not have to wait very long, lest I should get impatient.' She had convinced herself, after long and hard struggles, that she was about to be reunited with her children, and she was very glad to be able to shed her responsibilities. According to Barrie she said that for the first time in fifty years she had nothing on her mind. Denny could always have a home with her sister if necessary, and, as she explained in her last letter to Blackwood on 16 June, there would be enough to pay off her debts:

> Dear Mr Blackwood,
>
> I have looked at the title-page and made the last correction of the press that I shall ever be able to do. I can't tell you how sorry I am not to be able to revise the second volume....
>
> I am now lying, all possibility of work over, awaiting a very speedy end. You know that I have been working for a long time for daily bread. I will leave enough behind me to clear off everything, besides the literary remains, autobiographical, etc. I wish therefore to ask you as a last kindness to pay my bankers £100 to meet the expenses of the time, which will either be repaid to you by Denny as soon as my affairs are settled, or else subtracted from the price you may offer to her for these unpublished fragments. We are very old friends and have always I think worked along very comfortably together. Except for these matters I am very grateful to get away to 'the rest that remaineth', and very comfortable in my mind reposing on Our Dear Lord. Goodbye – my love to you all. Very truly yours,
>
> M. O. W. Oliphant.[42]

Robert Story had come to London for the Jubilee and called on her when he heard how ill she was. Over the last thirty years they had only met occasionally. Story was a happily married and successful man who had accumulated several honours – chaplain to the Queen in Scotland, Moderator of the General Assembly and Professor of Church History at Glasgow University. But he found that Margaret still had a profound effect on him:

> Her voice was still strong, with its old, familiar tone; her wonderful eyes were as lambent as ever; and her mind was as

> calm and clear as a summer's sea. 'I am dying', she said; 'I do not think I can last through the night.' Thinking of the *Little Pilgrim*, of the *Seen and Unseen*, and the many touching efforts her imagination had made to lift the impenetrable veil, I said, 'The world to which you are going is a familiar world to you.'[43]

Another visitor was Anne Thackeray Ritchie, who lived nearby and had seen her constantly in the last year. She reported that Margaret 'said to her girls, "Make things look *comfortable* after I am gone"', and that she was 'longing to go'.[44] But in fact Margaret lived a week longer than the doctors had predicted. She told Annie not to disappoint her husband by staying away from the Jubilee procession, promising that she would have no bad news on the twenty-second. Throughout the great day there were noisy bands and fireworks on Wimbledon Common, but she put up with it patiently. Her nieces read her Tennyson's poetry, including 'Crossing the Bar', and Lockhart's account of the death of Sir Walter Scott. Soon afterwards she began to lose consciousness. She died at twenty-five to twelve on the evening of Friday 25 June, according to Denny looking 'perfectly happy and peaceful'.[45] Her death certificate, which described her merely as the widow of Francis Oliphant, gave the cause of death as 'malignant disease of the colon', and exhaustion.

'I have lost a lifelong friend, and the world too', Anne Ritchie wrote four days later as she got ready to go to the funeral. 'She was to me one of those people who *make* life – so many un-make it.'[46]

She was buried at Eton cemetery next to the boys. It was a fine day; the streets were decorated with flags for the Jubilee and a band was playing in Windsor park. Howard Sturgis, who was there, noted that 'life was at its fullest, brightest, noisiest'.[47]

14 Aftermath

After the funeral Madge went back to Lochee so that her baby could be born at home. On 26 July she gave birth to a boy, named Francis Cyril Oliphant Valentine after her brother and cousin. But a few days later she developed malignant scarlet fever and died on 13 August, seven weeks after her aunt. 'I cannot imagine her feelings had she been still here', wrote Denny, 'thank God that was spared.'[1]

Meanwhile, Blackwood had been trying to get Margaret's pension transferred to Denny so that she could finish her art training, and she was in fact granted £75 a year for life. However, her brother-in-law was anxious that she should stay on in his home and look after the three small children, and it was obvious that there was nothing else she could do. Soon afterwards she and Annie Coghill began to go through Margaret's literary remains. Both women were in a state of shock, as Denny had lost the two people closest to her and Annie's husband had also died in the summer of 1897. Instead of the full-length autobiography which they had been expecting, they found two notebooks with entries written at long intervals, and with no real beginning or end. Some passages were too painful to print, and when these had been cut they were left with a very short manuscript. They added some of her letters to friends and publishers, with a tearful linking narrative by Annie, and the book, *The Autobiography and Letters of Mrs M. O. W. Oliphant*, was published in 1899. This was the first time the public had heard of Margaret's problems with her sons, and several reviews took the opportunity to discuss the relationship between her life and her art. The *Edinburgh Review* pointed out that she had gifts denied to Trollope, including a beautiful style, but that his reputation stood much higher:

Why with all these advantages does she get no further? What

> is it that sets the dividing line between her and George Eliot, or Charlotte Brontë?

The answer was – this critic felt – that Margaret had been less interested in her work than in motherhood. 'It may be an accident – but more likely it is not – that the women who have been great artists have been childless women.'[2]

Another critic, who had obviously known her well, wrote:

> To be closely related to her was to have a claim on her which overpowered every other.... Husband, brothers, sons, nephews, nieces, if they could not provide for themselves, it became in her eyes a duty to provide for them.... For them she abandoned the hope – or, as we believe, and as she believed – the certainty of being a great authoress on a level with George Eliot, and deliberately reduced herself, as she thought, to a manufacturer of saleable literature. The literature was far better than she feared, but that was her idea.... That Mrs Oliphant was a noble woman we have no doubt whatever. That she chose the noblest career we doubt very much.... We cannot agree that an author has a right for any object, however unselfish, permanently to lay aside his highest weapons.[3]

'No one even will mention me in the same breath with George Eliot', Margaret herself had written. 'And that is just.' Her reputation, such as it was, did not long outlive the century. The kind words of her contemporaries – that she had a strong sense of duty, that her writing was invariably pure and womanly – were not likely to make her attractive to the next generation, who had no way of knowing that in most respects she was profoundly un-Victorian.

However, after ten years enough money had been raised for a public memorial. On 16 July 1908 a large congregation came to St Giles' Cathedral, Edinburgh, where a plaque was unveiled near the memorial to Robert Louis Stevenson. J. M. Barrie gave the address, and Dr Cameron Lees prayed that it 'might keep her memory green in the hearts of her Scottish countrymen, and might bear to succeeding generations the praise of her many virtues'.

Denny was at the service with the Valentine children for whom she was now solely responsible, their father having died in 1907. She was more fortunate than Margaret for, although she lived into her late eighties, all of them survived her. Frank, the child born just before Madge died, became a distinguished chemotherapist. Margaret collected and arranged her great-aunt's papers and presented them to the National Library of Scotland in 1973.

Long before that time, Margaret Oliphant was practically forgotten. The *Autobiography* and most of her other books soon went out of print. *Salem Chapel* survived the longest, as an Everyman Classic, and *A Beleaguered City* and some of the supernatural stories were reprinted occasionally. The rest were torn up in thousands, practically disappearing even from the second-hand bookshops, and students of the Victorian age somehow got the impression that she had been an unimportant writer. In the 1930s Virginia Woolf looked at some of her 'innumerable faded articles', biographies and novels and found the effect depressing:

> Mrs Oliphant sold her brain, her very admirable brain, prostituted her culture and enslaved her intellectual liberty in order that she might earn her living and educate her children.... We have to applaud her choice and to admire her courage. But if we applaud the choice and admire the courage of those who do what she did, we can spare ourselves the trouble of addressing our appeal to them, for they will no more be able to protect disinterested culture and intellectual liberty than she was.[4]

The point Virginia Woolf was making – that women writers have special difficulties to face – is now generally accepted. But Margaret did not benefit from the new wave of interest in women's writing in the 1970s. On the strength of Annie's foolish remarks, she was written off as an anti-suffragist and a Victorian prude as well. Yet any woman today who tries to balance the needs of her family against her own need to work has a surprising amount in common with Margaret Oliphant.

'How I have been handicapped in life!' Margaret wrote, comparing herself with George Eliot. 'Should I have done better if I had been kept, like her, in a mental greenhouse and taken care of?' Perhaps, but if she had retreated into that greenhouse and concentrated on developing her own talents, the work might have been much less good after all. The bracing realism, the absence of smugness, the awareness of the rougher side of life could not have existed if the author of *Kirsteen* and *The Doctor's Family* had been a protected upper-middle-class lady. Howard Sturgis seems to have understood the paradox:

> By many writers almost a new gospel of selfishness is being preached to women – self-development, self-assertion, the right to be herself, to live her own life; it is always self in some form that is set as the ideal before the young woman of the day.
>
> Far other ideals had Margaret Oliphant.... She would have considered it pure waste of time solemnly to think out the lines along which her character ought to develop itself. As to letting it do so, at any cost to those she loved, the idea would never have found a moment's lodging with her.... The rule of her life was to spend and be spent for others ... and perhaps, after all, in this way she did find her own soul by losing it.[5]

It is not possible to write biographies of everyone who agrees to 'spend and be spent for others', which is probably what the majority of women have always done. The reason for studying Margaret Oliphant's life and work is simply that she was a great writer, who has been neglected for far too long. There are signs that more people are beginning to realise this, and that she may one day take her rightful place.

Notes and References

All quotations not otherwise identified are from the main published text of the *Autobiography*, but letters which appear in it have been identified by their dates. All books, articles and letters to publishers cited here are by Margaret, unless otherwise stated.

Abbreviations are as follows:

Annals: *Annals of a Publishing House: William Blackwood and his sons* (2 volumes, 1897). Volume 3, *The Life of John Blackwood* (1898) is by Mrs Gerald Porter.

A & L: Mrs Harry Coghill (ed.), *Autobiography and Letters of Mrs M. O. W. Oliphant* (1899).

Auto. MS: Manuscript of the *Autobiography*, now in the National Library of Scotland, Acc. 5793/9.

Blackwood's: *Blackwood's Edinburgh Magazine*.

Blackwood MS: Letters to the Blackwoods, now in the National Library of Scotland.

Colby: Vineta and Robert A. Colby, *The Equivocal Virtue: Mrs Oliphant and the Victorian Literary Market Place* (New York: Archon Books, 1966).

Macmillan MS: Letters to Macmillan, now in the British Museum.

NLS: National Library of Scotland.

Tulloch: *Memoir of the Life of John Tulloch* (1888) Page references are to the third edition (1889).

As a rule, I have identified quotations from novels by chapter (numbers in brackets in the text) and quotations from other books by page.

CHAPTER 1: OLIPHANTS AND WILSONS

1. Quoted in Hew Lorimer, *Kellie Castle* (Edinburgh: National Trust for Scotland, 1971).
2. 'Laurence Oliphant', *Blackwood's*, February 1889.
3. William Cobbett, *Tour in Scotland* (1833) p. 102.
4. 'Isabel Dysart', Chapter 1, in *That Little Cutty, and Two Other Stories* (1898).
5. ''Tis Sixty Years Since', *Blackwood's*, May 1897.
6. *Thomas Chalmers* (1893) p. 205.
7. *Royal Edinburgh* (1890) p. 455.
8. 'New Books', *Blackwood's*, April 1874.
9. *Tulloch*, p. 88.
10. ''Tis Sixty Years Since'.
11. *Ailieford* (1853) Volume 3, Chapter 11.

12. *John Drayton* (1851) Volume 2, Chapters 8 and 12.
13. George McGuffie, *The Priests of Etal* (fourth edition, Edinburgh, 1904), Chapter 11, 'The Literary Priest'.
14. Mrs Oliphant and F. R. Oliphant, *The Victorian Age of English Literature* (1892) Volume 2, Chapter 1.
15. *A & L*, 1881 section.
16. Auto. MS.
17. Margaret to Frank Oliphant, no day or month, 1852, NLS Acc. 5678/18.
18. *Athenaeum*, 24 November 1849.
19. Lord Jeffrey to Margaret, 5 January 1850, *A & L*.
20. The address given in her correspondence for 1851–52 is 24 Kenyon Terrace, Birkenhead, but the 1851 census gives the street number as 83.
21. George Wilson to Margaret, 21 May 1852, NLS Acc. 5793/3.
22. *Annals*, Volume 1, pp. 129–30.
23. Quoted F. D. Tredray, *The House of Blackwood, 1804–1954* (Edinburgh: Blackwood & Sons, 1964) p. 64.
24. 'John Blackwood', *Dictionary of National Biography*.
25. *Annals*, Volume 3, p. 21.
26. *Victorian Age of English Literature*, Volume 2, Chapter 8.
27. *Annals*, Volume 1, p. 316.
28. 'The New Exhibition', *Blackwood's*, June 1862, suggests that she had been to the 1851 Exhibition.
29. 'The Autobiography and Letters of Mrs M. O. W. Oliphant', anonymous article in the *Quarterly Review*, July 1899.
30. Margaret to Frank Oliphant, 1852, NLS Acc. 5678/18.
31. *Passages in the Life of Mrs Margaret Maitland of Sunnyside* (1849), Volume 3, Chapter 7.

CHAPTER 2: GENERAL UTILITY WOMAN

1. Baptism certificate of Francis Wilson Oliphant, Gateshead St Mary, 15 September 1819.
2. 'Francis Wilson Oliphant', *Dictionary of National Biography*.
3. *Annals*, Volume 2, p. 471.
4. Pugin's letters to Frank are in the National Library of Scotland. Acc. 5678/21.
5. Frank Oliphant to Major William Blackwood, 26 March 1856, Blackwood MS 4119.
6. Frank Oliphant to John Blackwood, 27 October 1856, ibid.
7. Francis Wilson Oliphant, *A Plea for Painted Glass* (Oxford 1855).
8. *At His Gates* (1872) Chapters 1, 44 and 45.
9. *Victorian Age of English Literature*, Volume 2, p. 186.
10. *Miss Marjoribanks* (1866) Chapter 11.
11. *For Love and Life* (1874) Volume 3, Chapter 15.
12. Mrs Wilson to Thomas Oliphant, 22 August 1852, NLS Acc. 5793/3.
13. Auto. MS.
14. Margaret to Mrs Maxton Graham, 6 April 1895, *A & L*.

15. 'Grace Greenwood' (Sara Jane Clarke Lippincott), *Haps and Mishaps of a Tour to Europe* (Boston 1854) quoted Colby, p. 28.
16. Blackwood MS 4106, 28 March 1854.
17. Ibid., 4 August 1854.
18. *Annals*, Volume 2, p. 475.
19. *Merkland* (1850) Chapter 15.
20. *Annals*, Volume 2, p. 470.
21. Ibid., Volume 2, p. 471.
22. Blackwood MS 4119, no day or month, 1856.
23. George Meredith, 'Contemporary Literature', *Westminster Review*, October 1857.
24. *Annals*, Volume 2, p. 472.
25. 'A Week in Florence', *Blackwood's*, November 1859.
26. Introduction to Gerardine Macpherson, *Memoirs of the Life of Anna Jameson* (1878).
27. 'The Seaside in the Papal States', *Blackwood's*, October 1859.
28. Blackwood MS 4141, 20 May 1859.
29. Ibid., 25 June 1859.
30. *A Son of the Soil* (1866) Chapter 31.
31. Betty Miller, *Robert Browning, A Portrait* (London: John Murray, 1952), Chapter 3.
32. *A Son of the Soil*, Chapter 33.
33. Blackwood MS 4725, 1 December 1859.

CHAPTER 3: THE SALT AND BITTER WAVES

1. Margaret to John Blackwood, 23 March 1860, *A & L*.
2. *At His Gates*, Chapter 16.
3. *Madonna Mary* (1867) Chapter 19.
4. Blackwood MS 4152, no day or month, 1860.
5. *The Life of Edward Irving* (1862) Chapter 6.
6. 'Edward Irving', *Dictionary of National Biography*.
7. *Annals*, Volume 2, p. 99.
8. Elma and Constance Story, *Memoir of Robert Herbert Story, by his daughters* (Glasgow, 1909) p. 43.
9. *Annals*, Volume 2, pp. 486–7.
10. *Tulloch*, p. 4.
11. A. K. H. Boyd, *Twenty-Five Years of St Andrew's* (1892) Volume 2, p. 27.
12. *Tulloch*, p. 480.
13. Ibid., pp. 161–2.
14. Colby, p. 79.
15. See *Agnes* (1865), *A Country Gentleman and his Family* (1886), and the title-story of *A Widow's Tale* (1898).
16. Blackwood MS 4163, no day or month, 1861.
17. *The Three Brothers* (1870) Volume 1, Chapter 17.
18. *Madonna Mary*, Chapter 14.
19. Blackwood MS 4163, 17 December 1861.

20. *Annals*, Volume 3, p. 73.
21. George Eliot to Sara Hennell, 23 April 1862, in Gordon S. Haight (ed.) *The George Eliot Letters, Volume 4* (London: Oxford University Press, 1956), p. 25.
22. Blackwood MS 4172, no day or month, 1862.
23. Ibid., no day or month, 1862.
24. Jane Carlyle to Margaret, no day or month, 1862, *A & L*.
25. William Tulloch, 'Mrs Oliphant', *The Bookman*, August 1897.
26. 'In the Garden', *Blackwood's*, August 1863.
27. *Tulloch*, p. 169.
28. Janet Leith Story long outlived Margaret, dying in 1926 at the age of ninety-eight. When in her eighties she published two very lively books of reminiscences.
29. Blackwood MS 4184, 12 December 1863.
30. Principal Tulloch to John Blackwood, Blackwood MS 4194, 13 February 1864.
31. Auto. MS.
32. 'The Life of Jesus', *Blackwood's*, October 1864.
33. Auto. MS.
34. *Tulloch*, 191–2.
35. Margaret to John Blackwood, 31 December 1864, Blackwood MS 4191.
36. Blackwood MS 4202, 8 March 1865.
37. Ibid., 11 June 1865.
38. Ibid., 22 December 1865.
39. Geddie Macpherson to Margaret, 21 April 1870, NLS Acc. 5678/20.

CHAPTER 4: THE MOST REMARKABLE WOMAN OF HER TIME

1. John Skelton, 'A Little Chat about Mrs Oliphant', *Blackwood's*, January 1883.
2. Howard Sturgis, 'A Sketch from Memory', *Temple Bar*, September–December 1899.
3. A. C. Benson, *Memories and Friends* (1924) p. 83.
4. 'On the Ebb-Tide', preface to *The Ways of Life* (1897).
5. Margaret to John Blackwood, no day or month, 1862, *A & L*.
6. *Innocent* (1873) Volume 3, Chapter 5.
7. *The Nonconformist*, 16 June 1869, NLS Acc. 5793/19.
8. J. I. M. Stewart, Introduction to W. M. Thackeray, *Vanity Fair* (Harmondsworth: Penguin English Library, 1968).
9. 'Miss Austen and Miss Mitford', *Blackwood's*, March 1870.
10. *The Doctor's Family* (1863) Chapter 12.
11. Ibid., Chapter 17.
12. 'Scottish National Character', *Blackwood's*, June 1860.
13. 'The Autobiography and Letters of Mrs M. O. W. Oliphant', anonymous article in the *Quarterly Review*.

14. A. C. Benson's diary, 17 January 1900, quoted in H. Montgomery Hyde, *Henry James at Home* (London: Methuen, 1969) p. 110.
15. *A Rose in June* (1874) Chapter 1.
16. 'Charles Dickens', *Blackwood's*, April 1855.
17. *The Railwayman and his Children* (1891) Volume 1, Chapter 15.
18. *Athenaeum*, review of *Margaret Maitland.*
19. Blackwood MS 4099, 4 February 1852.

CHAPTER 5: CHRONICLES OF CARLINGFORD

1. *The Perpetual Curate* (1864) Chapter 1.
2. *The Doctor's Family* (1863) Chapter 1.
3. 'Family History', *Blackwood's*, October 1856.
4. Margaret to John Blackwood, 20 September 1865, *A & L.*
5. Blackwood MS 4202, 11 October 1865.
6. Ibid., 19 April 1865.
7. Colby, p. 65.
8. Blackwood MS 4295, 22 October 1872.

CHAPTER 6: TWO FAMILIES TO SUPPORT

1. James Sime (1843–95) went abroad with Jessie soon after their marriage to study German philosophy and literature. On his return to England he published several studies of German writers and worked for the *Globe* and the *Pall Mall Gazette.*
2. Margaret to Mrs Tulloch, late 1865, wrongly dated 1866 in *A & L.*
3. Dinah Craik to Margaret, 2 October 1865, NLS Acc. 5793/5.
4. Margaret to Mrs Tulloch, late 1865.
5. Blackwood MS 4202, 12 September 1865.
6. *A Son of the Soil*, Chapter 1.
7. Jane Carlyle to Thomas Carlyle, 6 April 1866, in J. A. Froude (ed.) *Letters and Memorials of Jane Welsh Carlyle* (1883) Volume 3, p. 325.
8. See her poem, 'The Innermost Room', *Blackwood's*, March 1867.
9. Anne Taylor, *Laurence Oliphant* (Oxford: Oxford University Press, 1982) p. 142.
10. Blackwood MS 4225, 8 August 1867.
11. Ibid., no day or month, 1867.
12. See 'The Great Unrepresented', *Blackwood's*, September 1866.
13. Blackwood MS 4238, no day or month, 1868.
14. Ibid.
15. Ibid., 8 April 1868.
16. Queen Victoria's Journal, 14 March 1868. Reproduced by gracious permission of Her Majesty the Queen.
17. Sturgis, 'A Sketch from Memory'.
18. *Daily News*, 1 July 1869, NLS Acc. 5793/19.
19. *The Three Brothers*, Volume 2, Chapter 3.

20. Ibid., Volume I, Chapter 21.
21. 'Berkeley: The Philosopher', *Blackwood's*, January 1869. Reprinted in *Historical Sketches of the Reign of George II* (1869).
22. Margaret to John Blackwood, 18 August 1870, *A & L.*
23. Blackwood MS 4280, 2 December 1871.
24. Blackwood MS 4295, 30 March 1872.
25. *Annals*, Volume 3, p. 203.
26. *Innocent*, Volume 3, Chapter 14.
27. Margaret to John Blackwood, 13 May 1873, *A & L.*
28. Macmillan MS, 11 April 1877.
29. Sturgis, 'A Sketch from Memory'.
30. Benson, *Memories and Friends*, pp. 73–4.
31. Janet Leith Story, *Later Reminiscences* (Glasgow, 1913) p. 48.
32. *Annals*, Volume 3, p. 350.
33. Introduction to Gerardine Macpherson, *Anna Jameson*.
34. Margaret to Isabella Blackwood, 26 December 1874, *A & L.*
35. Margaret to John Blackwood, 16 July 1875, *A & L.*
36. Robert Gittings, *Young Thomas Hardy* (1975; Penguin revised edn, 1978) p. 275.
37. Winifred Gérin, *Anne Thackeray Ritchie* (Oxford: Oxford University Press, 1981; 1983 edn) p. 221.
38. Anne Thackeray Ritchie, 'A Discourse of Modern Sybils', *Cornhill*, March 1913.

CHAPTER 7: THE WOMAN QUESTION

1. *The Victorian Age of English Literature*, Volume 2, Chapter 5.
2. Margaret to John Blackwood, 16 August 1866, *A & L.*
3. *The Victorian Age of English Literature*, Volume 1, Chapter 3.
4. *Lucy Crofton* (1860) Chapter 8.
5. *Orphans* (1858) Chapter 19.
6. From Rhoda Broughton's *Cometh up as a Flower* (1867).
7. Blackwood MS 4349, no day or month, 1876.
8. 'The Grievances of Women', *Fraser's Magazine*, May 1880.
9. *The Literary History of England in the end of the Eighteenth and beginning of the Nineteenth Century* (1882) Volume 2, p. 248.
10. 'The Old Saloon', *Blackwood's*, October 1892.
11. *Diana Trelawney, The History of a Great Mistake* (1892) Chapter 13.

CHAPTER 8: PRODIGAL SONS

1. Margaret to Isabella Blackwood, 13 December 1875, *A & L.*
2. Margaret to Isabella Blackwood, 2 December 1875, *A & L.*
3. Lucy Poate Stebbins, *A Victorian Album: Some Lady Novelists of the Period* (London: Secker and Warburg, 1946) p. 185.

4. Blackwood MS 4337, no day or month, 1875.
5. Blackwood MS 4349, no day or month, 1876.
6. *In Trust* was published by Longman's in 1882 at the low price of 12s 6d, as an experiment, but failed to bring down the price of books.
7. Blackwood MS 4380, 5 June 1878.
8. Cyril to Margaret, 14 November 1876, NLS Acc. 5678/2.
9. Cyril to Margaret, 28 November 1876, ibid.
10. *Annals*, Volume 3, p. 353.
11. 'The Autobiography and Letters of Mrs M. O. W. Oliphant', anonymous article in the *Quarterly Review*.
12. A. W. Kinglake to Margaret, 20 June 1877, *A & L*.
13. Macmillan MS., 20 August 1877, wrongly filed as 1883.
14. Margaret to John Blackwood, 16 November 1877, *A & L*.
15. Introduction to Gerardine Macpherson, *Anna Jameson*.
16. 'Two Ladies', *Blackwood's*, February 1879.
17. Margaret to her nieces, 23 August 1878, NLS Acc. 5678/4.
18. Margaret to Cyril, 8 and 17 August 1878, NLS Acc. 5678/1.
19. Margaret to Cyril, August 1878, ibid.
20. Margaret to Cyril, 17 August 1878, ibid.
21. Margaret to Cyril, 20 August 1878, ibid.
22. Blackwood MS 4396, 16 March 1879.
23. Margaret to John Blackwood, 28 February 1879, *A & L*.
24. Blackwood MS 4396, 4 August 1879.
25. Margaret to Isabella Blackwood, 4 November 1879, *A & L*.
26. Margaret to Dinah Craik, 24 December 1879, *A & L*.
27. Margaret to William Blackwood, 24 December 1879, *A & L*.
28. *Fraser's Magazine*, January 1880.
29. Robert Louis Stevenson to Margaret, no date, NLS Acc. 5793/5.
30. Margaret to William Blackwood, 13 November 1884, *A & L*.
31. Margaret to Cyril, 31 December 1879, NLS Acc. 5678/1.
32. Margaret to Cyril, 2 January 1880, ibid.
33. Blackwood MS 4410, 18 February 1880.
34. Macmillan MS, 7 February 1881.
35. Ibid., 12 April 1882.
36. Margaret to Isabella Blackwood, Blackwood MS 4725, no date.
37. Janet Leith Story, *Later Reminiscences*, p. 49.
38. Blackwood MS 4437, 31 January 1882.
39. *The Wizard's Son* (1884) Chapter 1.
40. Ibid.
41. Margaret to Cecco, no date, NLS Acc. 5678/1.
42. Blackwood MS 4462, 1 July 1884.
43. Auto. MS.

CHAPTER 9: THE SEEN AND UNSEEN

1. *Memoir of the Life of Laurence Oliphant and of Alice Oliphant, his wife* (1891) p. 379.

2. Meredith Townsend, 'Mrs Oliphant', *Cornhill*, June 1899.
3. Most notably the Colbys.
4. Most recently in J. A. Cuddon (ed.) the *Penguin Book of Ghost Stories* (Harmondsworth: Penguin, 1984).
5. *Blackwood's*, January 1884.
6. The first two Little Pilgrim stories were published in *Macmillan's Magazine* in May and September 1882. They were followed by two small collections, *A Little Pilgrim in the Unseen* (1882) and *The Land of Darkness* (1888).
7. 'A Little Pilgrim in the Unseen'.
8. 'The Little Pilgrim in the Seen and the Unseen'.
9. First published in *Blackwood's*, January 1887.

CHAPTER 10: NEVER PENETRATING BEYOND THE THRESHOLD

1. Margaret to Annie Coghill, 7 September 1884, *A & L.*
2. Margaret to Cecco, 27 January 1890, NLS Acc. 5678/1.
3. 'The Old Saloon', *Blackwood's*, August, 1889.
4. Blackwood MS 4476, 18 May 1885.
5. Blackwood MS 4507, 8 April 1887.
6. Macmillan MS, 10 October 1885.
7. Margaret to Principal Tulloch, September 1881, *A & L.*
8. 'Principal Tulloch', *Blackwood's*, April 1886.
9. Margaret to Annie Coghill, 23 February 1886, *A & L.*
10. Blackwood MS 4490, 20 July 1886.
11. Margaret to Cecco, 24 August 1886, NLS Acc. 5678/1.
12. Margaret to Annie Coghill, 12 February 1887, *A & L.*
13. Cyril to William Blackwood, Blackwood MS 4507, 30 April 1887.
14. Blackwood MS 4507, 23 August 1887.
15. Margaret to Cyril, no date, NLS Acc. 5678/1.
16. Cecco to William Blackwood, 30 October 1887, *A & L.*
17. NLS Acc. 5793/13.
18. 'Mr Sandford', in *The Ways of Life* (1897) Chapter 7.
19. Blackwood MS 4507, 18 March 1887.
20. *The Second Son* (1888) was first published in the *Atlantic Monthly* with the American Thomas Bailey Aldridge named as co-author to avoid piracy, although this was not an accurate description.
21. Christina Rogerson was the daughter of Mrs Duncan Stewart, a friend of Henry James. *Kirsteen* is based on a story from her family. Christina had a stormy life which included a mental breakdown, an unhappy first marriage and the death of her second husband in the Boer War. She looked after disadvantaged children in her home at Hindhead. Her name was brought before the public in the famous divorce case involving Sir Charles Dilke, when it was alleged that she had been Dilke's mistress and written anonymous letters. It was after this that Margaret pointedly dedicated *Kirsteen* 'with love and respect to Christina Rogerson'.
22. Blackwood MS 4523, 8 October 1888.

23. Benson, *Memories and Friends*, p. 81.
24. Meredith Townsend, 'Mrs Oliphant'.
25. Blackwood MS 4540, 10 January 1889.
26. Margaret to Denny, 15 January 1889, NLS Acc. 5678/3.
27. Margaret to Cecco, January 1889, NLS Acc. 5678/1.
28. J. M. Barrie, Introductory Note to *A Widow's Tale and Other Stories* (1898).
29. Macmillan MS, 6 November 1889.
30. Margaret to Annie Coghill, 11 March 1890, *A & L*.
31. Madge to Denny, 30 March 1890, NLS Acc. 5678/11.
32. Margaret to Annie Coghill, 9 April 1890, *A & L*.
33. *Life of Laurence Oliphant* (1891) p. 334.
34. Madge to Denny, 7 May 1890, NLS Acc. 5678/11.
35. Cecco to Margaret, 29 August 1890, NLS Acc. 5678/2.
36. Margaret to Annie Coghill, 28 August 1890, *A & L*.
37. Auto. MS.

CHAPTER 11: THE GREAT NOVELS

1. *Fraser's Magazine*, May 1880.
2. Stebbins, *A Victorian Album*, p. 185.
3. *A House Divided* appeared in *Chambers's Journal* throughout 1885, while the agreement for *A Country Gentleman* was not signed (with Macmillan) until 28 August of that year. So it seems likely that the 'sequel' was actually the first book to be written.

CHAPTER 12: THE GREAT SHORT STORIES

1. J. M. Barrie, Introductory Note to *A Widow's Tale*.
2. 'Mr Sandford' was first published anonymously in the *Cornhill*, April–May 1888, and reprinted in *The Ways of Life* (1897).

CHAPTER 13: ON THE EBB TIDE

1. Auto. MS.
2. Margaret to Madge, 17 November 1890, NLS Acc. 5678/3.
3. Margaret to Madge 11 December 1890, ibid.
4. Auto. MS.
5. Ibid.
6. Madge to Denny, 11 June 1892, NLS Acc. 5678/12.
7. Margaret to Madge, 9 February 1891, NLS Acc. 5678/3.
8. Margaret to George Lillie Craik, 17 February 1893, *A & L*.
9. Margaret to Denny, 29 June 1893, NLS Acc. 5678/3.
10. Madge to Denny, 29 June 1893, NLS Acc. 5678/13.

11. Madge to Denny, 6 September 1893, ibid., and 26 January 1894, NLS Acc. 5678/14.
12. Madge to Margaret, 10 October 1893, NLS Acc. 5678/6.
13. Margaret to Denny, 13 October 1893, NLS Acc. 5678/4.
14. Margaret to Denny, 15 October 1893, NLS Acc. 5678/3.
15. Blackwood MS 4621, 27 July 1894.
16. Madge to Denny, 19 November 1892, NLS Acc. 5678/12.
17. Sturgis, 'A Sketch from Memory'.
18. Margaret to Annie Coghill, 13 September 1894, *A & L.*
19. Margaret to Annie Coghill, 2 October 1894, *A & L.*
20. Auto. MS.
21. Margaret to Emily Lawless, 25 October 1894, *A & L.*
22. 'Fancies of a Believer', *Blackwood's*, February 1895.
23. Margaret to William Blackwood, 26 August 1894, *A & L.*
24. Margaret to William Blackwood, 3 November 1894, *A & L.*
25. Blackwood MS 4621, 31 December 1894.
26. NLS Acc. 5793/16.
27. Barrie, Introductory Note to *A Widow's Tale.*
28. Blackwood MS 4621, 7 December 1894.
29. Margaret to Madge, 1 September 1895, NLS Acc. 5678/4.
30. First published in *Blackwood's*, January 1896, reprinted in *Stories of the Seen and the Unseen* (1902), and often found in collections of ghost stories.
31. 'The Anti-Marriage League', *Blackwood's*, January 1896.
32. Margaret to Madge, 19 November 1895, NLS Acc. 5678/4.
33. 'The Anti-Marriage League'.
34. 'The Old Saloon', *Blackwood's*, March 1892.
35. 'The Anti-Marriage League'.
36. Blackwood MS 4635, 28 November 1895.
37. Thomas Hardy to Grant Allen, 7 January 1896, in Richard Little Purdy and Michael Millgate (eds), *The Collected Letters of Thomas Hardy, Volume Two* (Oxford: Clarendon Press, 1980) p. 106.
38. Blackwood MS 4650, 26 April 1896.
39. Margaret to William Blackwood, 3 October 1896, *A & L.*
40. J. M. Dent, *Memoirs* (1938 edition) pp. 79–80.
41. 'On the Ebb Tide', preface to *The Ways of Life* (1897).
42. Blackwood MS 4664, 16 June 1897.
43. Elma and Constance Story, *Memoir of Robert Herbert Story*, p. 288.
44. Hester Ritchie (ed.) *Letters of Anne Thackeray Ritchie* (1924) pp. 242–3.
45. Denny Oliphant to William Blackwood, 26 June 1897, Blackwood MS 4664.
46. Ritchie, *Letters of Anne Thackeray Ritchie.*
47. Sturgis, 'A Sketch from Memory'.

CHAPTER 14: AFTERMATH

1. Denny Oliphant to William Blackwood, 2 September 1897, Blackwood MS 4664.

2. 'The Life and Writings of Mrs Oliphant', anonymous article in the *Edinburgh Review*, July 1899.
3. Meredith Townsend, 'Mrs Oliphant'.
4. Virginia Woolf, *Three Guineas* (1938) pp. 166–7.
5. Sturgis, 'A Sketch from Memory'.

Bibliography

1. General

Anderson, R. D., *Education and Opportunity in Victorian Scotland* (Oxford: Oxford University Press, 1983).

Benson, A. C., *Memories and Friends* (1924).

Boyd, A. K. H., *Twenty-Five Years of St Andrew's* (1892).

Brack, Alan, *The Wirral* (London: Batsford, 1980).

Clark, John Stock, 'Mrs Oliphant's Unidentified Social Novels', *Notes and Queries*, October 1981 (magazine published from Pembroke College, Oxford).

Clarke, Isabel, C., *Six Portraits* (1935).

Cobbett, William, *Tour in Scotland* (1833).

Cockburn, Lord, *Memorials of his Time* (Edinburgh: 1856).

Colby, Vineta, 'William Wilson, Novelist', *Notes and Queries*, February 1966.

Colby, Vineta and Robert A., *The Equivocal Virtue: Mrs Oliphant and the Victorian Literary Market Place* (New York: Archon Books, 1966).

Colby, Vineta and Robert A., 'Mrs Oliphant's Scotland: The Romance of Reality', in Ian Campbell (ed.), *Nineteenth-Century Scottish Fiction* (Manchester: Carcanet New Press, 1979).

Cunningham, Valentine, *Everywhere Spoken Against: Dissent in the Victorian Novel* (Oxford: Oxford University Press, 1975).

Daiches, David, *Edinburgh* (London: Hamish Hamilton, 1978).

Dent, J. M., *Memories of J. M. Dent, 1849–1926* (1928).

Drummond, Andrew L. and Bulloch, James, *The Scottish Church 1688–1843* (Edinburgh: Saint Andrew Press, 1973).

Drummond, Andrew L. and Bulloch, James, *The Church in Victorian Scotland 1843–74* (Edinburgh: Saint Andrew Press, 1975).

Drummond, Andrew L. and Bulloch, James, *The Church in Late Victorian Scotland 1874–1900* (Edinburgh: Saint Andrew Press, 1978).

Froude, J. A. (ed.), *Letters and Memorials of Jane Welsh Carlyle* (1883).

Gérin, Winifred, *Anne Thackeray Ritchie* (Oxford: Oxford University Press, 1981).

Gettmann, Royal A., *A Victorian Publisher* (Cambridge: Cambridge University Press, 1960).

Harrison, Martin, *Victorian Stained Glass* (London: Barrie and Jenkins, 1980).

Hollis, Christopher, *Eton* (London: Hollis and Carter, 1960).

James, Henry, *Notes on Novelists* (1914).

Lindsay, Maurice, *History of Scottish Literature* (London: Hale, 1977).

Macpherson, Gerardine, *Memoirs of the Life of Anna Jameson* (1878).

McGuffie, George, *The Priests of Etal, or Annals of Tillside* (fourth edn, Edinburgh: 1904).
Minto, W. (ed.), *Autobiographical Notes of the Life of William Bell Scott* (1892).
Moore, Katharine, *Victorian Wives* (London: Allison and Busby, 1974).
Oliphant, Cyril Francis, *Alfred De Musset* (1890).
Oliphant, Francis Romano, *Notes of a Pilgrimage to Jerusalem and the Holy Land* (1891).
Oliphant, Francis Wilson, *A Plea for Painted Glass* (Oxford: 1855).
Porter, Mrs Gerald, *The Life of John Blackwood* (Volume 3 of *Annals of a Publishing House*) (1898).
Ritchie, Anne Isabella, *From the Porch* (1913).
Ritchie, Hester (ed.), *Letters of Anne Thackeray Ritchie* (1924).
Saunders, L. J., *Scottish Democracy 1815–1840* (London and Edinburgh: Oliver and Boyd, 1950).
Showalter, Elaine, *A Literature of their own: British Woman Novelists from Brontë to Lessing* (Princeton: Princeton University Press, 1977).
Skelton, John, *The Table-Talk of Shirley* (1895).
Stebbins, Lucy Poate, *A Victorian Album: Some Lady Novelists of the Period* (London: Secker and Warburg, 1946).
Story, Elma and Constance, *Memoir of Robert Herbert Story, by his daughters* (Glasgow: 1909).
Story, Janet Leith, *Early Reminiscences* (Glasgow: 1911).
Story, Janet Leith, *Later Reminiscences* (Glasgow: 1913).
Story, Robert Herbert, *Memoir of the Life of the Reverend Robert Story* (1862).
Sturgis, Howard Overing, 'A Sketch from Memory', *Temple Bar*, September–December 1899.
Sutherland, J. A., *Victorian Novelists and Publishers* (London: Athone Press, 1976).
Taylor, Anne, *Laurence Oliphant 1829–88* (Oxford: Oxford University Press, 1982).
Terry, R.C., *Victorian Popular Fiction 1860–80* (London: Macmillan Press, 1983).
Trappes-Lomax, Michael, *Pugin, A Medieval Victorian* (1932).
Tredray, F. D., *The House of Blackwood 1804–1954* (Edinburgh: Blackwood and Sons, 1954).
Tulloch, John, *Movements of Religious Thought in Britain during the Nineteenth Century* (1885; reprinted Leicester: Leicester University Press, 1971 with an introduction by A. C. Cheyne).
White, Brian D., *History of the Corporation of Liverpool 1835–1914* (Liverpool: 1951).
Widdowson, Peter; Stigant, Paul and Brooker, Peter, 'History and Literary "Value", *Adam Bede* and *Salem Chapel*', in *Literature and History*, Spring 1979.
Williams, Merryn, *Women in the English Novel, 1800–1900* (London: Macmillan Press, 1984).
Wilson, Jessie Aitken, *Memoir of George Wilson* (Edinburgh: 1860).
Wolff, Robert Lee, *Novels of Faith and Doubt in Victorian England* (London: John Murray, 1977).

2. Books by Margaret Oliphant

* indicates that a book is good, or at least interesting. (W) indicates a novel attributed to William Wilson.

1849 *Passages in the Life of Mrs Margaret Maitland, of Sunnyside, written by Herself.*

1850 *Merkland, a Story of Scottish Life*

1851 *Caleb Field, A Tale of the Puritans*
John Drayton, the Liverpool Engineer (W)

1852 *Memoirs and Resolutions of Adam Graeme of Mossgray*
The Melvilles (W)

1853 *Ailieford, a Family History* (W)
Harry Muir, A Story of Scottish Life
**Katie Stewart, A True Story*, serialised in *Blackwood's*, July–November 1852.

1854 *The Quiet Heart*, seralised in *Blackwood's*, December 1853–May 1854.
Magdalen Hepburn, A Story of the Scottish Reformation

1855 *Lilliesleaf. Being a Concluding Series of Passages in the Life of Mrs Margaret Maitland*

1856 *Zaidee, A Romance*, seralised in *Blackwood's*, December 1854–December 1855.
Christian Melville (W)

1857 *The Athelings, or The Three Gifts*, serialised in *Blackwood's*, June 1856–June 1857.
The Days of my Life, an Autobiography

1858 *Sundays*
The Laird of Norlaw, A Scottish Story
Orphans, A Chapter in Life

1859 *Agnes Hopetoun's Schools and Holidays*

1860 *Lucy Crofton*

1861 *The House on the Moor*

1862 *The Last of the Mortimers, A Story in Two Voices*
**The Life of Edward Irving, Minister of the National Scotch Church, London*

1863 **The Rector and The Doctor's Family*, serialised in *Blackwood's*, September 1861–January 1862.
Heart and Cross
Salem Chapel, serialised in *Blackwood's*, February 1862–January 1863.

1864 **The Perpetual Curate*, serialised in *Blackwood's*, June 1863–September 1864.

1865 * *Agnes*

1866 **Miss Marjoribanks*, serialised in *Blackwood's*, February 1865–May 1866.
**A Son of the Soil*, serialised in *Macmillan's Magazine*, November 1863–April 1865.

1867 *Madonna Mary*, serialised in *Good Words*, January–December 1866.

1868 *Brownlows*, serialised in *Blackwood's*, January 1867–February 1868.
Francis of Assisi

1869 **Historical Sketches of the Reign of George II*, serialised in *Blackwood's*, February 1868–August 1869.
The Minister's Wife

1870 *John, A Love Story*, serialised in *Blackwood's*, November 1869–July 1870.
The Three Brothers, serialised in *St Paul's*, June 1869–September 1870.
1871 *Squire Arden*
1872 *At His Gates*, serialised in *Good Words*, January–December 1872.
Ombra
Memoirs of the Count de Montalembert, A Chapter of Recent French History
1873 *May*
Innocent, A Tale of Modern Life, serialised in *Graphic*, 4 January–28 June 1873.
1874 *A Rose in June*, serialised in *Cornhill*, March–August 1874.
For Love and Life
1875 **The Story of Valentine and his Brother*, serialised in *Blackwood's*, January 1874–February 1875.
Whiteladies, serialised in *Good Words*, January–December 1875.
1876 **The Curate in Charge*, serialised in *Macmillan's Magazine*, August 1875–January 1876.
Phoebe Junior, A Last Chronicle of Carlingford
Dress
The Makers of Florence: Dante, Giotto, Savonarola and their city
1877 *Dante*
Young Musgrave
Mrs Arthur
Carita, serialised in *Cornhill*, June 1876–August 1877.
1878 *The Primrose Path, A Chapter in the Annals of the Kingdom of Fife*
1879 *Molière* (with F. B. C. Tarver)
Within the Precincts, serialised in *Cornhill*, February 1878–April 1879.
The Greatest Heiress in England
1880 **A Beleaguered City, being a Narrative of certain Recent Events in the City of Semur*
He that Will Not when He May, serialised in *Macmillan's Magazine*, November 1879–November 1880.
Cervantes
1881 *Harry Joscelyn*
1882 *In Trust, the Story of a Lady and her Lover*, serialised in *Fraser's Magazine*, February 1881–January 1882.
**The Literary History of England 1790–1825*
A Little Pilgrim in the Unseen, serialised in *Macmillan's Magazine*, May and September 1882.
1883 *Sheridan*
**Hester*
It was a Lover and his Lass
**The Ladies Lindores*, serialised in *Blackwood's*, April 1882–May 1883.
1884 **Sir Tom*
**The Wizard's Son*, serialised in *Macmillan's Magazine*, November 1882–March 1884.
1885 **Two Stories of the Seen and the Unseen*
Madam, serialised in *Longman's*, January 1884–January 1885.
1886 *Oliver's Bride, A True Story*
**A Country Gentleman and his Family*
Effie Ogilvie, The Story of a Young Life

A House Divided Against Itself, serialised in *Chambers's Journal*, 3 January–5 December 1885.
1887 *The Makers of Venice: Doges, Conquerors, Painters and Men of Letters*
The Son of his Father
1888 **The Land of Darkness, along with some Further Chapters in the Experience of the Little Pilgrim*
Joyce, serialised in *Blackwood's*, May 1887–April 1888.
The Second Son (with Thomas Bailey Aldridge)
Memoir of the Life of John Tulloch
Cousin Mary
1889 *Neighbours on the Green, A Collection of Stories*
A Poor Gentleman, serialised in *Leisure Hour*, 1886.
**Lady Car, The Sequel of a Life*, serialised in *Longman's*, March–July 1889.
1890 **Kirsteen, A Story of a Scottish Family Seventy Years Ago*, serialised in *Macmillan's Magazine*, August 1889–August 1890.
The Duke's Daughter, and *The Fugitives*, serialised as *Lady Jane*, in *Good Words*, January–June 1882.
Sons and Daughters, serialised in *Blackwood's*, March–April 1890.
Royal Edinburgh: Her Saints, Kings, Prophets and Poets
The Mystery of Mrs Blencarrow
1891 *The Railwayman and his Children*
Janet
Jerusalem: Its History and Hope
A Memoir of the Life of Laurence Oliphant, and of Alice Oliphant, His Wife
1892 *The Cuckoo in the Nest*
**Diana Trelawney, The History of a Great Mistake*, serialised in *Blackwood's*, February–July 1892.
**The Marriage of Elinor*, serialised in *Good Words*, January–December 1891.
The Victorian Age of English Literature (with F. R. Oliphant)
The Heir Presumptive and the Heir Apparent
1893 *Lady William*
The Sorceress
Thomas Chalmers, Preacher, Philosopher, and Statesman
1894 *A House in Bloomsbury*
Historical Sketches of the Reign of Queen Anne
Who Was Lost and is Found, serialised in *Blackwood's*, June–November 1894.
The Prodigals and their Inheritance
Two Strangers
1895 *A Child's History of Scotland*
Sir Robert's Fortune, The Story of a Scotch Moor
The Makers of Modern Rome
1896 *Jeanne d'Arc: Her Life and Death*
The Unjust Steward; or, the Minister's Debt
The Two Marys
**Old Mr Tredgold*, serialised in *Longman's*, June 1895–May 1896.
1897 *The Lady's Walk, A Tale*, serialised in *Longman's*, December 1882–January 1883.

The Ways of Life, Two Stories
Annals of a Publishing House: William Blackwood and his Sons, their Magazine and Friends
1898 **A Widow's Tale, and other Stories* (with an Introductory Note by J. M. Barrie)
That Little Cutty, and Two Other Stories
1899 **The Autobiography and Letters of Mrs M. O. W. Oliphant*, arranged and edited by Mrs Harry Coghill
1900 *Queen Victoria, A Personal Sketch*
1902 **Stories of the Seen and the Unseen*

3. Modern Editions

Miss Marjoribanks (London: Chatto & Windus, Zodiac Press, 1969) with an introduction by Q. D. Leavis.
The Autobiography and Letters of Mrs. M. O. W. Oliphant (Leicester: Leicester University Press, 1974) with an introduction by Q. D. Leavis.
Hester (London: Virago Modern Classics, 1984) with an introduction by Jennifer Uglow.
Kirsteen (London: Dent, Everyman Classics, 1984) with an introduction by Merryn Williams.
The Doctor's Family and other Stories (Oxford: Oxford University Press, 1986) edited and with an introduction by Merryn Williams. The other stories are 'The Executor' and 'The Rector'.

4. Margaret Oliphant's contributions to *Blackwood's Magazine*

Katie Stewart	July 1852–November 1852
John Rintoul	March and April 1853
The Shadow on the Way	June 1853
The Quiet Heart	December 1853–May 1854
Mary Russell Mitford	June 1854
Evelyn and Pepys	July 1854
The Holy Land	September 1854
Zaidee: A Romance	December 1854–December 1855
Mr Thackeray and his Novels	January 1855
Bulwer	February 1855
Charles Dickens	April 1855
Modern Novelists, Great and Small	May 1855
Modern Light Literature:	
Theology	July 1855
Science	August 1855
History	October 1855
Travellers' Tales	November 1855

Modern Light Literature – *continued*	
Art	December 1855
Poetry	February 1856
Religion in Common Life	February 1856
Sydney Smith	March 1856
The Laws Concerning Women	April 1856
The Athelings	June 1856–June 1857
Macaulay	August and September 1856
Family History	October 1856
A New Una	October 1856
The Art of Cavilling	November 1856
A Christmas Tale	January 1857
Picture Books	March 1857
Charles the Fifth	July 1857
Modern Light Literature:	
Society	October 1857
From India	October 1857
Béranger	January 1858
The Condition of Women	February 1858
The Missionary Explorer	April 1858
Religious Memoirs	June 1858
The Byways of Literature	August 1858
Edward Irving	November 1858
Sermons	December 1858
A Winter Journey	April 1859
Felicita	August and September 1859
The Seaside in the Papal States	October 1859
A Week in Florence	November 1859
Scottish National Character	June 1860
Poetry	July 1860
The Romance of Agostini	September–November 1860
Social Science	December 1860
A Merry Christmas	January 1861
The Executor	May 1861
The Monks of the West	June 1861
Joseph Wolff	August 1861
Three Days in the Highlands	August 1861
Scotland and her Accusers	September 1861
The Rector	September 1861
Chronicles of Carlingford:	
The Doctor's Family	October 1861–January 1862
Among the Lochs	October 1861
Augustus Welby Pugin	December 1861
J. M. W. Turner, R. A.	January 1862
The Nation's Prayer	January 1862
Chronicles of Carlingford:	
Salem Chapel	February 1862–January 1863
The Lives of Two Ladies	April 1862
Sensation Novels	May 1862

The New Exhibition	June 1862
David Wingate	July 1862
Sermons	August 1862
John Wilson	December 1862
Henri Lacordaire	February 1863
Mrs Clifford's Marriage	March and April 1863
Marriage Bells	April 1863
Savonarola	June 1863
The Perpetual Curate	June 1863–September 1864
Novels	August 1863
In the Garden	August 1863
Amen in the Cathedral of St Andrew's	October 1863
Tara	November 1863
The Life of Jesus	October 1864
Life on an Island	January 1865
Day and Night	January 1865
Chronicles of Carlingford:	
Miss Marjoribanks	February 1865–May 1866
Josiah Wedgwood	August 1865
Leopardi	October 1865
French Periodical Literature	November 1865
General Lamoricière	February 1866
The Nile	August 1866
The Great Unrepresented	September 1866
Victor Hugo	December 1866
Brownlows	January 1867–February 1868
The History of Scotland	March 1867
The Innermost Room	March 1867
Elizabeth and Mary	April 1867
Novels	September 1867
A Royal Idyll	September 1867
A City of the Plague	October 1867
The Conversion of England	December 1867
The Queen of the Highlands	February 1868
Historical Sketches of the Reign of George II:	
The Queen	February 1868
Walpole: The Minister	April 1868
Chesterfield: The Man of the World	May 1868
The Latest Lawgiver	June 1868
Historical Sketches of the Reign of George II:	
Lady Mary W. Montagu	July 1868
Pope: The Poet	August 1868
The Young Chevalier	September 1868
Bunsen	September 1868
Historical Sketches of the Reign of George II:	
John Wesley: The Reformer	October 1868
Anson: The Sailor	December 1868
Berkeley: The Philosopher	January 1869
Richardson: The Novelist	March 1869

Historical Sketches of the Reign of George II – *continued*	
Hume: The Sceptic	June 1869
Hogarth: The Painter	August 1869
Charles Reade's Novels	October 1869
John	November 1869–July 1870
Saint Eloy sur les Dunes	November 1869
Mr Froude and Queen Mary	January 1870
Miss Austen and Miss Mitford	March 1870
Chatterton	April 1870
Count Charles de Montalembert	April 1870
New Books	May and August 1870
Piccadilly (review)	October 1870
Boating on the Thames	October 1870
New Books	November 1870, January and April 1871
Charles Dickens	June 1871
A Century of Great Poets: Cowper	June 1871
New Books	July 1871
A Century of Great Poets: Walter Scott	August 1871
Wordsworth	September 1871
American Books	October 1871
New Books	October 1871
A Century of Great Poets: Coleridge	November 1871
The Two Mrs Scudamores	December 1871–January 1872
A Century of Great Poets: Burns	February 1872
Voltaire	March 1872
A Century of Great Poets: Shelley:	April 1872
New Books	April and June 1872
A Century of Great Poets: Byron	July 1872
New Books	August 1872
William Smith	October 1872
A Century of Great Poets: Goëthe	December 1872
New Books	December 1872 and February 1873
In London	February 1873
Lord Lytton	March 1873
Kenelm Chillingley	May 1873
Alexandre Dumas	July 1873
A Century of Great Poets: Schiller	August 1873
A Visit to Albion	August 1873
New Books	September 1873

A Railway Junction	October 1873
New Books	November 1873
The Story of Valentine	January 1874–February 1875
The Indian Mutiny: Sir Hope Grant	January 1874
Fables in Song	February 1874
New Books	April and June 1874
Two Cities: Two Books	July 1874
New Books	August 1874
The Ancient Classics	September 1874
The Ancient Classics: Latin Literature	November 1874
Life of the Prince Consort	January 1875
New Books	May 1875
Art in May	June 1875
New Books	July 1875
Rivers	August 1875
Michael Angelo	October 1875
Lace and Bric-à-Brac	January 1876
A Century of Great Poets: Lamartine	February 1876
Thackeray's Sketches	February 1876
Eton College	March 1876
Norman MacLeod	April 1876
Macaulay	May 1876
The Royal Academy	June 1876
Molière	August 1876
Alfred de Musset	September 1876
The Secret Chamber	December 1876
New Books	February 1877
Lord Neaves	March 1877
Harriet Martineau	April 1877
A School of the Prophets	September 1877
The Opium-Eater	December 1877
New Books	March and June 1878
Englishmen and Frenchmen	August 1878
Three Days in Paris	October 1878
Novels of Alphonse Daudet	January 1879
Two Ladies	February 1879
Hamlet	April 1879
New Books	July 1879
An American Princess	November 1879
The Reign of Queen Anne	February 1880
Novels of Turgenev	May 1880
School and College	July 1880
New Novels	September 1880
Autobiographies	January, March, May, August and October 1881
A Few French Novels	December 1881
The Open Door	January 1882

Recent Novels	March 1882
The Ladies Lindores	April 1882–May 1883
Democracy	May 1882
Autobiographies	July 1882
American Literature	January 1883
Autobiographies	April 1883
James Fergusson	August 1883
An Italian Officer under Napoleon	September 1883
The Story of a Little War	October 1883
Old Lady Mary	January 1884
Sons of the Prophets	April 1884
The Duke of Albany	May 1884
Venice	July 1884
Three Young Novelists	September 1884
An Artist's Autobiography	November 1884
The Portrait	January 1885
A Soldier of Fortune	April 1885
London in May	May 1885
General Gordon	August 1885
A Scotch Physician	November 1885
London in January	February 1886
Scotch Local History	March 1886
Principal Tulloch	March and April 1886
Novels	December 1886
The Land of Darkness	January 1887
The Old Saloon	January, February, March and April 1887
Joyce	May 1887–April 1888
The Old Saloon	May 1887
The Rev W. Lucas Collins	May 1887
The Old Saloon	June–August 1887
Marco Polo	September 1887
The Old Saloon	November 1887 and January 1888
Pictures of the Year	June 1888
The Old Saloon	June and September 1888
On the Dark Mountains	November 1888
The Old Saloon	December 1888
The Emperor Frederick	January 1889
Laurence Oliphant	February 1889
The Old Saloon	March and April 1889
On the Riviera	May 1889
The Old Saloon	June, August, November, December 1889 and January 1890
Sons and Daughters	March and April 1890
The Old Saloon	March 1890
Lord Lamington	March 1890
The Holy Land	July 1890

The Old Saloon	August and November 1891
Diana	February–July 1892
The Old Saloon	February 1892
The Duke of Clarence	February 1892
The City of St Andrew's	March 1892
The Old Saloon	March and October 1892
Tennyson	November 1892
The Old Saloon	December 1892
A Visitor and his Opinions	April 1893
Marriage Bells	July 1893
Letters of Sir Walter Scott	January 1894
Dean Stanley	February 1894
Who was Lost and is Found	June–November 1894
The Looker-on	August 1894
An Eton Master	November 1894
The Looker-on	January 1895
Fancies of a Believer	February 1895
Men and Women	April 1895
John Stuart Blackie	April 1895
The Looker-on	June and December 1895
The Anti-Marriage League	January 1896
The Library Window	January 1896
The Heirs of Kellie	March 1896
The Looker-on	June and October 1896
The Verdict of Old Age	October 1896
J. G. Lockhart	November 1896
A Raid Among Books	December 1896
The Land of Suspense	January 1897
Recent Books	April 1897
'Tis Sixty Years Since	May 1897
22nd June	June 1897
Siena	July 1898

5. Other Sources

The Bentley Papers, British Museum.

Blackwood MS, letters 1851–97, National Library of Scotland.

Macmillan MS, British Museum.

Family letters etc., National Library of Scotland, Accs. 5678 and 5793.

'A Commentary from an Easy-Chair', articles in the *Spectator* from 7 December 1889 to 8 November 1890.

'Charlotte Brontë', in *Women Novelists of Queen Victoria's Reign: A Book of Appreciations* (1897).

'The Grievances of Women', *Fraser's Magazine*, May 1880.

Index